# An Irish Adventure with Food

## The Tannery Cookbook

## Paul Flynn

Food photography by Sally Kerr Davis

The Collins Press

First Published in 2003 by
The Collins Press, West Link Park, Doughcloyne, Wilton, Cork.

Finished dishes photographed by Sally Kerr Davis

© Photographs pages 6, 19, 27, 31, 55, 59, 63, 65, 73, 78, 95.101, 120, 141, 151, 186, 197, 213, 225, 231, plus author image and detail on spine, cover and title page Sally Kerr Davis.

© All other photographs Stuart Coughlan

ISBN: 1-903464-29-3

Printed in Ireland by ColourBooks Ltd.

Design & Typesetting by edit+

# Contents

# Introduction

I still remember the meal that turned me onto good food. I was fourteen and in France with the scouts. There was a welcome dinner for the Irish scouts – we were served roasted chicken legs in a white wine and tarragon cream sauce with pilaf rice. I took one mouthful of that chicken, with its flavours and textures which were so strange to me at that time, and I was hooked. Most of the boys wouldn't eat theirs so I helped and needless to say, I was like a little whale in my sleeping bag that night.

I went on to become a chef at seventeen, having somewhat neglected my education in the pursuit of girls and beer, and ended up in London, working for the tempestous Nico Ladenis in his two-star Michelin restaurant, Chez Nico, which was situated on Queenstown Road in Battersea. He expected a lot but he was very good to us, paid us well, and encouraged us to spend a large percentage of our wages on eating out in good restaurants for the purpose of education. After my first month working there he said to me, 'Hey

Oirish, where are you eating this weekend? You should try Hilaire. Book it'. This was not a man to be argued with, so that afternoon I made my first restaurant reservation: table for two, 8pm, Saturday night in the name of Flynn (we were very lucky to have Saturday nights off back then – 'I'm not opening Saturday nights', Nico used to say. 'Too many well-done bloody steaks'.)

I had another problem. Having confidently made the reservation for two, I had to find a woman. Thankfully someone took pity on me after numerous phone calls and desperate pleas. Next, having checked my wardrobe, which happened to be in my rucksack in the corner of the room, I discovered that I was seriously lacking in posh restaurant attire. I decided to buy myself a new suit – my old one being the one I wore for my confirmation. So I took the 137 from Clapham Common to Sloane Square and trawled the Kings Road for the outfit that would make me a man and transform my life. It cost £38 in a market beside the Chelsea Potters pub, black and white check, padded shoulders, drainpipe trousers and when you rubbed it, woolly bits came off! In restrospect, Duran Duran wouldn't have worn it for fear of it being too garish.

Saturday night finally came. It had been a hard week. Being the youngest in a tough two-starred Michelin kitchen was no picnic so the weekends were for serious revelry and as much debauchery as possible – forget about work until next week.

I had bought a bright red, narrow as a razor, tie to go with my suit but not wanting to overdo it I decided on a plain white shirt and exchanged my winkle-pickers for sober black shoes. I met my date outside South Kensington tube station and we walked up Old Brompton Road, not sure where I was going.

We eventually found it. By now, I was trembling. There was a lump in my throat and, wanting to obey the rules of etiquette, I let my date go first but my nerves had turned to panic and I almost pushed her through the door. I croaked my name to the very polite waiter who seated us by the window.

I felt like a goldfish. Suddenly I heard a voice booming across a packed restaurant. 'Hey Oirish, you made it!' I turned around and to my horror, there was Nico and his family at the other side of the restaurant. I gave a weak smile over to him and muttered to my date 'Jesus, he's here!!' When the waiter came along I felt like ordering a valium sandwich! Instead we studied the menu and talked about what we would choose. The menu was fine – at least it was printed in English (most high-class restaurant menus at the time were in French) – but when it came to the wine list I was flummoxed. It may as well have been hyroglyphics. Then I saw one I recognised – Sancerre. I had heard about that some-where. So I ordered, the waiter poured, I gulped.

I still remember what I had to eat that night. Pan-fried foie gras with glazed apples. Duck breast with cassis, followed by tarte tatin. I'm cursed with an appalling

memory for names and faces but I can remember every restaurant I have been to and what I had to eat.

We were on desserts when Nico and his family were leaving. He leaned over us with a rare beaming smile and boomed, 'You liked that Oirish, didn't you? Don't be hungover on Monday'. With that he left, and we could relax over a glass of Sauternes at the waiter's recom-mendation. I figured I was now broke. I beckoned the waiter to ask for the bill, only to be told that Mr Ladenis had taken care of it. A man of many surprises, he was just glad that I had chosen to spend my Saturday night educating my palate.

So, having left the restaurant unexpectedly flush with money, I hailed a taxi (flash!) and hit the Mean Fiddler in Harlseden. On Sunday, as far as my tastebuds were concerned, I may as well have spent Saturday night licking sandpaper.

I think my love affair with restaurants started that evening and I never cease to be fascinated by good ones and irritated by bad ones.

The chef in Hilaire that evening was Simon Hopkinson. Soon after that he joined forces with Sir Terence Conran to open Bibendum in the old Michelin building in Brompton Cross. Bibendum was the first of the Conran empire of restaurants. Simon Hopkinson doesn't cook there any more but he is still part owner. He is now a highly-respected food writer and hero of mine.

Nico Ladenis was my mentor. He gave me a chance when others wouldn't. He had an enormous reputation as a cook and was equally renowned for his thorny temperament. I knew nothing when I joined him in his Battersea restaurant, one of only four in the UK at the time holding two Michelin stars. I then worked in five of his restaurants over a period of nine years. He made me his head chef at 23 years old. I was in charge of fifteen chefs, a hugely responsible position. In retrospect, I think I was probably too young. However, it was the most important learning curve I could have had. He taught me about flavour and consistency, the two things that underpin my cooking now. These days I have my own style but my cooking is always rooted in the ethos of Nico's classical kitchen.

I occasionally look back on my time in London. It is scary to think it's twenty years since I first went there. I have many wonderful memories. I worked with lots of great and talented people. The code of the day was work hard, play hard – crazy nights and bleary-eyed mornings after a snatched few hours of sleep. People dropped out along the way to live normal lives – nights off with their families, happy to see their children for more than a few hours a day.

The talented people that made their mark at that time were dominated by Marco Pierre White, the colossus of the stoves.

I was privileged to be a witness to Marco's ascendancy in London during the late 1980s and early 1990s. For me, there has never been anyone like him. Even when he was in his early twenties he had acquired an almost mythical status in the London restaurant scene. A tall, gangly, half-starved whirlwind of talent that would work for the top chefs and absorb their knowledge for a few months, then cast them away like unwanted mistresses, leaving everyone in his wake feeling useless and inadequate.

I first met him when, in September 1985, I was sent up to Le Manoir aux Quat' Saisons in Oxford, one of the other Michelin two-star restaurants in the UK at this time, owned by Raymond Blanc. I was working as a commis chef at Chez Nico. These were the restaurants in which everybody with ambition aspired to work. There was a system between them of swapping staff to enable the chefs to learn from other kitchens and swap their ideas.

I was nineteen years of age and although I had been working in Nico's for over a year, this was a whole new ball game. Le Manoir was a much bigger restaurant. We, at Nico's, had five chefs – they had sixteen and most of them French – bad news for me as the French were noted for their arrogance and disdain for non-French cooks. So I figured nine days of scrubbing floors, washing pots and peeling potatoes lay ahead.

When I arrived I was introduced to the head chef who promptly dragged me over to a mangy looking giant who introduced himself as Marco. I stood there, quivering in front of this legend for what seemed like an eternity before he said 'You're Nico's boy. You stay with me for the rest of your stay.' I never left his side, chopping for him or cleaning up with him. During service he had me at the other side of the hot plate and was constantly feeding me with succulent bits of meat, spoonfuls of sauce and giving me a running commentary of how and why he was adding something or other to a sauce. He was like a boxer dancing around his ring, completely focused on his opponent. He moved faster than anyone else did, his food looked better than anyone else's and everyone feared him.

Marco used to try and sell Monsieur Blanc his ideas for dishes at £25 a shot! Whether he was taken up on the offer or not we will never know. At one point he challenged Monsieur Blanc to 'create the most wonderful dish from rabbit and langoustine'. The chefs were the judges and eventually ruled in Blanc's favour. I wonder was the fear of losing their jobs more scary than an ear bashing from Marco?

The chefs would start work at 8.30am and the whole place would be a flurry of activity, shouting, swearing, bread and croissants baking, stockpots on the boil, bones roasting ... Marco would have his work for lunch finished by 11.30 and this would leave him half an hour to do as he pleased. Most days he would walk in the garden smoking and drinking espressos or looking for flowers to garnish a famous dish they had on at the time, 'pigeon en sel croute with port jus'. These were whole squab pigeon, sealed in a pan and wrapped in a salt crust pastry that flavoured the bird and kept the moisture in. It was shaped exactly like a pigeon, with a beautiful glaze and pieces of truffles for eyes. This was served with a sauceboat of the jus and a fresh flower garnish, and carved at the table, the pastry discarded afterwards, inedible due to the salt content. All that work, just for show, but it was mesmerising to watch. One night during a particularly frantic service Marco roared at me to make him two pigeon en sel croute 'fast'. I ran to the fridge and proceeded to make him two gremlins with beaks. No matter what I did I could not get this stinking pastry to resemble a bird, let alone a pigeon! After five minutes he came thundering round the corner, pushed me out of the way and in what seemed moments, rustled up two perfect specimens that not only looked like pigeons but a pigeon fancier would have probably been able to tell the breed! He never lost his temper at my ineptitude because he had taken me under his wing but God help anyone who wasn't!

I witnessed his stunning talents in those nine days but also his ruthlessness, arrogance and impatience to those who didn't measure up. At night, on occasion, we went out with the other kitchen staff to the local pub. Marco used to dress in black leather dungarees and sunglasses. Picture this on a man that's 6'4" in a genteel English country inn! He just did not care what others thought. He was the star and we, his adoring public.

I learned a lot in my short time at Le Manoir but even then I knew I was seeing someone special. In the years to follow, Marco Pierre White has more than any chef changed the face of cooking in Britain. Along the way he made cheffing sexy and respectable. When he started his career, chefs were perceived as lowly paid, undereducated, faceless workhorses. At the end of his career he has probably single-handedly inspired, driven and trained countless young men and women to carry on his tradition.

From the back of his book *Wild Food from Land and Sea* comes the telling quotation: 'At six I wanted to be a chef, at seven Napoleon and my ambitions have been growing ever since' – Salvador Dali.

Being let loose in my own kitchen when I was used to the dominant hand of a great chef was a daunting experience. Like anyone that's just flown the coup I wanted to prove myself on my own terms and not live under someone else's shadow. I wanted the freedom to cook good sausages and mash with onion gravy or fish and chips as much as the upmarket dishes I was used to cooking. I am ten years back in Ireland this year: I live in a small country town on the south coast of Ireland; I drive a battered old jeep, for naturally my wife has the good car; life is good. But as much as I try to relax in other ways, cooking good food remains a challenge. One off day and a customer might not darken your door for a year. In a place where passing trade is negligible, that can be a very serious issue. Consistency is the key. This book rarely give whole recipes for dishes. It will mostly give you ideas, a little repertoire to make simple things a whole lot better. I wanted the book to be one that you could take to bed with you, and maybe have a little chuckle before dozing off. Running a restaurant is no joke so I always try to see the lighter side of things. And I hope you do too.

I don't know anyone who doesn't like apple tart ... A good baker is given almost iconic status ... Crisp, sweet pastry, oozing with tart melting apples. Served up with cream or ice-cream or custard ...

I have this image of myself trundling around in a wax jacket, green wellies and soil underneath what's left of my fingernails. Good honest work, out in the fresh air, tending to the herbs, pruning, digging, weeding and enjoying the fruits of my labour. Anyone who has seen 'The Good Life' knows what I mean. The reality, of course, is quite different. Our garden resembles 'Jurassic Park'. The apple, plum and pear trees that were planted (not by me, I might add) have all but disappeared behind a forest of dock leaves. I never realised that such a variety of weeds existed or grew so fast. Professional help is definitely required. I must say though, I still love the romantic notion of picking apples off my own trees and cooking with them at the restaurant.

I don't know anyone who doesn't like apple tart. For us Irish, it's a telling dish. A good baker is given almost iconic status in the country. In baking everyone has their forté: some excel at Christmas cakes, some at puddings, some at pavlovas and then there is the apple tart. There is nothing better than crisp, sweet, pastry, oozing with tart melting apples. Served up with cream or ice-cream or custard. I'm a cream man myself but I have seen people go for all three.

Years ago I came home from London one Christmas, proudly brandishing a copy of Nico's cookbook. I explained to my family that this was what it was all for. The hours, the pressure, the work. I gleefully passed the book around, sweetbreads, quail, Muscat grapes. 1984 in rural Ireland was not a place you would readily find these alien ingredients but yet the colours and artistry leapt from the pages. My intensity was palpable. It was important they understood. They were appreciative, if a bit bemused. My eldest brother was now leafing through the book. He settled on the picture of the apple tart, a wafer thin circle of pastry spread with almond cream, then covered with slivers of apple delicately arranged and caramelised in a hot oven with butter and sugar, surrounded by a rich caramel sauce. 'What kind of a feckin' apple tart is that?' is all he could say. 'I made that you big ignoramus,' I mumbled, and snatched the book from him. I was wounded.

It's funny but that apple tart was almost a symbol of my achievement. Look what I can do, I wanted to say. I've come full circle. That tart was different but maybe no better than the ones we loved as children. The pleasure and appreciation derived from both styles may be the same but it did take me a while to learn that the essential difference was only the style and perhaps the surroundings it was served in.

We were in Glasgow recently and ate in Gordon Ramsay's restaurant, Amaryllis. Of course the food and service were impeccable, the restaurant hushed and reverential. On the dessert menu was a tarte tatin for two with caramel sauce and vanilla ice-cream. Unfortunately it was late and the last one had just gone. The table next to us had been luckier and we enviously watched a crispy caramelised tarte tatin being majestically held aloft inside a gleaming copper pan. Well, I tell you. I don't know what stopped me from rugby tackling the waiter. It was ceremoniously divided between two plates regally sauced with a mahogany caramel sauce. We felt as though we were watching a piece of theatre. In the meantime our desserts arrived and were duly ignored while we freaked out the couple on the other table who must have thought they had gastro-stalkers next door. A swift finger in the ribs brought me back to earth and my cheese.

We do of course use apples in other recipes too. I like to make an intensely flavoured apple sauce for my pork. We also make a delicious fruity vinaigrette; and I fry chunks of peeled apples in butter and brown sugar to go with duck or chicken livers, lamb's liver or some pâtés and terrines. This is also good with pheasant, quail and goose. To give a little boozy bite, splash the pan with brandy, quickly remove the apples and keep in a warm place.

# Apple and Cinnamon Butter

Serve this cold with game or with smoked duck or chicken. A great dish would be to thin it down with some cream or chicken stock and run it through some warm pappardelle with savoy cabbage and sautéed chicken livers.

Melt the butter until foaming add the cinnamon, cook for one minute and throw in the apples. Cook over a medium heat for five minutes. After three more minutes add the cider, then cook for another 15 minutes. Finally add the sugar until you get a nice sweet/sour balance. Purée with a hand blender. It will be quite runny and a nice cinnamon colour. Allow to cool and store in the fridge for up to two weeks.

**This makes 3 450 g / 1 lb jars**

200 g / 7 oz butter
900 g / 2 lb cooking apples, peeled, cored and diced
2 tablespoons ground cinnamon
120 ml / 4 fl oz dry cider
demerara sugar to taste

# Apple Jelly with Blackberry Cream

Soak the gelatine in cold water. Remove and squeeze out the excess water. Warm the cidona, whisk in the gelatine and then add the apple juice. Pour into ramekins and chill for 24 hours. (This does not necessarily have to be served with blackberries. Out of season feel free to serve it with a caramel or vanilla ice-cream.)

Mix together the blackberries, crème de mûre and caster sugar and allow to stand for a few hours. When you are ready to serve, whip the cream and fold through the blackberry mixture. Arrange the jellies by turning them onto a place. Spoon the blackberry mixture beside the jelly and garnish with some mint.

**Serves 4**

**For the jelly:**
4 leaves gelatine
120 ml / 4 fl oz cidona (If Cidona, a sparkling apple juice, is unavailable substitute with apple juice.)
600 ml / 1 pint apple juice – Crinnaghtaun if possible

**For the blackberry cream:**
2 punnets blackberries
30 ml / 1 fl oz crème de mûres (A blackberry liqueur. If this is unavailable use Cassis blackcurrant liqueur)
pinch caster sugar
300 ml / 1/2 pint cream

## Caramelised Apple Filo Parcels

**Serves 4**

8 small Granny Smiths, peeled and cored

pinch cinnamon

2 tablespoons brown sugar

1 x 400 g / 14 oz packet filo pastry

110 g / 4 oz butter melted

Chop the apples and toss with a pinch of cinnamon and the sugar.

To make four parcels, butter a baking tray and lay out the filo pastry sheets alternately too form a star shape, brushing with melted butter as you go. Repeat for the next three. You will probably have a little of the filo pastry left over.

Place the apple mixture in the centre, bring up the edges and pinch to form a parcel. Don't worry if they do not look perfect, in fact the rougher looking the better. Brush the parcels liberally with melted butter and place in a preheated oven 180°C/Gas 4 for 15–20 minutes until golden brown. Halfway during the cooking, remove the baking tray and sift a little icing sugar over the parcels. Finish cooking and allow to cool a little. Serve with vanilla or caramel ice-cream with a drizzle of maple syrup.

## Apple and Lemon Vinaigrette

**This makes about 600 ml / 1 pint**

150 g / 5 oz caster sugar

juice of one large lemon

120 ml / 4 fl oz white wine vinegar

1 teaspoon Coleman's mustard powder or 1 tablespoon
    Coleman's English Mustard

300 ml / ¹/₂ pint peanut or sunflower oil

120 ml / 4 fl oz olive oil

120 ml / 4 fl oz Crinnaghtaun apple juice or the best
    apple juice you can get

black pepper

This apple and lemon vinaigrette is extremely versatile. Primarily used as a dressing for leaves, I also fold it through warm new potatoes with celery leaves and chopped shallots to go with smoked chicken or duck. I marinate little goats cheeses in this too and they are delicious spooned over leaves with roasted peppers. Warm it gently, add a touch of cream and chopped chives and it becomes a sauce for poached fish.

Boil the sugar, lemon juice and white wine vinegar until the sugar has dissolved. Do not reduce. Remove from the heat. Whisk in the mustard powder, oils and apple juice. Season with plenty of black pepper. It will keep in your fridge for three to four weeks.

## Apple Compôte

Dissolve the sugar in the butter. Add the apple and cloves. Simmer until apples are cooked and allow to cool.

4 Granny Smith apples, diced finely
75g / 3 oz butter
150 g / 5 oz brown sugar
2 cloves

## Apple Doughnuts

These are not doughnuts in the classical sense but an apple compôte that is sandwiched between two slices of bread dipped in batter and fried.

Butter the bread. Place the apple compôte in the middle. Sandwich the bread together with another slice and cut into 7 cm rounds (with a scone cutter). To make the batter, whisk the flour, 25 g of sugar and the cider together. Dip the bread rounds into the batter and deep fry at 180°C until golden brown. Remove and dip in the remaining sugar mixed with the cinnamon.

**Serves 4**

8 slices white bread
50 g / 2 oz butter (soft)
110 g / 4 oz self-raising flour
110g / 4 oz caster sugar
150 ml / ¼ pint dry cider
150 g / 5 oz apple compôte
oil for deep frying
generous pinch cinnamon

## Apple and Cinnamon Punch

I had this on Christmas Eve last. You can have it with or without bacardi, it is equally delicious. The recipe comes by way of Julia Keane, the maker of Crinnaghtaun Apple Juice, the best apple juice I know.

Warm these together until the sugar has dissolved and the spices have time to infuse. Do not boil. Pour into glasses with a dash of bacardi if you like and sip away.

**Serves 4 – 6**

750 ml / 1 ¼ pint apple Juice (the best you can find)
2 tablespoons demerara sugar
2 teaspoons cinnamon (optional)
10 cloves
bacardi to taste

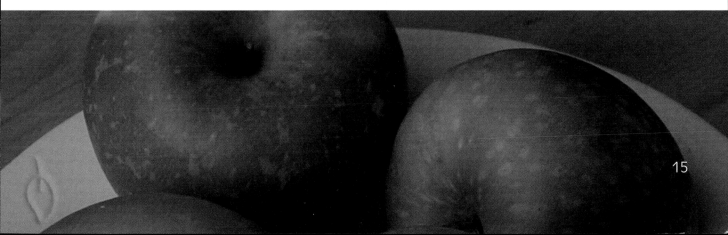

# Asparagus has a very delicate flavour and cannot be bullied. The season for Irish asparagus is short, so make the most of it.

The bottom line with asparagus is don't muck about with it. The thicker stuff is best. It has more flavour. Trim off the brown woody stalk and with a peeler take off the rest, starting a couple of inches from the tip down towards the base. Speed peelers are the ones with flexible blades. They generally take off less than fixed peelers. This is crucial with asparagus because if you peel off too much, you are left with nothing. Lay the asparagus on a chopping board. Be gentle and take care not to press too hard, turning the asparagus with your free hand. The result should be nice and rounded, just as nature intended.

Cook these in boiling salted water. The tips are extremely fragile and will disintegrate with too much cooking so test with a small knife every thirty seconds or so. When the knife meets little resistance in the stem, put them into iced water. Tongs are good for this job.

Now, in the past I have served asparagus with my tomato and avocado salsa and parma ham. At the moment, we have it on the menu gratinated with crayfish and bearnaise sauce (see eggs), but my favourite way to serve it is with Parmesan fritters, rocket and roasted tomatoes, maybe dressed with some balsamic vinegar and olive oil.

Asparagus has a very delicate flavour and cannot be bullied. The season for Irish asparagus is short, so make the most of it. If you are serving it for dinner, cook and cool it as before and heat it up in a pan with a little butter just before serving. This allows you to control the cooking. Here are some suggestions with this basic method.

Melted butter, lemon juice, cracked black pepper and Maldon sea salt cannot be beaten. For those of you who fancy the challenge of a hollandaise, fold a little whipped cream into it and there you have what's called a sauce mousseline. You could either gratinate this under the grill or leave it alone. Either way it's delicious. It's lovely with boiled ham cut into thick slices with new potatoes and mayonnaise; or with poached salmon, boiled eggs and capers. Try it served with chopped eggs, toasted bread crumbs, parsley, paprika and melted butter (à la Polonaise), or scrolled in super fresh sliced bread, the crusts taken off and buttered very lightly. This is very elegant finger food.

## Asparagus with Ham Hock, Soft-Boiled Eggs and Mayonnaise

One of my favourite cuts of meat is the hock of ham: sticky, unctuous and bursting with flavour. All you need are some soft-boiled eggs and maybe some freshly boiled potatoes to make a perfect tea. A large dollop of mayonnaise, homemade if you can but buy it if you don't have the time or the inclination.

Peel off the fat and prize the meat from the bone with a spoon for best results. There should be rough lumps, not stringy bits. Arrange all the ingredients on 4 plates and serve.

Serves 4 although there will be some ham hock left over for sandwiches.

2 ham hocks – boiled for 2 hours or so or until tender and allowed to cool
1 bunch asparagus – peeled, trimmed, cooked and refreshed under cold water
1 or 2 soft-boiled eggs per person – boiled for 5 minutes, then peeled
mayonnaise
boiled potatoes
salt and pepper
dollop of English mustard

## Asparagus with a Fondue of Crozier Blue

Crozier blue is a lovely Irish sheep's cheese, not so strong it overpowers the asparagus, complementing it just right. This is a great starter for a dinner party. It couldn't be simpler. Your ramekins can be prepared hours earlier, only to be stuck in the microwave when your guests are seated. Serve with a little bread if you want but dipping the asparagus into the fondue could be quite enough.

Mix the cheese, wine, cream, chives, salt and pepper and divide between 4 ramekins.

Turn your cooked asparagus in the hazelnut or olive oil. Arrange it on plates. When serving, microwave the ramekins on high for 90 seconds. Remove, stir and microwave again for 30 seconds until hot and bubbly.

Serves 4

225 g / 8 oz Crozier blue (or your favourite cheese – not too strong)
90 ml / 3 fl oz sweet wine
90 ml / 3 fl oz cream
1 large pinch chopped chives
milled black pepper
salt
1 bunch Asparagus, peeled, trimmed, blanched, refreshed under cold water and drained
1 tablespoon hazelnut oil or olive oil

# Asparagus and Parma Ham Rolls with Sauce Gribiche

**Serves 4**

8 slices super fresh wholegrain bread
butter for spreading
4 generous slices Parma ham
8 large cooked asparagus spears

Cut the crusts off the bread and butter them. Lay the ham on top, taking care not to go over the edges. Place one asparagus spear in the centre of each slice, allowing the tips to protrude, then roll tightly. Skewer with some cocktail sticks, two should do, and refrigerate for 30 minutes while you make your sauce. Divide the sauce, remove the sticks from the bread and place on the sauce gribiche.

## For the Sauce Gribiche

2 hard-boiled eggs, shelled
the same weight each of capers and gherkins chopped
$1/2$ tablespoon chopped tarragon
$1^1/2$ tablespoons chopped parsley
2 generous tablespoons olive oil.

Weigh the eggs out of their shells and then measure out the same weight of both capers and gherkins.
Separate the yolks from the whites, sieve the yolks and finely chop the whites
Chop the capers and gherkins. Mix together in a bowl. Add the fresh chopped herbs to the mixture and pour in the olive oil, mixing just to bind. You might need another drop of olive oil but the texture should be a paste, not runny.
This sauce gribiche is also lovely with salmon.

# Warm Asparagus with Smoked Chicken

**Serves 4**

1 bunch of asparagus, trimmed and peeled
1 breast smoked chicken, thinly sliced
4 tablespoons tomato and avocado salsa (see Avocados)

Assembling snazzy dishes in a restaurant can just be a case of assembling a few basic preparations that we always have around. This dish came about when our veg man brought us some beautiful asparagus. I looked around the fridge. We had some salsa. The horseradish cream was simple and the smoked chicken was there. It was just a matter of putting them together.

## For the horseradish cream

90 ml / 3 fl oz lightly whipped cream
1 teaspoon creamed horseradish (mixed together)
milled black pepper

Cook the asparagus in boiling salted water until soft. Don't let them go too far or the tips will disintegrate. Drain and divide between 4 warm plates. Divide the smoked chicken. Spoon over the salsa and drizzle over the horseradish cream.
To finish, sprinkle with sea salt and milled pepper.

warm asparagus with smoked chicken

# I got so many hard avocados thrown at me in Nicos, I should have worn a helmet. I know about avocados. Be gentle with them. They bruise easily.

I got so many hard avocados thrown at me in Nicos, I should have worn a helmet. I know about avocados. Be gentle with them. They bruise easily. To test an avocado don't squash it, just apply some gentle pressure to the thin end. If there is some give, it's ripe. Squeeze a little lime or lemon juice over it to stop it discolouring, not too much as it easily overpowers the delicate taste of the avocado. Peel it at the last possible minute and season it well. We all know that avocados are beautiful with prawns, real prawns that is, not the horrible frozen rubber variety. Same for crab, and they are a natural partner for trout, smoked trout, parma ham or smoked chicken.

The following recipe is hugely useful. I serve it with tomato and pepper soup, over scallops and calamari. Try it with seared salmon, spoon it over mussel and saffron risotto or grilled prawns with crème fraîche. It's fresh, and zingy, colourful and it envigorates any dish. Try it as a dip with tortilla chips for your Saturday night TV viewing. This is a staple in my kitchen provided that tomatoes are in season.

## Tomato and Avocado Salsa

Place all the ingredients in a bowl. Mix gently so as not to break up the avocado pieces. Leave for two hours before serving, the flavours will get better. This will keep for 2 days in the fridge, the lemon and lime keeping the avocado bright.

**Serves 4**

4 ripe plum or vine tomatoes, deseeded and diced
1 large avocado, diced
1 small red onion, diced
1 clove garlic, finely chopped
60 ml / 2 fl oz good olive oil
squeeze lemon juice
60 ml / 2 fl oz lime cordial
Half bunch coriander, stalks and all, roughly chopped
Salt and pepper to taste

## Guacamole Cream

I use this primarily with crab during the summer. We chefs have all sorts of moulds to make things look special: darioles, tians, ramekins and the like. However, they never make anything taste nicer so I really wouldn't worry about them. A dollop of this with some crab meat, garlic bread and good tomatoes would impress me just as much. The ripeness of the avocados is of paramount importance. If they are not right don't bother making this.

If you prefer a chunky effect just fold in some chopped red onion, more avocado and some tomato.

Put all the ingredients in a food processor and blend until completely smooth. Refrigerate with clingfilm placed across the surface of the purée to stop it oxidizing.

**Serves 4**

2 ripe avocados
2 tablespoons crème fraîche
1 teaspoon chilli sauce
salt
juice of 1 lime
fresh coriander (optional)

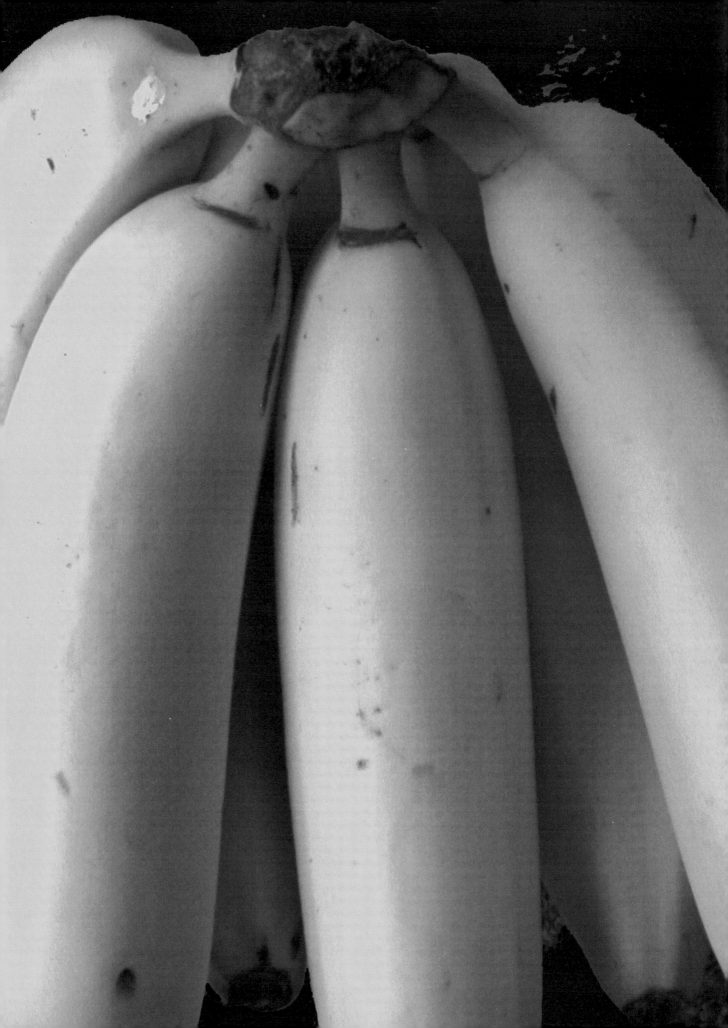

# Take the banana fritters of the Chinese variety. Who hasn't crunched through them to discover fiery hot **banana** burning your tongue? At times, I have been half tempted to submerge myself in the fish tank, head–first ...

There were always bananas hanging around in varying degrees of ripeness in Tommy Powers, our local bar/grocer. I remember buying tobacco for my father, eyeing up the old boys leaving the shopping list with the girl at the counter to put in a box ready for their departure, nicely merry after a couple of large bottles and drops of whiskey. They talk about millennium men! These boys were doing the shopping decades ago and not one bit of credit did they get for it.

At school, the country lads would always have an auld banana sandwich, sprinkled with icing sugar. The smell of ripe bananas permeated the classroom so much it smelt like a veg shop. Not very conducive to learning Portia's lines from *The Merchant of Venice*, a part I aspired to in the school play but I was relegated to the background as a comely wench.

Around that time I remember a dish called Chicken Maryland: breadcrumbed chicken with deep fried bananas and rashers of bacon. Deep-fried bananas have their place but there would have to be money involved for me to eat them with chicken! Take the banana fritters of the Chinese variety. Who hasn't crunched through them to discover fiery hot banana burning your tongue? At times, I have been half tempted to submerge myself in the fish tank, head–first to cool myself down. Another dessert which it seems you only see in Chinese restaurants these days is banana splits. Layers of banana, cream, strawberry and chocolate sauce. I am thinking of reworking that classic in a contemporary manner to serve in the restaurant during the summer.

These days I serve banana fritters without

the crispy sugar coating but with coconut ice-cream and a hot rum syrup. The banana's best buddy is caramel and a variation on the theme would be butterscotch or fudge, all of the above we serve in the restaurant from time to time. A fudge and yoghurt ice-cream with caramelised bananas goes down well, the yoghurt lightening the heaviness of the fudge; and another favourite is banoffi ice-cream: caramelised chunks of banana and buttery biscuit folded through a toffee ice-cream. This gives a really chunky result reminiscent of Ben and Jerry's Chunky Monkey without the nuts.

## Banoffi Ice-cream

### Serves 8

1 vanilla pod
600 ml / 1 pint full fat milk
600 ml / 1 pint cream
175 g / 6 oz caster sugar
10 egg yolks
1 tin sweetened condensed milk, simmered unopened
    for 3 hours and allowed to cool

### For the caramel

25 g / 1 oz butter
75 g / 3 oz caster sugar
4 bananas, sliced
110 g / 4 oz digestive biscuits, crushed

Split the vanilla pod and scrape the seeds into a pan with the milk and cream. You can leave the pod itself in the mixture but remember to take it out before putting the custard into the ice-cream machine. Boil the milk and cream. Whisk the sugar and eggs together. Pour the milk and cream mixture over the eggs. Put on a very low heat, stirring all the time until thick. While the mixture is still warm add in the tin of condensed milk which should have turned into fudgey toffee. Pour the mixture into an ice-cream machine and churn for 45 to 50 minutes. This varies from machine to machine. Meanwhile, in a pan place 25 g butter and 75 g sugar. Bring to the caramel stage. Pour over the sliced bananas and allow to cool.

The ice-cream is ready when it is very thick and you will be able to see that it is quite frozen. At the end, fold in 110 g roughly crushed digestive biscuits and the cooled caramel bananas. Transfer into a container and place in the freezer.

If you don't have an ice-cream machine, this is a little more difficult but possible. Place the custard into a roomy container and put in the freezer. Every 10–15 minutes or so, whisk it so that large ice crystals don't form. If you have children, this is a great job for them. When semi-set, fold in the bananas and biscuits as above.

# Banana Compôte

A lot of success in cooking is having a repertoire of little recipes that you can call on to make a complete dish. This is one, a simple Banana Compôte. This is lovely served warm with some vanilla or caramel ice-cream or if you have rum in the compôte a creamy coconut ice-cream would be fantastic. Present this well and you have dessert any restaurant could serve.

In a large saucepan dissolve the sugar with the water over a low heat and bring to the boil. Wash down the inside of the pan with a pastry brush dipped in cold water to prevent crystals forming. Cook the sugar until it turns a deep amber colour. Take off the heat and carefully whisk in the cream bit by bit. At this point add the dark rum and the bananas and allow to cool. If you like, do this a day in advance. Just warm it up in a pan or the microwave when you want it.

**Serves 4**

**For the caramel sauce**
75 g / 3 oz caster sugar
90 ml / 3 fl oz water

30 ml / 1 fl oz cream
2 teaspoons dark rum (optional)
3 bananas, diced into 1 cm cubes

# Glazed Bananas

We serve these with a spoonful of vanilla cream and a drizzle of maple syrup on warm banana gingerbread. Choose very ripe bananas and run them through the oven for a couple of minutes once they have been caramelised. We use a gas gun but you can grill them. They are good on their own with some ice-cream, maple syrup and a few toasted pecans.
Peel the bananas, cut them in half lengthways and half them again.
Cover the cut side of the bananas with the sugar and slowly caramelise with the gun or glaze under the grill until all the sugar has turned to caramel.

**Serves 4**

4 ripe bananas
2 tablespoons demerara sugar

## Banana Gingerbread

(This makes one 900 g / 2 lb loaf tin.) **Serves 8**

225 g / 8 oz self-raising flour
1 teaspoon ground ginger
110 g / 4 oz treacle
110 g / 4 oz butter
110 g / 4 oz demerara sugar
175 g / 6 oz golden syrup
1 egg
3 ripe bananas

This is a combination of bananabread and gingerbread. It freezes superbly. It's great for an afternoon tea and it's light enough to be used as a dessert, which we do in the restaurant.

Preheat the oven to 160°C/Gas 2$\frac{1}{2}$. Mix the flour and ginger in a bowl. Melt together the treacle, butter, sugar and golden syrup. Beat the egg and mash the bananas well. Mix all the ingredients in a bowl.

Bake for 45 minutes to 1 hour. Leave to rest for 10 minutes in the tin before turning out on a wire tray.

This is delicious with some whipped cream and a dash of maple syrup. If you want to go a little further, caramelise some bananas, as in the previous recipe, and sprinkle with sesame seeds.

To reheat, slice and place in the microwave for a very short time: a few seconds should do it.

The smell of ripe bananas permeated the classroom so much it smelt like a veg shop. Not very conducive to learning Portia's lines from *The Merchant of Venice*, a part I aspired to in the school play but I was relegated to the background as a comely wench.

warm banana gingerbread with maple syrup and glazed bananas

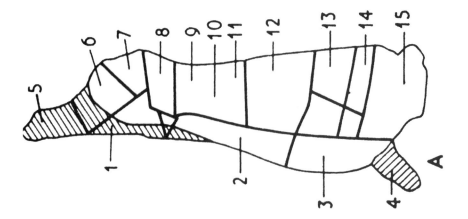

Why is it that fillet and sirloin steak are the only cuts of beef that the general public seems interested in eating? As much as I enjoy a good steak, I get far more pleasure in both cooking and eating other much less popular cuts. They take a little more work but if you enjoy cooking, that can be part of the pleasure. You can't beat an osso bucco of beef. A piece of shin, cut across the bone, braised with vegetables and red wine and served with honey roast carrots, mash, and its own juices, reduced to a sauce consistency.

I was recently asked to do a cookery demonstration for the West Waterford Good Food Tree, a worthy grouping of food producers, restaurants and guesthouses in the west Waterford region who are endeavouring to raise the standard of food in the area and in the process encourage tourism. I decided to be controversial and do a number of dishes featuring ox cheek. Ox cheek is usually used for daube of beef, a classical French beef stew that is garnished with button mushrooms, onions and lardons of bacon, served with either potato purée or buttered noodles.

The search for this cut of beef began a week or so in advance. Many butchers could not procure it for me as it is generally considered unsellable in one piece by the meat factories and usually ground down to mince for burgers. I finally managed to get some and tried my daube and was blown away by the result. Meltingly delicious and as rich as Bill Gates. Now I can rescue as much as I want from the blades of the mincer, providing I give plenty of notice to my butcher.

So on Monday morning last I was on a stage, brandishing a 14oz piece of jaw meat being scrutinised by 100 or more pairs of sceptical eyes. After an hour or so of awkward stage-craft I produced the following three dishes. I know I didn't convince everyone, since the work involved might put off anyone who is not a keen cook, but I can guarantee that the results are very satisfying.

As I drove away from the beautiful Nire Valley I felt that in my own way I had stood up for the much maligned, mistreated and neglected fellow, the ox cheek.

# The search for this cut of beef began a week or so in advance ... The result ... meltingly delicious and as rich as Bill Gates.

## Braised Ox Cheek

Trim all the sinew from the ox cheeks, dust with flour and fry in hot oil turning periodically until brown all over. Remove from the heat and reserve.

Chop the onion, celery and carrot finely and cook in the butter in a large pan. Add the flour and cook until golden brown, then add the red wine and stir over moderate flame until no lumps are present. Add the stock, herbs and peppercorns. Bring to a simmer making sure the flour does not stick to the bottom of the pan. Place the meat in the liquid, top up with water to cover if neccessary, and cook over very low heat for approx. 1¹/₂–2 hours until meat is very tender.

When cooked strain the stock, remove the meat and reduce the stock by half, leave to cool and place the meat back in the stock and refrigerate.

This is the basis for the next three dishes.

**Serves 4**

4 ox cheeks approx / 400 g / 14 oz untrimmed
¹/₂ bottle of red wine
2.4 l / 4 pints light chicken stock (cubes will do)
1 medium onion
¹/₃ head of celery
4 carrots
4 rashers smoked bacon
4 cloves of garlic
110 g / 4 oz butter
75 g / 3 oz flour
75 g / 3 oz flour for dusting
90 ml / 3 fl oz oil for frying
4 bay leaves
1 sprig thyme
1 pinch black peppercorns

# Parsley Crusted Daube of Beef with Spiced Pepper, Red Bean & Tomato Stew

Serves 4

### Herb Bread Crumbs

110 g / 4 oz breadcrumbs

50 g / 2 oz parsley

50 g / 2 oz assorted herbs, thyme/sage

1 clove of garlic, crushed

25 g / 1 oz melted butter

### Pepper Stew

4 ox cheeks

25 g / 1 oz creamed horseradish

1 large onion, finely sliced

2 red peppers, finely sliced

50 g / 2 oz butter

2 cloves of garlic, finely chopped

1 chopped red chilli

1 tin chopped plum tomatoes

$1/2$ chicken stock cube, crumbled

1 pinch cumin

1 pinch of paprika

1 tin of kidney beans drained

salt and pepper

Bar the butter, put all the ingredients for the crumbs into a food processor and blend until an even texture and a deep green colour.

Remove ox cheeks from the cooking liquor. Brush with horseradish cream, smother with herb breadcrumbs and drizzle with the melted butter. Reserve.

### Pepper Stew

Cook the onion and peppers in the butter until soft and golden, add the chopped garlic, chilli and cumin cook for 2 more minutes before adding the tinned tomatoes, stock cube, kidney beans and paprika. Cook slowly for $1/2$ hour over a low heat. Season and reserve. The end result should be syrupy and fairly solid.

### Assembly

Place ox cheeks on a roasting tray in a moderate oven until golden brown and crispy (about 15 minutes), serve on top of the pepper stew. I would serve this with mashed potatoes.

# Warm Salad of Ox Cheek, Red Onion, Radish and Butterleaf Lettuce

Thinly slice the ox cheeks at a 45-degree angle and assemble, overlapping each other in order to cover the entire plate similar to a carpaccio.

Whip up the cream into a soft mound and fold in the creamed horseradish, salt and pepper and reserve.

Whisk the olive oil, sherry vinegar, garlic, salt and pepper and reserve.

### Assembly

Place the sliced ox cheeks on plates in the oven for 2 minutes at a moderate heat, all you want to do is warm them as they are already cooked.

When warm, spread a thin layer of horseradish cream over the meat. Toss the butterleaf lettuce in the dressing. Place in the middle of the plate and scatter the assorted vegetables around the outside of the plate. Place half a boiled egg on the top of the lettuce and serve.

Serves 4

2 ox cheeks
90 ml / 3 fl oz cream
25 g / 1 oz commercial creamed horseradish
30 ml / 1 fl oz olive oil
dash of sherry vinegar
clove of garlic crushed
1 head butterleaf lettuce
6 radishes thinly sliced
1/4 cucumber cut into thin batons
1 red onion, sliced thinly into rings
1 tablespoon capers
flat leaf parsley chopped
2 boiled eggs, cooked for 8 minutes from boil

# Beetroot

I used to hate beetroot. One mouthful of that vinegary jarred stuff put me off it for a good ten years. Only a visit to Roscoff in the mid-1990s converted me to its possibilities. It was more like a gentle caress than a slap in the face. Then last year I ate a salad of roasted baby beets with herb crème fraîche in Charlie Trotters, Chicago (am I name dropping or what?). Not only was it delicious but it felt so healthy while I was eating it I thought I was in a negative calorie situation. It's a pity I couldn't be in that place more often! So now I use it quite a lot, and although I'll never be caught settling down to watch a video with a bowl of them, let's say we have come to an understanding. For starters, you have to love the colour. Boil them if you like, taking care not to trim off too much either end but for best results, scrub them, leave them in their skins, wrap them in foil and bake them in a moderate oven for at least 2 hours. This concentrates the colour and flavour and you can keep them in the fridge for 2-3 days.

It can be difficult to get produce in the country and I feel that when cooking requires such careful planning it can sometimes take the spontaneity out of it. So when I got some beautiful organic beetroot recently, I went on a blitz. I blended creamy St Maure goat's cheese with olive oil and Crinnaghtaun apple juice to make a dressing akin in consistency to Caesar dressing. I used this to coat some little gems and piled it on top of some thinly sliced beetroot scattered with roasted walnuts. It was a best-seller. I also diced the beets and dropped them into brown sauce with some port and all-spice for pheasant, and mixed them with walnut oil, capers, parsley and a splash of honey for a salsa for perch. All of the above in one week. It was a close call whether they made an appearance on the dessert menu! Stop chef, that's a bridge too far.

## Pickled Beetroot with Honey

This is a homemade version of the vinegary jarred stuff I was talking about. Infinitely superior and perfect for a salad on summer days.

Mix all ingredients together in a bowl. This will keep for 3–4 days in fridge. Lovely with a dollop of crème fraîche on top.

Serves 4–6

4 beetroot, oven-cooked as before, peeled and cut into 1 cm dice
30 ml /1 fl oz olive oil
30 ml / 1 fl oz sunflower oil
30 ml / 1 fl oz red wine vinegar
1 tablespoon capers
Juice of 1 orange
1 tablespoon honey

## ... not only delicious but so healthy ... I thought I was in a negative calorie situation.

## Smoked Duck with Beetroot Fritters and Celery Leaf Yoghurt

If you didn't fancy making a batter for this, no problem. The dish will work without it.

Mix the flour and salt into the cider until you have a smooth thick batter. Preheat a deep pan of oil to 180°C./Gas 4 Season the beetroot wedges and dust with flour. Coat with batter. Drop into the hot oil and fry for a few minutes until crisp and golden. Remove and salt lightly.
Divide your duck on four plates. Divide your fritters. Mix celery leaves into yoghurt and spoon on the side.

**Serves 4**

450 g / 1 lb self-raising flour
salt
300 ml / 1/2 pint cider
oil for deep frying
12 x 2 cm cooked beetroot wedges
1 smoked duck breast, thinly sliced
1 bunch chopped celery leaves
6 tablespoons thick natural yoghurt
salt and pepper

## Roasted Beetroot with Goat's Cheese Mousse and Pickled Cucumber

Peel the beetroot. It helps if you use some kitchen towel or rubber gloves. The skin will come off without a knife. Slice as thinly as you can into perfect circles. If you have a mandolin this is just the job. Place the beetroot into a bowl, add the hazelnut or olive oil and season. Arrange the beetroot on 4 plates in an over-lapping circle leaving a well in the centre of the plate. Place the cucumber on top of the beetroot in a similar fashion and pipe the goat's cheese mousse into the centre forming a peak. Drizzle the remaining hazelnut oil around the beetroot and serve with garlic crumbs on the side. (see Garlic)

This is an ultra simple combination of fresh crisp vegetables, vibrantly colourful beetroot and creamy goat's cheese. I would serve this with just some garlic bread.

**Serves 4**

2 medium beetroot – scrubbed, wrapped in foil and roasted in a slow oven for 1 to 2 hours. They are done when you can stick a knife or skewer in to them and meet no resistance. I know 2 beetroot look silly all on their own for that long in an oven so you could always do more. They will keep for 2–3 days in the fridge.
2 tablespoons hazelnut oil or olive oil
goat's cheese mousse (see Garlic)
pickled cucumber (see Cucumber)

... **blackberries** are different. I love 'em. Everything about them. The colour, shape, taste, even the pips ... I've gone around with a big purple mouth in blackberry season, looking like a child that's eaten too many wine gums ...

Nothing makes me appreciate living in the country more than watching the blackberries getting plumper on the hedgerows. Life is so hectic now, it's hard to stop for a moment and take stock of things. Boys fishing lazily from Twomile Bridge, their bikes flung haphazardly into the ditch. The abundant fuchsia which creates a crimson corridor to our house. These are the afternoons I make time to pick blackberries before the birds get them. The dog, cat and kitten follow me up the path, chasing the butterflies. I'm so glad I left those Dublin traffic jams behind.

I'm not really a fruit person. I wish I were. Gooey calorific desserts are far more my thing but blackberries are different. I love 'em. Everything about them. The colour, shape, taste, even the pips don't bother me. I've gone around with a big purple mouth in blackberry season, looking like a child that's eaten too many wine gums. Of course nobody would tell me, letting me make a fool of myself in front of customers.

There's a wonderful liqueur in the same vein as cassis only made from wild blackberries called crème de mûre. Good off-licences should stock it or at least be able to order it for you. It is fantastic with chilled Beaujolais made in the same way as a kir: a little drop in your glass and the red wine poured on top. It's like sipping sheer heaven and it's called a Cardinale. This same nectar drizzled over blackberries with a little caster sugar makes this fruit altogether more elegant. My favourite way to eat blackberries is with fluffy cream into which some lemon curd has been folded. Crumble some meringue on top and you have one of the most delicious desserts imaginable. At the restaurant, we get a little flashy with the same combination by alternating little meringue discs with lemon curd cream and blackberries in the middle. I like taking classics apart and putting them together in a different format. A blackberry trifle would become blackberry jelly with a little jam and cream sponge and a compôte of fruit. Now you might say, why bother go to that trouble but I do think it's important to give people something they wouldn't ordinarily make at home.

We all know that apples have a particular affinity with blackberries but with the exception of the old crumble or Eve's pudding I don't mix them that much. I'm too fond of the blackberry flavour itself but I do realise that they can be expensive to buy in large quantities or extremely time consuming to pick, even if you have the inclination to do so. So you must pardon me for getting all country life on you. It's just that sometimes I need to be reminded that the simple things are the best.

## Blackberry Jelly

Serves 4–6

500 g / little over 1 lb blackberries
225 g / 8 oz sugar
300 ml / ½ pint water
6 leaves gelatine
120 ml / 4 fl oz port
2 tablespoons crème de mûre or homemade blackberry liqueur.

Boil the blackberries, sugar and water together for 10 minutes. Blitz with a hand blender and place in a fine mesh sieve with a clean teatowel lining it over a basin. This should take approximately 2 to 3 hours to drain completely. If it's not ready, give a gentle squeeze to the teatowel (not too much as it may go cloudy). Discard the pulp.

Soak the gelatine in a couple of spoonfuls of cold water until completely soft. Heat the port without boiling and whisk in the gelatine. Remove from the heat. Stir the port and crème de mûre into the blackberry juice. Pour everything either into individual moulds or one large pudding basin. Allow to set overnight in the fridge.

To turn out, immerse briefly in hot water and serve with some fresh berries and good vanilla ice-cream.

## Blackberry and Apple Eve's pudding

Peel, core and slice the apples. Add the sugar and water and cook to a fairly firm purée. Pass through a sieve and spread on a large buttered baking dish. Scatter the blackberries over the apple purée.

Place the butter and sugar in a bowl and cream until light and creamy in colour. Add the eggs and beat well. Sieve the flour, baking powder and salt and fold into the creamed mixture, together with the milk.

Spread a layer of the mixture evenly over the apple and blackberries.

Place in the oven at 190°C/Gas 5 and bake for 35-40 minutes.

Serve hot with custard or whipped cream.

Serves 6–8

**For the apple purée:**
1 kg / 2.2 lb apples
250 g / 9 oz sugar
120 ml / 4 fl oz water

275 g / 10 oz blackberries

**For the pudding mixture:**
150 g /5 oz butter
150 g / 5 oz sugar
3 eggs beaten
225 g / 8 oz flour
1 heaped teaspoon baking powder
pinch salt
30 ml / 1 fl oz milk

## Blackberry Liqueur

This is beautiful for deserts or in white wine or champagne.

Crush the blackberries slightly in a large bowl. Add all the ingredients and let the fruit macerate, covered for at least 6 weeks in a cool place (maybe in the garage). Strain the liquid through a sieve lined with a double layer of muslin over a bowl. Transfer into bottles.

If you can't get crème de mûre this is an alternative but it is taking slow food very seriously. However, you will have your crème de mûre for next year!

450 g / 1 lb blackberries
1 cinnamon stick
2 cloves
75 g / 3 oz sugar
350 ml / 12 fl oz vodka

I was in love and eager to please so I duly wrapped some **Brussel sprouts** in foil after Christmas dinner in my home to bring down to my future wife whose house was only 15 miles away but totally sproutless. So like that hero, the Cadbury's Milk Tray man, I drove like a maniac down frosty country roads, my eyes streaming from eau du sprout, to deliver the package to my lady.

'Bring some sprouts down with you, Mam doesn't allow them into the house because of the smell.' This was Christmas morning some years back. I was in love and eager to please so I duly wrapped some sprouts in foil after Christmas dinner in my home to bring down to my future wife whose house was only 15 miles away but totally sproutless. So like that hero, the Cadbury's Milk Tray man, I drove like a maniac down frosty country roads, my eyes streaming from eau du sprout, to deliver the package to my lady. Now there's an economical and original gift for you. No 'Happy Christmas' for me just 'where are they?' while simultaneously rifling my pockets for sprouts to be quickly smothered in gravy, in lieu of dessert. That's Brussels sprouts. You either love them or loathe them. It's simple to avoid that dead, foul smell that lingers around every inch of your house leaving you no choice but to open windows and shiver to get rid of the smell before the visitors start to call.

I recently got an e-mail that tells me that by adding some bay leaves to the water while cooking sprouts or cabbage, you can eliminate the stinky smell around the house.

Follow one rule. DON'T OVER COOK THEM. There is a very fine line here between intensely flavoured little cabbagey balls or a stinky mush, and a couple of minutes on the wrong side can make the difference.

I'm going to come clean here. I have been known to include Brussels sprouts in a turkey and stuffing sandwich, lathered with cranberry sauce. Now I know this will never become a best-seller in sandwich bars worldwide but if you like sprouts, you'll love it. Dunk it into the cooking juices of the turkey and away you go.

For Christmas Day, peel them as usual. Slice them lengthways four or five times. Place into a pot with a few knobs of butter and cover with chicken stock, (bouillon will do). Add salt and pepper. Cover with a butter wrapper or tin foil, and cook till the liquid is absorbed ensuring all the flavour stays in the pot and not down the sink. If not quite cooked, you can always add a little more liquid.

If you have an empty nest, how about this alternative Christmas dinner for two. It combines all the ingredients of a traditional Christmas lunch with a fraction of the trouble. Ask your butcher for some turkey escalopes. Place the escalopes between two sheets of cling and bash it even thinner with a meat mallet or rolling pin. Beat some eggs, add some grated lemon zest, sage, salt and pepper and some grated Parmesan or even better, Gabriel cheese. Flour the turkey. Brush off any excess flour. Dip in the egg mixture and place in a hot pan foaming with butter. Cook on either side for a couple of minutes until golden brown. Remove, drain on a paper towel and repeat the process. Accompany this with the sprouts and some creamy mashed potatoes strewn with crispy bacon. Of course cranberry sauce is a must.

Brussels sprouts, with their emerald richness and distinctive nutty flavour, would be delicious with linguini, some shredded smoked duck or chicken and toasted chestnuts or walnuts turned in a sage and onion butter. Try them mashed with potato and served with gammon or pork. A soup would not be crazy as long as sprouts play a support part and are not the leading role, such as with potato and horseradish, garnished with crispy black pudding.

So you guys, forget hip and trendy bars and clubs, fumbling for words that you instantly regret saying. Just carry a little foil packet of sprouts with you everywhere over the festive season. Offer them with confidence and panache and see what happens.

## Bubble and Squeak

Quantities vary according to your taste and how many you are feeding.

finely chopped or sliced onion
generous lump of butter
some cooked potatoes (mashed)
some cooked sprouts or cabbage (shredded)
salt and pepper
splash milk

For those who are not aficionados this should be a revelation. The Bubble and Squeak refers to the noise this conglomeration makes in the pan while it is cooking. For me it's a perfect brunch dish when you are a little delicate from the night before. It can be sort of a kitchen sink job, but I like to be a little bit more selective than that. Serve it with bacon or gammon and a fried egg on top.

Fry the onion in butter in a shallow pan. Meanwhile mix the cooked potatoes and sprouts in a bowl. Add the seasonings to taste. Mix well. If it's a little too dry, add the milk. Fry over a high heat pan, mixing as you go along. Cook until crispy brown bits appear. Mix some more then cook again. It should have a crunchy and soft texture at the same time. Serve with fried egg and bacon on top.

## Brussel Sprout and Cheddar Purée

I sometimes serve this with boiled ham and even fervent sprout haters have been known to come around. Sometimes by changing the physical appearance of something it can make people more amenable. Dilute the flavour and you are even another step closer. I also serve this with pork but I usually omit the cheddar.

Cook the sprouts in boiling salted water until soft but still retaining their colour. Drain and transfer them to a food processor and process for 1 minute. Add the cheddar, garlic butter, nutmeg, salt and pepper, honey, a little lemon and the mustard and process until a little chunky.

Note: If you don't have garlic butter, just use butter and a small clove of garlic.

275 g / 10 oz Brussel sprouts
75 g / 3 oz mild cheddar cheese
2 tablespoons of garlic butter (see Garlic)
1 pinch of nutmeg
salt and pepper
1 teaspoon honey
squeeze of lemon
half teaspoon of English mustard

## Creamed Brussel Sprouts with Smoked Bacon

This is just another adaptation of the horseradish béchamel that I use in the cabbage chapter. It is good for pork or chicken and, of course, turkey.

Cook the sprouts in boiling salted water until just soft. Drain and refresh under cold water. Sauté the bacon strips in a little oil until crispy. Strain the oil and tip the bacon into a bowl. Drain the sprouts and add them to the bacon together with the sage. Stir in the horseradish béchamel. If it is too thick add a little chicken stock and heat up when required.

450 g / 1 lb Brussel sprouts, cut into quarters
110 g / 4 oz rindless smoked bacon, cut into thin strips
150 ml / 1/4 pint horseradish béchamel (see cabbage)
1 tablespoon chopped sage or marjoram
1 tablespoon sunflower oil

The emerald green richness of summer cabbage entices me. I love everything about this variety. Red cabbage is a good wintery staple. But I am never too fond of the cannonball-like white, even the cutting of it is annoying. It almost requires a Samurai master's deftness with a sword. The curls and folds of summer cabbage, as pretty as a picture, just need to be washed, de-stalked and shredded. Cook this lightly in a little butter and stock. Add salt and pepper and a little sugar to temper any bitterness and you will have a flavour hit like nothing else.

My formal cheffy training has instilled a sense of form in my cooking. A little package here, a dariole mould there. Shredded cabbage, sautéed in butter with finely sliced onion, carrot and parsnip, all stuffed inside a blanched outer cabbage leaf is an attempt to render your dinner visually beautiful and in theory nothing like you would do at home. I'm well aware that this fiddlyness does not make a good cook. Taste is the thing. In fact, this style with no substance is the rock that a lot of chefs perish on. A hefty slab of hairy bacon, cabbage and steaming spuds is still the stuff of my dreams. A little silky white sauce lubricating the lot, butter oozing from the spuds. You see, you can take your boy from the country but never the country from the boy.

Colcannon is rarely off my menu. Whether it's with crispy confit of duck, shank of lamb, daube of beef, it sits towering over the plate just waiting to be scooped up with an unctuous sauce and meltingly tender meat. Colcannon is a cinch to make and dispense. No pretty pictures here. It's too earthy for that.

Oriental flavours go particularly well with cabbage. They are robust enough to stand up to its own unique flavour. A favourite in the restaurant is Oriental duck broth with noodles, cabbage, ginger and spring onion. When you confit duck legs, it's normal to use the same fat two or three times. A by-product of this is an intense ducky jelly that when simmered with a little water and some flavourings, in this case star anise, soy sauce, coriander, orange and garlic makes an intensely flavoured broth.

I blanch some noodles and shred spring onions, carrots, lots of cabbage, pickled ginger, chillies and beansprouts. Stir-fry the lot in sesame oil. Meanwhile deep fry the confit duck leg. Place the duck leg on top of the noodles and spoon over the broth. Then I scatter some chopped ripe plums, coriander and sesame seeds on top. A crunchy, superbly flavoured but still very light dish.

Here are three cabbage dishes that I am particularly fond of.

Taste is the thing ... style with no substance is the rock that a lot of chefs perish on. A hefty slab of hairy bacon, **cabbage** and steaming spuds is still the stuff of my dreams. A little silky white sauce lubricating the lot.

## Spicy Oriental Cabbage

**Serves 4**

1 large pinch salt

1 head summer cabbage, stalked, shredded very finely, washed and patted dry

60 ml / 2 fl oz sesame oil

1 red chilli pepper sliced (you can use less if you don't like it too hot)

20 g / 3/4 oz fresh root ginger, finely diced

50 ml / 2 fl oz white wine vinegar

25 ml / 1 fl oz sweet sherry

60 g / 2 oz raisins, preferably blonde

30 g / 1 oz pickled ginger, sliced

1/2 tablespoon icing sugar

salt and pepper

This is another recipe from the old days in London. Nico used to serve this with salmon and a plum sauce. It goes beautifully with scallops, lobster, monkfish or duck. The addition of raisins is the key element here. This dish is easy to prepare and keeps for 2-3 days in the fridge.

Sprinkle the salt over the cabbage. Mix in well and leave for 2 hours. This will take the excess liquid from the cabbage resulting in a crispier texture. Rinse well in cold water and pat dry.

Heat up the sesame oil. Then quickly fry the chilli and fresh ginger. Toss in the cabbage and quickly fry for one to two minutes. Add in the white wine vinegar, sherry, raisins and pickled ginger and fry for one more minute. Then add in the icing sugar, allow the liquid to dissolve and the cabbage slightly caramelise. This should take no more than two minutes over a high heat. Season with salt and pepper.

When first prepared at Chez Nico this spicy cabbage was served with pan-seared salmon. Salmon is still the best with it, even served with just a drizzle of dark soy sauce over the salmon, but scallops are also particularly fine. Comfit of duck is a winner carrying on the Chinese tradition.

## Baked Cabbage with Ham and Ardrahan Cheese

Serves 4

half head summer cabbage, stalked, shredded and
      blanched
200 g / 7 oz chunky boiled ham
150 g / 5 oz Ardrahan cheese
1 teaspoon English mustard
120 ml / 4 fl oz cream
black pepper

Whisk the mustard into the cream. Divide the rest of the ingredients into four gratin dishes with the cheese on top. Sprinkle some freshly ground black pepper over each and then pour over the cream.

Bake in a preheated oven 180°C/Gas 4 for 10–15 minutes or until golden brown and creamy. Serve as a starter for four with brown bread or as a supper dish for two with some new boiled potatoes.

## Creamed Cabbage with Smoked Duck and Crumbled Chestnuts

Serves 4 as a starter

For the horseradish béchamel
25 g / 1 oz butter
25 g / 1 oz flour
120 ml / 4 fl oz milk
60 ml / 2 fl oz cream
half tablespoon commercial creamed horseradish
1 pinch nutmeg

1 head summer cabbage, washed, stalked and shredded
1 smoked duck breast
half a packet of vacuum packed chestnuts (approx 50 g
      / 2 oz - if you can't get chestnuts, substitute
      toasted whole almonds)

Melt the butter and add in the flour. Cook for 2-3 minutes over a low heat, then add in your milk, whisking vigorously to a smooth cream. Cook for 10 more minutes. Then add in the cream, horseradish, salt, pepper and nutmeg.

Blanch the cabbage for 2 to 3 minutes, then drain and refresh under cold water. Squeeze out any excess water, then fold in the horseradish béchamel through the cabbage. You may not need all of it. Stop when the cabbage is thoroughly coated but not sloppy. This can be warmed through when you want it. If your duck is not sliced already, slice it as finely as you can, trimming off any excess fat.

Distribute the cabbage amongst four warmed plates. If the sauce seems a bit too thick, thin it down with a little stock beforehand (a stock cube will do if you haven't any stock to hand). Arrange the sliced smoked duck on top. Then crumble the chestnuts on top again. Rustic but extremely tasty.

If you want to use this as a main course, just omit the smoked duck and replace with a duck breast per person.

# Pappardelle with Chicken Livers, Cabbage, Garlic and Sage Butter

Pappardelle goes well with meaty and strong flavours, perfect for chicken livers and just right for winter. You can have your pasta cooked off ahead of time, just reheat in boiling water for one minute, drain and add to the rest of the ingredients at the last minute.

Heat the oil in a frying pan. When very hot, add the chicken livers making sure they are nice and dry. Cook for 2–3 minutes depending if you like them pink or not. Throw in the sage straight away. Add the sherry vinegar. De-glaze the pan, season and scrape into a bowl on the side. Keep warm. Melt the garlic butter in the same pan and allow to foam taking care not to burn. Add the mustard powder and cabbage. Cook for 1 minute, then add the hot pasta and season. Divide into four warm bowls, top with the chicken livers and pan juices, sprinkle over the almonds and serve.

Serves 4

2 tablespoons sunflower oil
275 g /10 oz cleaned chicken livers cut into 1 cm dice
1 generous pinch shredded sage
splash of sherry vinegar
75 g / 3 oz garlic butter (see Garlic)
pinch Colman's English mustard powder
handful shredded and blanched cabbage
450 g / 1 lb dried pappardelle
2 tablespoons toasted almonds
salt and pepper

# Bacon and Cabbage Soup with Mustard Cream

Sweat the onion in the butter in a large pot. Add the potato and cabbage. Cook for another 2 minutes. Add the ham or chicken stock and bay leaves. Bring to the boil and cook as quickly as possible until the potatoes are soft. Liquidise or blend with hand blender. Add ham or bacon. Season and remove the bay leaves. Divide between 4 bowls and spoon the mustard cream on top.

Serves 4–6

This a lovely winter soup generally made when you have leftovers of ham.
1 medium onion, finely diced
110 g / 4 oz butter
2 large potatoes, peeled and diced
450 g / 1 lb savoy or spring cabbage (1 small cabbage)
600 ml / 1 pint ham or chicken stock
175 g / 6 oz cooked ham or bacon
4 bay leaves
salt and pepper

**mustard cream:**
60 ml / 2 fl oz cream, lightly whipped
1 teaspoon English mustard
1 tablespoon chopped chives

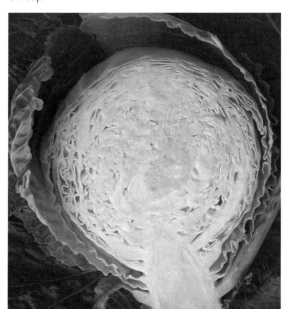

# carrots ... their sweetly caramelised crunch deviously decadent while emitting that 'I'm crunchy so I'm healthy' vibe.

A big dirty carrot will satisfy me any day. My earliest memories of them are mashed with parsnips at Sunday lunch. We all know that one. Honey roasted we are all now familiar with, thanks to our ever broadening palates. When we are so familiar with something we take it for granted and finding new ways with it rarely crosses our minds. Try glazing carrots with sesame oil and brown sugar for an oriental touch to go with chicken, lamb or beef. You can serve them the same way with a swarthy couscous, drizzled with some minted yoghurt, their sweetly caramelised crunch deviously decadent while emitting that 'I'm crunchy so I'm healthy' vibe.

Try a carrot soup with the addition of some unsweetened chestnut purée for an earthy twist and top this with a dollop of crème fraîche.

A crunchy vibrant carrot salad will be made if you peel strips from a carrot and mix with some English mustard, crème fraîche and chives. This I serve with succulent corned beef which I get from McGraths butchers in Lismore. It's also very good with hot or cold ham or gammon or simply as part of a summer salad. I love dippy things so I'll give the recipe for a roast carrot, pumpkin and feta cheese dip which is lovely with little toasts for any soirées you may have coming up. The acidity of the feta cuts through the sweetness of the carrots. One of the most prominent memories I have of carrots is of a sauce I used to make 14 years ago at Chez Nico to go with sweetbreads. The meat was crispy on the outside and soft as butter inside, the aroma rich and heady from many glazings with the best madeira. This, combined with some spinach and the most fabulous sauce made with carrots and Sauternes was one of the most delicious things I have ever eaten. I know people's penchants for offal may have waned with all that's been going on in the last few years but the sauce is to die for. Serve it with a slowly roasted leg of lamb and you'll be everyone's favourite. Alternatively if you just wanted to liven up an ordinary carrot for your Sunday roast, there's a recipe below. I will say though, there is one carrot road I won't go down

again. On one of our Chicago sojourns we were a little ropey from the night before so my sister-in-law took us into a health juice bar where I was persuaded to have a carrot and wheatgrass drink. Well, by Jesus. How it didn't come straight back up again I will never know but I left the juice bar twice as queasy as I went in. Maybe my body rejected something unabashedly healthy , not being used to it and all!

## Carrot Sauce with Sauternes

**Makes approx 600 ml / 1 pint**

450 g / 1 lb carrots
300 ml / ½ pint chicken stock
sprig thyme
1 clove garlic, sliced
salt and pepper
300 ml / ½ pint cream
90 ml / 3 fl oz Sauternes

If you cannot find Sauternes use another sweet wine or cider.

Dice the carrots and place in a pan with the stock, thyme, garlic, salt and pepper. Simmer for one hour. Remove the thyme and add the cream. Return to a low heat and cook very slowly (taking care not to allow the sauce to stick to the bottom as it would burn and taint the flavour) for another 20 minutes. Add the sweet wine and cook for another five minutes. Liquidise well and serve.

## Carrot, Raisin and Mustard Salad

**Serves 4 as a side salad**

2 large carrots, washed and peeled
2 tablespoons crème fraîche
1 teaspoon English mustard
dessertspoon raisins
pinch finely chopped chives
a little salt and pepper

This is a refreshing crunchy salad I serve with corned beef to compliment the unctuous meat with some crunch. It would be good with ham or chicken or with a cold meat platter.

Soak the raisins in some boiling water and allow to plump up, then strain after half an hour or so.
Peel the carrots into strips, top to bottom with a veg peeler. Into a bowl, add the rest of the ingredients and mix well. This will keep in the fridge for two days.

## Roast Carrot, Pumpkin and Feta Purée

This can be served cold as a dip or warm as an accompaniment, particularly with lamb.

Preheat the oven to 180°C/Gas 4. Place the prepared vegetables and garlic cloves into a roasting pan. Sprinkle over the spices and drizzle over the olive oil and sugar. Roast for 30 minutes or until the vegetables are soft and caramelised. Remove to cool. Once cold, purée the vegetables and oil in a processor with the feta cheese. Season to taste with salt and pepper.

**Serves 4**

1/4 small pumpkin, peeled and cubed
2 large carrots, peeled and cubed
6 cloves garlic, peeled
1 teaspoon cumin seeds
1 teaspoon paprika
60 ml / 2 fl oz olive oil
1 tablespoon brown sugar
110 g / 4 oz feta cheese

## Braised Carrots with Chick Peas, Orange and Rosemary

Preheat the oven to 170°C/Gas 3. Place the butter in a roasting tray and melt over a low heat. Add all the remaining ingredients except the stock and turn in the melted butter, cooking for around 10 minutes. Add the stock and cover the tray with some tin foil to make a lid. Cook for another 20 to 25 minutes until the carrots are soft. Remove the rosemary and serve.
if you have any leftovers add some more chicken stock, bring to the boil, liquidise and you will have a fab soup for the next day.

**Serves 4**

110 g / 4 oz butter
3 large carrots, peeled and cut into 1 cm sticks
2 cloves garlic
2 sprigs rosemary
peel of 1 orange
1 teaspoon ground cumin
1 standard tin chick peas, drained and rinsed
salt and pepper
200 ml / 7 fl oz chicken stock (cube will do)

# When we are so familiar with something we take it for granted and finding new ways with it rarely crosses our minds.

# "cauliflower... cabbage with a college education"

In Mark Twain's words, 'cauliflower is nothing but a cabbage with a college education'. A cauliflower can be smelly if you over cook it. Does everyone think of cheese when they think of cauliflower? I would venture that a lot of people do. I wanted to make my version of cauliflower cheese with a cheese that would do the cauliflower justice. I often find that a quick phonecall to an expert can save time and money so I called Kevin Sheridan of Sheridan's Cheese. I was looking for something sweet that melts easily to offset the bitterness of cauliflower. He came up with two different types. Cantal, a Swiss mountain cheese and Bras in France. In due course, two samples arrived and not wanting to make a traditional béchamel in all its gloopiness, I opted for a light and frothy sabayon made with our local Crinnaghtaun apple juice. You can dress this up with shavings of smoked turkey, smoked chicken, or ham, smoked or not.

# Gratin of Cauliflower with Cantal Cheese

This is just a posh cauliflower cheese.

Place the egg yolks and apple juice in a stainless steel or glass bowl over a lightly simmering pot of water. Whisk continuously until the mixture starts to thicken. At this point add the cheese and chopped chives. Cook carefully for one more minute. Too much and the mixture will scramble. The end result should be frothy and mousse like.

Pre heat the grill. Arrange the florets of cauliflower in the centre of a plate. Spoon over the cheese sabayon and brown under the grill. Scatter the smoked turkey shavings around and toss the toasted almonds on top.

**Serves 4**

4 egg yolks

120 ml / 4 fl oz Crinnaghtaun apple juice (or the best apple juice you can find)

110 g / 4 oz crumbled or grated cheese (preferably cantal but I recommend people use their favourite cheese, as long as it melts, bang away)

handful chives, chopped

1 cauliflower cut into florets and lightly boiled

shavings of smoked turkey, chicken or ham (optional)

toasted almonds to garnish

# Indian Potato and Cauliflower Soup with Fresh Dates, Yoghurt and Almonds

The idea for this came from the Indian dish Alloo Gobi. It's a particularly good soup. The flavours really pick up the cauliflower and smacks it around a bit.

Sweat the onions in the butter, for 2-3 minutes, until soft and translucent. Add the garlic, ginger and spices and cook for two more minutes, then add the potatoes, cauliflower and stock. Bring swiftly to the boil and cook until tender. Season. Blitz with a handblender or liquidiser and pass through a sieve. Serve with the chopped fresh dates, yoghurt, coriander and almonds.

**Serves 6–8**

1 medium onion

110 g / 4 oz butter

2 cloves of chopped garlic

2 cm / 3/4" fresh ginger, peeled, then chopped

1 teaspoon curry powder

1 pinch cumin

1 pinch turmeric

8 cardamom pods, crushed

2 large potatoes, washed peeled and diced

1 small cauliflower, outer leaves discarded, then cut into 2 cm pieces

1.8 l / 3 pints light chicken stock

6 fresh dates roughly chopped

4 tablespoons natural yoghurt

1 pinch chopped coriander

toasted almonds

salt and pepper to taste

# Chestnut

I am still amazed when seasoned customers express surprise upon finding out that the restaurant kitchen begins work at 9 am. Late finishes and early(ish) starts are the order of the day until I can convince people to have just one huge meal at around four o clock in the afternoon. That would make my life a lot easier although I am not sure what I would do with my spare time. There's always darts, I suppose.

The bulk of a kitchen's work is done in the mornings and there is barely enough time to get everything done before lunch service begins. Soups, stocks and sauces being made. Ice-creams being turned, pasta being rolled paper thin to make raviolis. Herbs are picked, fish pin boned and meat trimmed. Confits of duck, daubes of beef and simmering cauldrons of crubeens. The chutneys need to be made and the salads picked and washed. There is a race for space and pots.. This hive of activity gets cleaned by 12.15 and an air of calm descends. Concentration must now be focused on getting the food to the customer as it is intended.

With the limited time available to us, I eschew the butchering of carcasses, leaving that to the butchers, and the filleting of fish, leaving that to the fishmongers. These rough ungainly jobs are best left to the profession-als, leaving us free to make sauces, dressings, sabayons and soufflés. There are those who would say perhaps correctly that I am taking some of the craft from my profession harking back to years gone past when in regal hotel kitchens there were sauciers, pattissiers, rottissiers and garde – mangers in their indi-vidual sections. Their attendant commis would teem around the stoves and preparation areas like a small obedient army.

Small kitchens such as ours are streamlined with everyone a jack of all trades. There are four of us now in the kitchen and there is a lot to do. So when I find a new product that is prepared in such a way as to cut out extra work for us, I jump at it. Chestnuts are one particular God given pre-prepared item. I have attempted to roast my own. They always end up burnt, hard and seemingly uncrackable leading to my intense frustration. I use chestnuts in four different forms. Cooked and vacuum packed which I find indispensable, sweetened purée flavoured with vanilla, unsweetened purée and chestnut flour. So rather than froth rabidly from the mouth whilst trying to emulate the authentic Parisian chestnut roasters, I serenely and happily snip open my packet. Hey presto, stress free cooking. That's the name of the game. I serve them in a French onion broth that's spooned over a mousseline of cèpes (wild mushrooms). I chop them through red wine sauces, pungent with juniper and served with pheasant or woodpigeon, and I've stuffed duck with them, alongside sausagemeat and mashed potato, some lightly cooked onions and pineapple sage completing the mixture. The juice of the duck moistens and mingles deliciously. A blob of redcurrant or a swathe of horseradish cream on top of crispy roast potatoes and some gently steamed broccoli. Open a bottle of red wine and you have a feast.

The purée is something of a mixed bag. The sweetened purée is unbelievably sweet and flavoured with vanilla. Like the fabled and luxurious marron glacé, it is for some an acquired taste. I make a chestnut parfait with some punchy cognac but I usually use some unsweetened purée with the sweet to spare any extra visits to the dentist. The alcohol also detracts from the sugary rush. My most recent discovery of chestnut flour delights me the most. Coeliacs may be very interested in this flour as a substitute on a gluten free diet. It has a subtle nutty flavour and is coarser and more robust than plain flour. We use this to make our warm fruit muffins, which we serve on our early bird or Sunday lunch menus with a ball of smooth vanilla ice-cream and maybe a fruit coulis. I have also made some chestnut flavoured tagliatelle which I served with smoked duck and Brussel sprout leaves, drizzled with a Gewürtzraminer cream and crispy onions. Try and buy chestnut flavoured pasta from a specialist food shop. The flour might prove a bit more elusive to find but as always, if you don't ask you don't get. The chase will be worth your while. It's often available in health food shops because of its gluten free properties.

## Armagnac Chestnut and Chocolate Ripple Parfait

A parfait is essentially a light ice-cream. The method negates the need for an ice-cream machine. It takes just a little practice and a good eye. A sugar thermometer is a great help when making the meringue but you can get away with it with the method described here. We chefs, the butch lot that we are, stick our fingers in. Aren't we mad? Don't try this at home.

This mixture should fill two 450 g/1 lb loaf tin. These will need to be lightly buttered and lined with clingfilm with enough cling overlapping the sides so we can cover the top of the parfait. It keeps for ages in the freezer. Just turn it out and cut with a hot knife.

Firstly whip your cream to a soft peak in your mixer. Remove into another bowl. Clean your mixing bowl and put in your egg yolks. Start to whip on $3/4$ speed, then up to full. Bring your sugar and water to the boil and start to reduce. Get a bowl of iced water and a pastry brush. If you see any crystalisation starting on the side of the pot, brush it into the sugar. You need to bring the sugar to soft ball or 121 degrees celcius if you have a thermometer. If not dip the pastry brush into the iced water, then into the sugar, then back into the iced water. The sugar should condense into a little ball between your fingers. Then it is ready. Turn your mixer up to full. Pour the sugar syrup little by little onto the eggs and whip until almost cool. At this stage it should be pale and frothy. Gently fold in your chestnut purée and the armagnac, then fold in the cream until combined. Fill $1/3$ of each loaf tin with the mix and drizzle over half of the melted chocolate. Fill another 1/3 in each and drizzle over the rest of the chocolate. Finally add the last layer of chestnut mixture. Cover with the clingfilm and freeze.

### Serves 10–12

600 ml / 1 pint cream

10 egg yolks

225 g / 8 oz caster sugar

300 ml / 1/2 pint water

250 g / 9 oz sweet chestnut purée

armagnac to taste

200 g / 7 oz chocolate, melted (this can be done in the microwave – finely chop your chocolate and put on low setting)

# Raspberry and Chestnut Muffins

**Makes 10–12 muffins**

We use various fruits in these muffins: strawberries, raspberries, cherries, blueberries or blackberries. If any of these are not in season, frozen or tinned fruit will be fine but if using tinned, make sure the juice is well drained.

225 g / 8 oz butter

75 g / 3 oz chestnut flour (available in health shops due to its gluten-free qualities)

75 g / 3 oz ground almonds

195 g / 6$\frac{1}{2}$ oz icing sugar

180g / 6 oz egg whites

150g / 5 oz raspberries (or fruit of your choice)

Boil the butter until it turns a nutty brown and allow to cool. Sieve the chestnut flour and icing sugar into a bowl. Add the ground almonds. Add the nut-brown butter. Whisk the egg whites until stiff and smooth. Add to the mixture. Cover and leave in a fridge overnight. The next day, fold in the fruit.

Preheat the oven to 160°C/Gas 2$\frac{1}{2}$. Spoon the mixture into well buttered muffin moulds. Bake for 20 to 25 minutes until golden brown. Serve warm with vanilla ice-cream.

# Caramelised Onion, Chestnut and Cider Sauce

**Serves 4–6**

110 g / 4 oz butter

30 ml / 1 fl oz sunflower oil

2 large Spanish onions, finely sliced

1 sprig thyme

200 ml / 7 fl oz dry cider

1 splash sherry vinegar

1 drizzle of honey

400 ml / 14 fl oz chicken stock

cooking juices from your joint

vacuum-packed chestnuts, crumbled

I like to get the best flavour possible out of every ingredient. Quite often it can mean adding very little to a dish but understanding what's going on during the cooking process. This is a lovely sauce for pork. I usually roast and caramelise a belly, confit or roast a boneless neck end which for me is the nicest cut of pork.

Sometimes I omit the liquid once the onions are caramelised, instead stirring in a couple of spoons of crème fraîche and some thyme. I spread this into a pre-baked pastry case on top of some shredded confit duck or pork and serve it with some béarnaise sauce. In a heavy pot with a lid melt the butter and oil until foaming, then add onions and thyme. Cover with lid and let them cook over medium heat for about 20 minutes, stirring occasionally. They are meant to steam without browning. Remove the lid, turn up the heat and cook for a further 20 minutes, frequently scraping the bottom of the pan to bring colour and flavour back onto the onions until the point that the onions are a deep caramel colour. Deglaze the pan with the cider and sherry vinegar, scraping the bottom of the pot to remove any colour and reduce by half. Add honey, chicken stock and roasting juices if available. Cook for a further 10-15 minutes until it takes on a thick consistency. Add the chestnuts and season.

raspberry and chestnut muffin

# Travelling to other countries, seeing different styles of food, new restaurants and ingredients excites me. Travel truly broadens the mind ... Chick peas

Cooking for me is about spontaneity. It's a way of expressing myself but every now and again I need inspiration. Travelling to other countries, seeing different styles of food, new restaurants and ingredients excites me. Travel truly broadens the mind and every year I return with a list of dishes for the kitchen to try. I can see the dread in my chefs' faces. 'Oh God, what is he going to get us to do now? Isn't there enough work already?' I know I will drive them crazy.

One such trip some years back to Restaurant Daniel in New York gave rise to one of my favourite discoveries ever: chick pea fritters. These are so good I almost wasn't going to share the recipe for fear of seeing them everywhere. They are simple to make and go with meats, especially lamb, with a spicy twist, or fish by substituting the cumin for fennel seeds and a little grated orange zest. The chick pea or gram flour can be a little hard to get although health food and oriental supermarkets should stock it.

## Lemon Hummus Cream

**Makes about 450 g / 1 lb**

1 x 350 g / 12 oz chick peas, drained
3 tablespoons crème fraîche or natural yoghurt
1 tablespoon honey
1 chopped clove garlic
juice of one lemon and 50 g / 2 oz sugar, brought to the boil and cooled

A spoonful of this is delicious with spiced roast lamb or chicken. Crème fraîche gives a thicker result than the natural yoghurt.

In a food processor, put the chick peas, crème fraîche or yoghurt, honey and garlic. Blend until smooth and add the cooled lemon syrup, salt and pepper to taste. This could also be used as a dip for raw vegetables. It can be converted quite easily with some chicken stock into a light sauce to be served with whatever takes your fancy..

## Chick pea Fritters with Raita

Place the milk in a pan with the olive oil, butter, garlic and cumin seeds and bring to the boil. Slowly add the gram flour, stirring to combine. Stir over a medium heat for 10 minutes until thickened.

Line a deep roasting tin with non-stick parchment paper. Spoon in the fritter mix, then level the top with the back of a spoon, cover with clingfilm and chill overnight to set. Using a sharp knife, cut out the fritters and roll in the polenta to coat.

Deep-fry the fritters for 2–3 minutes until golden and crispy. Drain on kitchen paper and arrange on serving plates. Spoon the raita into small bowls and set on the side to serve.

Serves 4

600 ml / 1 pint milk
2 tablespoons olive oil
1 tablespoon softened unsalted butter
1 garlic clove, finely chopped
pinch cumin seeds
150 g / 5 oz gram flour (chick pea flour)
polenta, for coating
vegetable oil, for deep frying
salt and freshly ground black pepper
1 quantity raita (see Cucumber)

## Chick pea Soup with Olives, Orange and Coriander

Sweat the chopped vegetables in the butter and sesame oil until soft. Add the cumin, garlic, rosemary and chick peas. Cook softly for one more minute and cover with the chicken stock. Bring to the boil and cook for 5 more minutes. Liquidise and season the soup. Serve with a dollop of natural yoghurt and the olive and orange dressing.

For the dressing, simply mix all the ingredients together.

Serves 4–6

3 stalks celery, finely chopped
1 leek, finely chopped
2 carrots, finely chopped
1 onion, finely chopped
25 g / 1 oz butter
30 ml / 1 fl oz toasted sesame oil
1 teaspoon cumin
1 clove garlic
1 sprig rosemary
2 tins strained chick peas
1.8 l / 3 pints chicken stock

Olive, orange and coriander dressing
8 olives roughly diced (black and stoned are the easiest to cut up but not necessarily the best olives)
1 bunch shredded coriander, stalks and all
25 g / 1 oz toasted flaked almonds
1 orange segmented, then each segment cut in three
30 ml / 1 fl oz good olive oil

# *Provençale Couscous with Chick peas*

**Makes 4–6**

The Stock:

600 ml / 1 pint chicken stock

1 pinch turmeric

1 sprig rosemary

1 pinch paprika

1 pinch cumin

1 pinch chilli powder

1 pinch sugar

salt and pepper

120 ml / 4 fl oz tomato juice

zest and juice of 1 orange


350 g / 12 oz instant couscous

3 red onions, peeled and cut into 1 cm cubes

60 ml / 2 fl oz olive oil

2 red and 2 yellow peppers, cut into 1 cm cubes

2 garlic cloves crushed

2 courgettes, cut into 1 cm cubes

1 tin chick peas, rinsed and drained

100 g / 4 oz stoneless dates cut into 3


**The Dressing**

30 ml / 1 fl oz olive oil

30 ml / 1 fl oz sunflower oil

handful fresh parsley

good pinch fresh coriander

good pinch fresh mint

juice 1 lemon

splash white wine vinegar

I love couscous and use it frequently with my main courses. It's supremely tasty. I usually serve it with a ginger marinated chicken (see Ginger) but it's equally good, if not better, with lamb. It's perfect for vegetarians and although the recipe calls for a lot of ingredients it's very satisfying once it's made. This is great served cold with some pitta bread and lemon hummus cream or cucumber raita. I want to draw attention to a ready-made mix called couscous spices that I have come across recently. It may be available in some supermarkets so buy it, as it will save you a lot of hassle if you are intimidated by the recipe.

Bring the stock, spices, tomato juice, orange juice and zest up to the boil and cook gently for 10 minutes. If it is a little bit bitter add sugar. Put the couscous into a large bowl and pour $1/3$ of the stock over it. Stir, cover completely with clingfilm and allow to steam for 10 minutes. Break up the couscous with a fork and pour in another $1/3$ of the stock. Cover with clingfilm once more and let it rest for 10 more minutes. Again loosen the couscous with a fork. If it is soft to the bite it is ready, just season. If not, repeat the process with a little more stock. Cook the onions for 2–3 minutes in olive oil, then add the peppers and garlic. Cook for 2 more minutes, then add the courgettes. After 3–4 minutes add the chick peas and dates. Season and mix in with the couscous.

This is used to bind and give fresh flavour to the couscous and vegetables.

Put all of this into a liquidiser and process until smooth. Pour on top of couscous and mix.

chicken marinated with cumin on provençale couscous

One mouthful of the curry I had ordered and I almost cried. My eyes streamed, my nose was running. It felt as if a swarm of bees were having a disco in my mouth. My meal was ruined. My ego deflated.

At first I thought they were picking on me for some reason and flung in a few extra **chillis** for the fun.

We had just arrived in Bangkok, my white freckly legs stuck into flip flops, the rest of me thrust into most unbecoming shorts and a fake Calvin Klein t-shirt (doesn't everyone in Bangkok?). We grabbed a tuk tuk, pointed to a supposedly snazzy restaurant address and travelled awestruck around the frenzied streets. There were mounds of glistening crispy creatures on every street corner that we subsequently found out were deep-fried locusts. A tasty snack but we declined. We came to a halt outside a very dodgy go-go bar. No, no I gesticulated wildly to the page on my Fodors guide but the driver wasn't having any of it. This was either his mate's place or he was getting commission to bring mugs like us there. He must have thought I would be better off sampling some of the other delicacies of Thailand where a No. 27 does not refer to a position on a menu but the young lady gyrating in front of you. Luckily I had my Christian Brothers values (?) and my wife to steer me clear and insisted that he took us to the restaurant. That's where I had my first taste of real Thai food, none of the namby pamby toned-down flavours that we westerners are used to. One mouthful of the curry I had ordered and I almost cried. Even Máire looked worried for me. My eyes streamed, my nose was running.

It felt as if a swarm of bees were having a disco in my mouth. My meal was ruined. My ego was deflated.

At first I thought they were picking on me for some reason and flung in a few extra chillis for the fun. That's paranoia again I know, but I soon found out this amount was quite normal so, at every other meal, while gagging to taste everything, I meekly had to ask for the extra mild version.

Too much chilli can ruin a meal is the moral of that story, especially if you are not used to it. A little can envigorate and stimulate but always err on the side of caution. I occasionally have one or two dishes on the menu with a little Thai orientation.

One of my favourite things in the world is a bouillabaisse of seafood with those Thai flavourings, a little hint of chilli and ginger. The mild creaminess of coconut is offset by the sharpness of the lime, a deliciously fragrant, flavourful, silky sauce that will transport you to some faraway place. This is used to poach mussels, prawns and monkfish or you could use seabass or salmon, whatever you like. Throw in some roughly chopped spring onion, chopped coriander and cherry tomatoes and ladle over a mound of basmati rice. This is light, almost broth like and bursting with flavour.

# Poached Seafood in a Ginger, Chilli and Coconut Broth

This makes around 2 litres but you need this to comfortably poach the fish. Use the rest as a soup.

### Broth

1 onion, finely chopped

3 stalks celery, finely chopped

2 tablespoons sesame oil

2 cloves garlic, finely chopped

2 cm fresh ginger, finely chopped

10 cardamom pods, crushed

half tablespoon of cumin seeds, roasted and crushed, powdered is ok but use less

half teaspoon coriander seeds roasted and crushed, powdered is ok here too

1 tablespoon mild curry powder

2 l / 3 ½ pint of chicken stock (Knorr bouillion is fine)

150 ml / ¼ pint cream

2 x tins 350 ml / 12 fl oz tins coconut milk

100 ml / 4 fl oz lime cordial or juice of 2 limes

pinch caster sugar

sweet chilli sauce to taste

lots of chopped coriander and basil

### Fish

400 g / 14 oz mussels, scrubbed and de-bearded

225 g / 8 oz monkfish fillet, cut into chunks

225 g / 8 oz salmon fillet, cut into chunks

400 g / 14 oz raw Dublin Bay prawns, peeled and cleaned

8 spring onions trimmed, washed and cut into 2 cm / 1" pieces

1 punnet of cherry tomatoes

lots of chopped coriander and basil

Sweat the onion and celery slowly in sesame oil. After two minutes add the garlic, ginger and spices. Cook for 2–3 more minutes, then add the stock and reduce by half. Add the cream, coconut milk, lime and sugar to taste. Do not boil further. Then add the sweet chilli sauce to taste. This is a good way to control the heat. Pass the sauce directly through a sieve into a large pan with a ladle to extract all the flavour.

This stage can be done earlier in the day if you like.

Bring the sauce up to a simmer. Drop in the mussels and monkfish. Do not boil. After one minute add the salmon, then after another minute the prawns, spring onions and cherry tomatoes. Cook for one more minute, then add the coriander and basil. Add salt and pepper and transfer into a best bowl. The fish will be cooking all the time so it's important to eat it straight away. I like to eat the broth first, then the fish with plain steamed rice.

poached seafood in a ginger chilli and coconut broth

## Chilli Glazed Pineapple with Minted Yoghurt

**Serves 4**

1 large pineapple
1 red chilli, deseeded and finely diced
2 tablespoons demerara sugar
50 g / 2 oz butter
pinch chopped mint
200 ml / 7 fl oz natural yoghurt

Preheat the grill.

Top and tail the pineapple, peel with a serrated knife, slice into 1 cm slices and place on a non-stick tray. Scatter the chilli evenly over the slices, then sprinkle with the demerara sugar and finally drop a knob of butter on each. Place under the grill for about 5 minutes or until glazed.

Mix the chopped mint with the yoghurt. Divide the pineapple between plates. Pour over any excess juice and top with a dollop of yoghurt for a delicious dessert.

## Chilli, Coriander and Yoghurt Dressing

$\frac{1}{2}$ l / 1 pint thick natural yoghurt
1 medium red chilli, deseeded and finely chopped
1 handful of picked coriander, finely chopped
$\frac{1}{2}$ teaspoon mint sauce or fresh mint

This is a spicy little dressing that gives freshness to an otherwise rich dish. I use it with risotto of curried peas served with a sliver of grilled salmon. It is also good with chicken, lamb, scallops or prawns, especially if the main ingredient has a slightly spicy twist.

Mix all ingredients together and dollop over your dish.

## Red Pepper Relish

**Makes 750g /1 $\frac{1}{4}$ lb approx.**

50 g / 2 oz caster sugar
60 ml / 2 fl oz white wine vinegar
5 red peppers, deseeded and finely chopped
1 small red chilli, deseeded and finely chopped
1 small piece stem ginger, peeled and finely chopped
1 clove garlic, peeled and crushed
2 x 350 g / 12 oz tins whole plum tomatoes, puréed
2 leaves or 1 sachet of gelatine

This is an absolute essential in our kitchen. It goes with practically everything. It has a nice mildly hot sweet and sour note. The colour is stunning. It has been served with our Cannelloni Goats cheese for the last two years.

Bring the sugar and vinegar to the boil. Add diced peppers and cook for 2 minutes. Add the chilli, ginger and garlic, then the tomatoes and cook for a further 15 minutes. Remove from the heat. Soak the gelatine in cold water. When soft stir in well, allow to cool and put in sterilised jars to refrigerate. The result should be a vivid red light jelly.

red pepper relish

# All you want is a beautiful chocolate tart or pudding and if you are overly concerned with percentages of cocoa solids, you need to find a hobby

I know there are a few of you out there who can take or leave chocolate, but the vast majority of us love the stuff. It is part of our culture. As a nation our taste in chocolate comes from Britain, whether we like it or not. Sweet and milky and low in cocoa which means it is not as pure as say the French or Belgians would like.

I once saw a programme where the TV people were offering Parisians a taste of some of our sweets, everyday stuff that we see all the time. The majority thought it disgusting and not chocolate at all, their preference being for the darker, purer, less sweet chocolate. Fair enough. The adage of old dogs and new tricks applies to me I'm afraid. I don't like chocolate too bitter. Does that make me a pleb? There are people out there who would think so. Chocolate snobbery is rife amongst chefs. 55%, 60%, 65%, 75%. The higher the percentage of cocoa solids, the purer the chocolate and the more bitter. This also means the more expensive.

Valrhona is the Rolls Royce of chocolate. Many chefs print Valrhona on their menus leaving us in no doubt as to the pedigree of their Marquise au Chocolat. I don't use it myself. There are plenty of good alternatives that are cheaper, such as Belgian Callbaut and French Cacao Barry. Not that it should matter to you if you are coming to us for dinner. All you want is a beautiful chocolate tart or pudding and if you are overly concerned with percentages of cocoa solids, you need to find a hobby or you are in danger of becoming a terminal bore. I'm happy with 55% myself but avoid the cheap stuff in supermarkets if at all possible.

# Chocolate Truffle Cake

Melt the butter and crush the biscuits. Mix together and press into a 10" springform tin. Place in fridge for 20 minutes.

**For the cake mixture**

Melt the butter and cocoa powder in a bowl set over hot water until cocoa has dissolved.

Whip the cream and icing sugar together to a thick ribbon stage. Melt the chocolate carefully in a bowl over hot water and mix it through with the butter and cocoa. Meanwhile, whisk the egg yolks and caster sugar until thick and creamy. Fold in the cocoa mixture, then fold in the cream. Fold through until you get an even consistency and colour.

Tip the chocolate mixture into the tin smoothing the top. Refrigerate for at least 3 hours before cutting. Cut with a hot knife for nice sharp edges.

**12 generous servings**

I like to serve this with some prunes and Armagnac or with raspberries in summertime. Try the poached pears in white wine (see Pears) with this and a little whipped cream.

400 g / 14 oz unsalted butter

200 g / 7 oz cocoa powder

600 ml / 1 pint cream

75 g / 3 oz icing sugar

10 egg yolks

350 g / 12 oz caster sugar

200 g / 7 oz chocolate (minimum 55% cocoa solids)

Biscuit base

275 g / 10 oz digestive biscuits

75 g / 3 oz melted butter

# Chocolate and Hazelnut Cookies with Special Hot Chocolate

Beat together the butter and sugar. Add the hazelnuts, flour, baking soda. Beat until the mixture comes together. Add the chocolate chips. Divide in two halves and roll in clingfilm into a sausage shape to refrigerate for one hour. When ready to use, peel away the clingfilm. Cut in half centimetre slices and place on a greased baking tray. Bake in a preheated oven 170°C/Gas 3 for 20 to 25 mins until golden brown. If you wish you can freeze this mixture to be taken out when you fancy.

**Makes 25 cookies (approx)**

150 g / 5 oz butter

75g / 3 oz caster sugar

75 g / 3 oz ground hazelnuts

300 g / 11 oz flour

pinch baking soda

225 g / 8 oz small chocolate pieces of good quality plain chocolate

# Special Hot Chocolate

Boil the milk, pour on top of the chocolate and whisk until smooth. Add sugar to taste. This can be laced with your favourite liqueur. Try Tia Maria, Cointreau, Amaretto or Brandy.

You don't need to serve much of this as it is quite heavy.

**Serves 4**

600 ml / 1 pint milk

225 g / 8 oz good quality plain chocolate, chopped

sugar to taste

## Doughnuts and Dips

10 portions of two small doughnuts

300 ml / ¹/₂ pint warm milk
75 g / 3 oz butter
1 teaspoon fresh yeast or one sachet dried
450 g / 1 lb flour
1 teaspoon salt
1 egg beaten
4 tablespoons caster sugar

## Dips

I love homemade doughnuts. My wife suggested serving mini doughnuts with an assortment of dips (something for everyone!) after a visit to Burger King, of all places. I use these in the restaurant, alternating the dips. The following are some suggestions that are easy.

Hazelnut – add some Nutella into the chocolate sauce below

Chantilly cream – whipped cream with vanilla and sugar

Cheesecake cream – whipped cream, cream cheese, sugar and vanilla

Compôte of berries – berries turned in their own coulis

Lemon curd – see Lemons

Fruit coulis of any kind

Heat milk and butter till all the butter is dissolved. Add in yeast and beat. Add all the dry ingredients together and slowly mix. Add the egg, then allow to prove for 45 minutes in a warm place. 'Proving' allows the yeast to work, whereby the dough will rise to twice the volume, aerate, and therefore lighten.

Knock back (knock the air out of them so they return to their original size), shape into 25 g / 1 oz balls and prove for 25 minutes in a warm place covered loosely with clingfilm. You can freeze these at this stage to be taken out and proven when you need them. If not freezing, then place the balls on a lightly floured tray with some clingfilm draped over the top and proved to double their size. This should take about 20 minutes. Then deep fry at 160°C/Gas 21/2 until golden and roll in the sugar. (If you like put a pinch of cinnamon through the sugar for a different flavour.)

Note: If at any time the mix seems too wet, add a little more flour. When kneading and shaping, flour your board very well as the doughnuts can be quite sticky.

# Chocolate Sauce

Mix together the chocolate and butter. Boil the milk, cream and sugar and pour onto the chocolate mix. Stir the mixture until completely melted, but do not allow it to re-boil. The chocolate sauce is now ready. Serve warm or cold – the cooler the temperature, the thicker the sauce.

200 g / 7 oz good quality plain chocolate, finely chopped
25 g / 1 oz unsalted butter, chilled and diced
150 ml / 1/4 pint milk
2 tablespoon double cream
25 g / 1 oz caster sugar

# Over to the Table Hot Chocolate Pudding

I serve this easy but delicious pudding in coccotte dishes. Wider and shallower than ramekins, they allow me to place a scoop of ice cream on top of the pudding when it comes out of the oven. The centre of the pudding should be a little liquid – that's the sauce. The rest will have baked into a deliciously light sponge.
Note: Ramekins will do - just serve the ice cream on the side. When filling the moulds allow for space as the pudding will double in size.

Beat the eggs, egg yolks and sugar in a mixer until pale in colour and light and fluffy. Melt the chocolate and butter together in a bowl over a pot of gently simmering water.
Fold the egg mixture and chocolate together. Then fold in the flour very gently and pour into your buttered moulds. You can place these in the fridge until later. These will also freeze very well.
Cook for 10 minutes in a 180° / Gas 4 oven and serve immediately with ice cream.

Makes 4–6

250 g / 9 oz solft butter, unsalted if possible
5 whole eggs and 5 egg yolks
125g / 4 1/2 oz caster sugar
250g / 9oz dark chocolate
50g / 2 oz sieved flour
Butter for greasing the dishes

Widely used in Spanish cooking, chorizo is a coarsely textured, strongly flavoured pork sausage with paprika and garlic, either mild or hot. I would recommend the mild one unless you have masochistic tendencies.

I'd like to tell you that I discovered chorizo as a young boy when I wandered down the back streets of a tiny village in Andalucia, the smoky seductive smell drawing me to a tiny restaurant where I ate chorizo sausage simmered in Rioja wine with potatoes. I saw the light. In an instant I knew my life's calling, to cook. That would be my life's passion and all the rest of it. But I would be telling porky pies, to use Jamie Oliver speak. In truth, I began to see chorizo appear more and more on restaurant menus, almost becoming as dangerously common as that old trollop, basil.

I wanted to know more about it so I ordered it from my supplier, did a bit of reading, tried it in various guises and I don't think it has been off my menus since, always lurking under something or other. It lends itself to many different dishes. I usually cut it into half centimetre cubes and fry it quickly to disperse the fat and bring out the flavour, sometimes adding marjoram or chopped flat leaf parsley to the pan. I may spoon the whole lot over mash or breast of chicken to give the bird a little kick up the bum that it often needs.

The most common chorizos available to us are from Spain and are available at delicatessens. These are air dried and suitable for slicing or cutting into chunks to be used in a dish or eaten raw like salami, although I never use it raw as I think it is too fatty.

I used to scoff at the notion of mixing meat and fish until I ate paella and that shut me up. Now I put a few fried slices in my seafood stew as a beautiful counterpoint to salmon and mussels and serve with saffron rice. A bit of a saucy paella if you like.

I often make little chicken sausages, studded with raisins, pistachios and ruby-like chorizo served with buttered spinach. You can try a jazzed up tomato and mozzarella salad. Alternate slices of tomato, chorizo (finely sliced) and buffalo mozzarella. Place on a large plate. Warm the plate through the oven or under the grill for a short while. Scatter with sliced red onions and olives, drizzle with good olive oil and eat with garlic bread – though, I hasten to add, wait until tomatoes come into season for this number.

You could try it diced again and fried over a warm potato salad, topped with a poached egg and your favourite leaves for a light lunch or even with some scrambled egg and spring onion for brunch. Dried chorizo keeps for ages in the fridge. It is one of those 'musthaves' for any keen cook's larder. So now I have saved you a trip to Spain, although you may not thank me for that.

## Dublin Bay Prawns Poached in Saffron and Chorizo Cream

Chorizo and saffron for me are one of the most beautiful flavour combinations. The addition of cream adds a luxurious velvety finish. It makes for a rich dish but this is tempered with some fragrant basmati rice. I don't like cream sauces to be reduced to the point where they become almost cloying. I tend to stop them somewhere in between a broth and that stage, allowing you to get a spoon out or a piece of bread to mop up the sauce.

Sweat the onion in the olive oil until soft and transluscent. Add the chorizo, then the garlic and cook for one more minute until the chorizo releases its oil. Add the wine, stock and saffron and reduce by half. Then add the cream, rosemary, orange peel and cardamom and cook slowly for 10 to 15 minutes or until it achieves coating consistency. Add the prawns and cook for a further 2 to 3 minutes. Remove the rosemary. Add the peas, give a squeeze of lemon juice and serve with some steaming basmati rice.

This could easily become a bouillabaisse with any fish you like in it. Just don't reduce the sauce much so that it's nice and soupy. If you added some chicken, it would become very similar to a paella in flavour.

**Serves 4**

1 small onion, finely chopped

4 tablespoons olive oil

110 g / 4 oz chorizo, diced into quarter centimetre pieces

2 cloves garlic

100 ml / 3–4 fl oz white wine

100 ml / 3–4 fl oz chicken stock (cube will do)

saffron, 1 pinch of strands or 1 sachet of powder

300 ml / 1/2 pint cream

1 sprig rosemary

2 pieces orange peel (from a peeler)

6 cardamom pods, lightly crushed

700 g / 1$^1$/$_2$ lb cleaned fresh prawns (out of the shell)

100 g / 3–4 oz blanched peas (frozen)

squeeze lemon juice

I'd like to tell you that I discovered chorizo as a young boy when I wandered down the back streets of a tiny village in Andalucia ... But I would be telling porky pies, to use Jamie Oliver speak

# Warm Chorizo and Butterbean Salad

**Serves 4–6**

5 tablespoons olive oil

200 g / 7 oz chorizo sausage, thinly sliced

3 medium red onions, peeled and chopped

1 large red pepper, cored, deseeded and sliced

3 garlic cloves, peeled and finely chopped

1 teaspoon cumin seeds

450 g / 1 lb butterbeans

1 generous handful chopped fresh coriander

juice of one lemon

salt and freshly ground black pepper

a few sprigs of coriander to garnish

This is as good cold as hot; on its own or as an accompaniment to meat, especially lamb or chicken or more robust fish such as monkfish, hake or cod.

Heat 1 tablespoon of the olive oil in a non-stick frying pan and cook the chorizo over a medium heat for 1–2 minutes or until lightly browned. Remove with a slotted spoon, transfer to a bowl and set aside.

Fry the onion in the oil remaining in the pan for 10 minutes or until browned. Add the red pepper, garlic, cumin and butterbeans and cook for a further 5 minutes, stirring frequently to prevent sticking. Add to the chorizo.

Add the chopped coriander, lemon juice and remaining olive oil. Season well and serve immediately, garnished with coriander.

# Linguini with Chorizo, Kidney Beans, Parsley and Pecorino Cheese

**Serves 4 to 6**

500 g / 1.1 lb dried linguini

1 tablespoon olive oil

50 g / 2 oz chorizo, diced into half centimetre cubes

2 cloves garlic, peeled and crushed

1 standard tin kidney beans (rinsed under cold water)

100 ml / 3–4 fl oz cream

100 ml / 3–4 fl oz chicken stock (cube will do)

handful flat parsley (washed and roughly chopped)

salt and pepper

75 g / 3 oz grated pecorino (or parmesan)

This is very tasty, with Spanish overtones. If you wanted to upgrade it, you could pair it with some roasted monkfish or some grilled hake, in which case omit the pecorino. Pecorino is an Italian hard sheep's cheese. Look out for it in good delis. Parmesan will also do instead.

Cook the pasta according to the packet instructions. In another heavy-based pan, heat the olive oil and fry off the chorizo, then the garlic, taking care not to burn. Add the kidney beans and mash them a little with a potato masher or the back of a spoon. Add the chicken and cream stock and start to reduce. When the sauce reaches a coating consistency add the cooked pasta and the parsley, salt and pepper. Divide into warm bowls and scatter over the pecorino.

linguini with chorizo, kidney beans, parsley and pecorino cheese

# Cosmopolitan Christmas parties

If I were to advise you on how to impress your friends at your Christmas gathering it would be to start with a Cosmopolitan cocktail. Máire is an avid fan of the TV series 'Sex and the City', and at our recent house-warming she simply had to make them because 'it's what Carrie drinks' you see. So our friend Kevin, who is in the business, made the real McCoy, burning the orange peel to release its natural oils into the alcohol. Now I have to tell you the end result is pink and for the full effect you really need to serve them in the Martini glass. We have now made friends with quite a few farmers and their wives, but try offering a pink cocktail to a man who has just spent his day up to his eyes in cow poo and is looking forward to a feed of pints! I had to say, don't worry, we're all friends here, and your secret penchant for pink cocktails is safe with me. The Cosmopolitans went down a treat and the fact that they are lethal came into evidence later when the ubiquitous 'Bat out of Hell' was played and we were catapulted into the 1980s, taking the party outside by way of a human train. Oh, those were the days.

The next day while making an attempt to cook breakfast for the overnighters I gave out to them for not using coasters under their tea. They were incredulous as the girls had been dancing to Spandau Ballet's greatest hits on the table in their stilettos the night before, and now I was worried about their hot mugs. Needless to say, I conceded. The point of all the above is that for a delicious and glamorous start to your party, you need Cosmopolitans.

As for food, there is only one golden rule. Keep it simple. Preparation is everything and it is important not to get too stressed out. Remember, people are coming to socialise and the food is only part of that. A stressed host or hostess will only make the guests feel uneasy. The chances are that if you do that end of it right, the food plays a diminished role in proportion to the general shenanigans. The biggest decision to make depends on the number of people you have coming and how well you know them. Either way, the best approach is to keep hot dishes to a minimum. Start with soup or a cold starter, followed by a hot main course and cold pudding or else something you can pull out of the oven and pour custard or cream over. It's also important not to try to be too obscure in your choice of food. I myself fell into this trap at the self-same party deciding to do a cassoulet because it is one of my all-time favourite things. Well, what a disaster! My beans were undercooked, my pork overcooked and stringy. I was flustered and embarrassed. After all, this is what I do for a living. People were hungry and I had no choice but to give it to them. Most people were polite and consoled me but my closest friends proclaimed it rotten and tried to feed it to the dog who wasn't even interested. 'Hey Flynny, do you have anything we can put in a sandwich, I'm starving? Is there a McDonalds in Dungarvan?' Some friends, huh? I was disconsolate so I had to have another Cosmopolitan and put on Billy Idol's 'Dancing with Myself', pretending it was all a bad dream. So I learnt my lesson the hard way. It's bangers and mash for the next party.

Having said all that, it is my function to be of some benefit to you when preparing for your party. Try and have as much as you can

arranged in advance, leaving you to swan around in your stilettos mingling with your guests and amusing friends with your witty repartee.

Here's the Cosmopolitan recipe, to keep the guests happy!

## Cosmopolitan

**For 4 people**

In a cocktail shaker over ice:
4 measures Absolut vodka
4 measures Cointreau
juice of one orange
Fill up with Cranberry juice
Shake well

Fill four martini glasses and have a twist of orange peel ready. Hold the orange peel over a lighter or the gas ring for approximately 10 seconds until you see the oil emerging. Garnish the glasses with the peel and a slice of orange if you wish. Enjoy!

75

# crab

Auntie Peggy comes home once a year. As children, we always looked forward to her arrival. We would gather in anticipation at my granny's house because she always brought lots of exotic sweets. She went to England to be a nun in the 1930s at the age of sixteen and when she came home we tried to pack as much into her three weeks as possible: day trips and spins galore to see relatives around the county.

The first time I saw crab was on a trip to Helvick Head when I was about seven. Peggy and I strolled along the pier, stopping to chat to fishermen who seemed respectful to this formidable lady. They gave her a plastic bag full of crab claws. She was reluctant to take them but I gave her plenty of encouragement, curious as ever. What I remember of that evening more than anything was the mess. Our attempts to prise the meat out of the claws with a hammer and some forks were almost futile. My father wrestled determinedly and gave up, settling instead for tripe and onions. That experience sort of put me off crab for a while as I associated it with a lot of work for very little reward. To this day I don't like fiddly food, preferring to leave the preparation to the cooks.

With the advent of picked crab meat we can now buy 500g packets of hassle free deliciousness. As with anything, the quality varies. You have to look for a creamy whiteness, chunks of reasonably whole meat that you can pick through yourself to ensure there is no stray shell. If you are stuck you can use frozen crab, just avoid that grey opaque colour as the taste will be insipid and the meat stringy. An important note if you are using frozen crab is not to squeeze too much juice out as the flavour tends to be in this liquor and tipping it away can leave the crab with no flavour at all.

There will be howls of derision from some quarters when I say that except for soups I don't use brown crab meat. I find it too fishy. But that's just me. At the moment we have crab on the menu in two formats: suspended in a creamy savoury custard and gratinated with some sesame seeds so it resembles a crème brûlée. This we serve with melba toast and pickled cucumber, the perfect foil for the creaminess of the custard. We also serve double fillets of lemon sole, stuffed with a salmon mousse with flaked crab, ginger, spring onions and raisins. I will also for Sunday lunch roast some crab claws, give them a gentle bash and lather them in ginger, chilli and garlic butter and let the punters pick away at their leisure. Surely that's what Sundays are for?

Crab and mayonnaise are bedmates that will never tire of each other. Cream sauces beg to be poured over crab. I know I have eaten fabulous crab dishes in Chinese restaurants with soy, ginger and spring onions but somehow there is always something missing, that silky blanket of cream seems just right. I know that no one will ever ask me to write a diet book but I can only cook it the way I like to eat.

During hot weather I like to put a gazpacho of crab on the menu: chilled spicy tomato soup with a fluffy cloud of crab mayonnaise. Or gratin of crab with baby courgettes: egg yolks whipped over a water bath with some white wine and Dijon mustard until fluffy. Fold in some crab meat and chopped chives. Spoon some over tender courgettes and grill until golden brown. If you like replace the courgettes with asparagus for a simple summer starter. That's the beauty of crab. It comes cooked ready to eat and all you need is imagination.

## Crab Crème Brûlée with Pickled Cucumber and Melba Toast

This is one of the most popular starters in the restaurant. Years ago I came across a recipe for Mrs Beeton's potted crab in a magazine. It interested me and so we tried it, adapting along the way. It has oriental overtones with the pickled ginger and garlic. The ginger enhances the crab and cuts through the cream. It's really very easy to do, and perfect for a dinner party as it can be prepared in advance.

Mix all the ingredients together and allow the flavours to infuse for 15 to 20 minutes. Preheat the oven to 150°C/Gas 2. Ladle the mixture into the ramekins. Prepare a bain marie by filling a roasting tray with water and warming it on the stove. Place the ramekins in the bain marie. The water should come halfway up the sides of the ramekins. Place the bain marie in the oven for 40 minutes. When cooked through, the mixture should wobble just a little in the centre. Remove from the bain marie and allow to cool. These should be served not quite chilled but definitely at room temperature. When ready to serve, sprinkle a thick layer of sesame seeds on top of each ramekin and brown under the grill. Serve with some melba toast, a wedge of lemon and pickled cucumber (see Cucumber).

**Serves 4 (in ramekins)**

450 ml / 16 fl oz cream
1 egg plus two egg yolks
150 g / 5 oz picked white crab meat
25 g / 1 oz drained chopped pickled ginger
2 green stems spring onion, finely chopped
1 clove garlic, peeled and crushed
salt and pepper
50 g / 2 oz sesame seeds

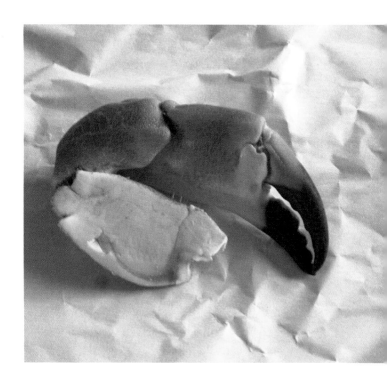

roasted crab claws with garlic, ginger and chilli butter

# Roasted Crab Claws with Garlic, Ginger and Chilli butter

We had this on our summer Sunday lunch menu. People enjoyed picking away at their leisure. Patience is definitely required while eating this. You can now buy cooked and cracked crab claws which really convenient, as long as they are good, of course. We are lucky we have a plentiful supply of crab claws when the season permits. If you are really stuck this butter will even enliven those mean little crab toes. However, you should really try to get the big manly crab arms with the toes still attached. There is really no measurement I can give you for crab. It all depends on the size of the crab and how much you like it. The butter below will be sufficient for 4 generous portions. The crab really needs to be awash with it.

Let the butter go soft at room temperature. Put in a food processor with the garlic and ginger and pulse it 4–5 times making sure it is well amalgamated.

**Makes 4 servings**

For the butter
200 g / 7 oz butter
4 large cloves garlic, roughly chopped
50 g / 2 oz pickled ginger
1 red chilli, deseeded and finely chopped (use sweet chilli sauce if you wish)
1 bunch coriander, roughly chopped
2 spring onions, chopped

Remove to a bowl and fold in the chilli. At this stage, add the chopped coriander and spring onion. Roll it in clingfilm into a sausage shape and refrigerate or freeze, depending on when you want it.

All you have to do is warm the crab through the oven (assuming it's cooked). Remove the clingfilm, then melt the butter gently and lather it over the crab. Serve with some lemon wedges.

# Angel Hair Pasta with Crab, Lemon and Rosemary Cream and Garlic Crumbs

As we all know, lemon and crab have a natural affinity. I have found that this lemon and rosemary cream makes an ideal sauce to serve with crab and pasta. Once you have made the lemon cream, this dish is a cinch to assemble. Simply cook the angel hair pasta according to the packet instructions. Be careful with angel hair though. You must spend your time with some tongs to separate the strands while it's cooking. It is so fine that really it's cooked as soon as the water comes back up to the boil after adding the pasta. Once the pasta is drained, mix carefully with the lemon cream and the crab meat. Chop some parsley and fold through the pasta for colour. This can be served warm or it's a lovely summer salad served cold. Simply sprinkle over some crunchy garlic crumbs. Season and that's it.

**Serves 4–6**

500 g / 1.1 lb angel hair pasta
lemon and rosemary cream (see Lemons)
450 g / 1 lb picked white crab meat
handful chopped parsley
sprinkling of garlic crumbs (see Garlic)

# cucumber

Cucumbers are funny things aren't they? I'm glad they sell them in halves now. Halves are sensible. No more will they lurk, tired and unwanted in the depths of the fridge. I have a complaint though. You see I have no nails, bitten to the quick I'm afraid, so trying to take one of those plastic jackets off a cucumber without cutting the cucumber is a feat of intense frustration. I won't have them in the kitchen. I haven't got the patience. It's a naked cucumber zone only. I reckon some sadist who wanted to get his own back on truculent chefs probably invented those little jackets.

Mad dogs and English men. Cricket, Henley, straw boaters, crazy striped jackets and Pimms. There is something quintessentially English about cucumbers and cucumber sandwiches with the crusts cut off. Personally speaking, I would rather eat my own underpants than a cucumber sandwich and I don't know anyone who loves them that much (not that they would be volunteering to have a munch on my smalls either) but I do think cucumbers have their uses.

I always pickle them gently in sugar, vinegar and chilli for they are a perfect foil for rich food. Of course, one of my staples in summer is cucumber raita, a mixture of yoghurt, mint and finely sliced salted cucumber. This I serve with spicy chicken and couscous. This mixture seems to aid the digestion and lighten anything it is served with.

One of the most fabulous things I ever ate was on holidays in Greece: a lamb souvlaki, slathered in tsatziki. Rather like a kebab but with a Greek version of raita. I can still taste it now. On the same holiday, I tasted a proper Greek salad for the first time. Awash with colour and healthy vibrancy, no matter how I try I can never recreate the freshness of those holiday flavours. Produce lingering in cold rooms around the country can never compare to freshly picked vegetables ripened in the sun. Forgive me for practically turning into an Ambassador for Greece but it was in my island hopping youth.

Peeled, deseeded and diced cucumbers are lovely run through a light cream sauce or mayonnaise with dill, served with fresh or smoked salmon. My favourite crispy aromatic duck with pancakes and plum sauce would be unthinkable without them. Most of the time, I peel them as the skin can be bitter and a little chewy. The seeds tend to release water so if you are making raita or tzatziki, take them out or they will dilute the creaminess of the finished dish.

## Cucumber Raita

This is indispensable with smoked salmon, mildly spiced chicken or lamb, or with couscous.

Peel and quarter lengthways, then deseed the cucumber. Slice finely and sprinkle with the salt and work it all in. Allow to rest at room temperature for one hour, then rinse under cold water. Pat dry with a tea towel and place in a bowl. Fold in the yoghurt and mint. This will keep for 3–4 days in the fridge. Use with chicken, lamb, curries, or try it with smoked salmon and pitta bread.

**Makes approx 500 ml or just under 1 pint.**

1 cucumber
1 pinch salt
250 ml / under ½ pint thick natural yoghurt
good pinch chopped mint

## Pickled Cucumber

I use this with my crab crème brûlée, my goat's cheese mousse and through green salads. For a sweet and sour, slightly hot bite, crispy duck in the Chinese style is lovely with this and some shredded spring onions.

Slice the cucumber as thinly as you can. A mandolin is perfect for this job. Salt, rest and rinse the cucumber as before. While the cucumber is resting, bring the sugar, vinegar and chilli sauce to the boil and reduce for 30 seconds. Take off the heat and allow to cool completely. Dry the cucumbers, place in a bowl and add the liquid. This will keep in the fridge for 2–3 days. Any more and the cucumber loses its colour.

1 cucumber
1 pinch salt
50 g / 2 oz caster sugar
60 ml / 2 fl oz white wine vinegar
1 teaspoon sweet chilli sauce

## *Chilli Squid with Raita and Baked Cherry Tomatoes*

This is just simple grilled squid, cherry tomatoes and raita. Serve with some rocket leaves for a nice light starter.

**Serves 4**

2 tablespoons toasted sesame oil

2 tablespoons sunflower oil

2 level teaspoons chilli powder

450 g / 1 lb baby squid

12 cherry tomatoes

squeeze lemon juice

salt and pepper

Firstly make the chilli oil. Heat the oil until it is hot but not smoking. Then remove from the heat and count to 30 before mixing in the chilli powder. Leave until cold and strain thorough kitchen paper.

Wash the squid. Trim off the head taking care not to split the tentacles and then cut the tentacles in two. Cut down each squid body and flatten out. Score a diamond pattern on both sides with a sharp knife, then cut into strips. Pat dry, then marinade in the chilli oil.

Take a griddle pan and put it over a medium heat. Grill the squid pieces for 2 to 3 minutes, turning over once. Just before it's cooked, throw on the cherry tomatoes and leave for 30 seconds. Remove them and the squid. Season and serve with the raita and a wedge of lemon.

## *Cucumber, Olive, Tomato and Feta Cheese Salad*

**Serves 4**

1 cucumber, peeled deseeded and cut in $1/2$ cm dice

4 plum tomatoes, deseeded and diced like cucumber

10 black olives, stoned and cut into quarters

20 toasted pine nuts

8 mint leaves shredded

4 tablespoons olive oil

75 g / 3 oz feta cheese, diced

2 tablespoons white wine vinegar

salt and pepper

I use this as a garnish for my tomato soup. Really all it is, is a little Greek salad. It can be served as a starter with some basil oil or put into some warm pitta bread as a sandwich.

Mix all ingredients together. If you like, substitute basil for mint. This will keep for a couple of days in the fridge.

# Cucumber and Dill Beurre Blanc

For me, Beurre Blanc is the singularly most impressive sauce in cooking. It was the first proper sauce I learned to make and if ever you learn to make only one sauce let this be it. Indispensable with fish, it can be adapted in lots of different ways to give it different twists. Rosemary is a particularly good flavour with this. Just add some into the liquid when you are reducing it and pass it out at the end. I also serve a ginger and cumin version of this with mackerel. Here I'm making the sauce and at the last minute adding diced cucumber and chopped dill for colour, flavour and texture, which is perfect for salmon.

This sauce cannot be refrigerated. Once it's made it must not be boiled. It can be made an hour or two in advance, to be reheated when you need it.

Cook the shallots slowly in one knob of the butter so they are soft and translucent. Add the pepper, vinegar, white wine and chicken stock. Reduce to a syrup. Add cream. Bring to the boil quickly and add the butter bit by bit amalgamating with a whisk as you go along. When the butter is well incorporated, season, add the sugar and the lemon and pass through a sieve into another pot. If it's a little bit thick add a splash of milk. Stir in diced cucumber and dill.

**Makes 600 ml / 1 pint**

6 small shallots, finely chopped
300 g / 11 oz butter cut into slices
1 teaspoon cracked black pepper
90 ml / 3 fl oz white wine vinegar
150 ml / 1/4 pint white wine
75 ml / 3 fl oz chicken stock
50 ml / 2 fl oz cream
salt
pinch of sugar
squeeze of lemon
1/2 cucumber, peeled, deseeded and cut into 1/2 cm dice
good pinch of chopped dill

**Cumin** is one of those spices that really gets around. I used to think it was unique to Middle Eastern cuisine until I found it in recipes for north African couscous. In the Canaries, it flavours fish soup and in Spain it's indispensable with chick peas.

The smell of freshly roasted cumin almost makes me dizzy. It is an unmistakable heady aroma that tantalises me like no other. I don't really remember the first time I encountered it.

Cooking is like building blocks – you try different combinations and at first nothing goes right but gradually you acquire the knowledge to build things right.

The first time I cooked with cumin I was making a tomato sauce for grilled red mullet. Tomato sauces I had made before but never with cumin and lots of ginger. I was given detailed instructions by my boss. These special assignments could make or break you in his eyes but fortunately it worked fine first time (harrumph): the plump fillet of mullet served on sweet and sour cabbage with the new tomato sauce, brick red in colour slathered all round it. We tried some in the kitchen and the combination blew my mind.

I've since eaten and used it an awful lot. My favourite pairing of all time has to be a tender lamb shank that's been cooked in a cumin and tomato broth with lots of garlic, served with chick peas and a dollop of mint yoghurt. I use cumin in soups, batters, sauces and stews. I would go so far as to say there are times that I use too much of it, forgetting that my love of it might not be shared by everyone else in the world. Almost religiously I see it as my duty to convert the unbelievers, sceptics and confirmed 'plain eaters'.

But I must make you aware of the difference between seeds and powder. Sure you can use the powder for convenience. I'm all for that but when you roast some seeds in a dry pan for 2 minutes, then tip them into a pestle and mortar, give them a good bashing and take a whiff – that is the only drug I will ever need.

Cumin is one of those spices that really gets around. I used to think it was unique to Middle Eastern cuisine until I found it in recipes for north African couscous. In the Canaries, it flavours fish soup and in Spain it's indispensable with chick peas. Hop across the Atlantic to Mexico and it's part of the background of chilli con carne. Incidentally, I have found that orange goes marvellously well in conjunction with cumin, either in dark stews or even tomato sauces, made with a hint of orange peel.

These little subtleties make a difference. Cumin is used also in the preparation of Munster cheese. Now this, I'm sorry, is the outer limit of my love for cumin. There aren't many things I wouldn't eat but along with that festering, foul smelling cheese, Époisse, Munster is one of them so let's think nice things and go to happy land again.

Nice things to do with cumin – now, the following are not meant to be done together unless you are planning a cumin festival chez vous. If you wish to serve the smoked salmon as a starter, to be followed by the pork, leave the cumin out of the blinis.

## Smoked Salmon on Raisin and Cumin Blinis, Spring Onion Yoghurt

**Serves 4**

2 spring onions, finely chopped
120 ml / 4 fl oz natural yoghurt
300 g / 11 oz sliced smoked salmon
pinch fresh coriander roughly chopped

**For the blinis**
150 g / 5 oz plain flour
pinch salt
1 sachet dried yeast
two eggs, separated
200 ml / 5 fl oz milk
50 g / 2 oz soaked raisins
pinch cumin powder
sunflower oil for frying

The warmth of cumin perfectly matches the smokiness of the salmon and coolness of the yoghurt. These little pancakes are light and fluffy and extremely versatile. Mix the flour, salt and yeast together. Make a well in the centre and add the egg yolks and milk. Gently bring the mix together until it is a smooth batter. Add the raisins and cumin. Beat the egg whites to a peak and fold into the mixture.

Heat a little sunflower oil in a non-stick frying pan. Drop the mixture one spoonful at a time onto the pan to form a little pancake. Brown on each side. Drain on kitchen towel. Set aside and keep in a warm place.

Meanwhile mix the chopped spring onions into the natural yoghurt

Arrange the smoked salmon on a warm blini with a tablespoon of the yoghurt on top. Garnish with the chopped coriander.

# Candied Roast Pork with Cumin

Preheat the oven to 180°C/Gas 4. Take a roasting tray big enough to accommodate the meat and drizzle half the oil on the bottom. Arrange the onions in a line and sit the pork on top, then scatter evenly with the cumin, sugar, salt and pepper. Add the water, garlic and rosemary to the tray. Cover with tin foil making sure it's tightly crimped at the sides, then place in the oven for 45 minutes. Remove the foil and baste. Cook for another 45 minutes basting every now and then. This steaming, roasting technique makes for very juicy meat. The end result should be sticky and caramelised. Allow to rest in a warm place for 20 minutes or so before carving.

I would serve this with buttered spinach (see Spinach), sweet and sour creamed onions with sage (see Onions) and some roast potatoes.

I cooked one of these for staff lunch the other day and was mightily impressed with this joint of meat (a tournados is a Waterford term. For your butcher it's called a boneless and rindless neck end). Nicely juicy and tender and feeds six hungry people.

60 ml / 2 fl oz sunflower oil
one large onion cut into 2 cm discs
1 tournados of pork 1.2 kg to 1.4 kg / approx 3 lb
1 tablespoon cumin powder
pinch demerara sugar
pinch rock salt
pinch cracked black pepper
half cup water
4 cloves of garlic
2 sprigs of rosemary

# Chicken Marinated with Cumin, Garlic and Yoghurt

Yoghurt is a great tenderiser. I serve this chicken on top of the chick pea couscous (see Chick peas) with a tomato and orange sauce (see Tomato). The spices give a depth of flavour without being overpowering. Marinate your chicken for up to 3 days and it will melt in your mouth.

Whisk all the ingredients together and immerse the fillets completely. When cooking place on a buttered baking sheet with some extra butter on top of the chicken and put into a 180°C/Gas 4 preheated oven for 18–20 minutes.

This would also be nice with the chick pea fritters (see Chick peas) and cucumber raita (see Cucumber).

An extra dish strongly featuring cumin is the braised lamb shanks (see Lamb).

**Serves 8**

4–6 chicken fillets, skinned
570 ml / 1 pint thick natural yoghurt
juice 1 lime
1 teaspoon ground ginger
1 teaspoon ground cumin
½ teaspoon turmeric
1 cloves of garlic, crushed
1 tablespoon icing sugar

# Emperor Hirohito of Japan made a meal of No. 423,900 on 3 October 1971 and a few years ago they celebrated duck No. 500,000.

I know I shouldn't be saying this but I even like bad duck. We have all eaten it. A dodgy Chinese fatty duck late at night after too much alcohol because the craving is there for aromatic duck with pancakes and it has to be sated. I can never roll my pancakes fast enough and afterwards I feel like I need an industrial dose of liver salts. That's not to say, of course, that there aren't good versions. That's the trouble, you get one good one and you're hooked. You will spend forever trying to get one as good again. It's like chasing the Holy Grail. Fortunately for me. our local Chinese restaurant is good.

You see that's my absolutely positively favourite way of eating duck, followed closely by a good confit leg and thirdly by roast. A crispy and succulent duck leg cooked in its own fat for a couple of hours with herbs, garlic and spices is hard to beat. It may sound iffy but anybody who likes it loves it and to everybody else I say 'what's wrong with you?!' When the duck legs are cooked you can keep them in the fridge, covered in fat, for 2–3 weeks. They only get better. To cook, scrape off the excess fat. Place them on a tray skin side down in a hot oven for 10 to 15 minutes until crispy and serve them on some creamed lentils with cabbage and mash. Then I thank God for the French. It is possible to buy confit duck legs, already cooked and vacuum packed in good delis. Confit duck is rarely off our menu and if I may say so I make a mean one: unctuous, gooey and bursting with flavour. At the moment I am serving it with creamed peas and bacon. Béarnaise sauce is just heavenly with it or our mini versions (female legs) we serve as a starter on ginger blinis with hoi sin sauce, curry oil, cucumber and spring onion, my humble homage to the Chinese version.

Roast stuffed duck is proper comfort food par excellence. As much as I use spices and flavourings myself, I'm a sucker for a good plain stuffing. I believe that lightness of hand is essential and I have a preference for bread based ones.

To achieve crispy skin, succulent flesh and tender legs makes roasting whole ducks a tricky business but when you serve it with a little gravy from the juices, roast potatoes and lovely vegetables, you would wonder why would anybody do it any other way. Sadly not too many restaurants do this any more.

I haven't spoken about types of duck yet. Wild ones spend their life waddling around marshland in search of food whereas the domestic bird has a soulless existence and seldom tastes of anything. If you know anything about me by now, you know that I am not a food snob but do try and get hold of mallard, teal or widgeon, and you won't regret it.

I have a keen interest in great classic restaurants and without a doubt, the grande dame of them all must be the Tour d'Argent on the banks of the Seine, overlooking Notre Dame. I have a beautifully illustrated book called the *Gourmet Guide to Paris* and the photo on the cover depicts a table laden with roast duck looking out onto the Eiffel Tower. This restaurant is world-renowned and centuries old. It was on this site that Henri III ate heron pâté in 1520. They started to count and number their ducks in 1890 and the Grand Duke Vladimir ate duck number 6,043 in 1900. The future queen Elizabeth feasted on No. 185,937 in 1948. Emperor Hirohito of Japan made a meal of No. 423,900 on 3 October 1971 and a few years ago they celebrated duck No. 500,000. Now that's what I call special duck!

# Duck Liver Parfait

Pre-heat the oven to 160°C/Gas 2½ and line a 450 g / 1 lb loaf tin with clingfilm. Use oil and a pastry brush to ensure it gets in all the corners. Leave some overlapping clingfilm to cover the top of the mixture afterwards. Preheat a bain marie in a roasting tray, (to about 80°C, very hot but not simmering). The water is to come halfway up the loaf tin. In a small pan, bring the port and brandy up to the boil with the shallots, garlic and thyme and reduce until almost dry. Add this to the chicken livers and liquidise. When this is nice and smooth, add the eggs and butter, then the salt and pepper. When completely amalgamated, pass the mixture through a sieve into a warm container so the butter doesn't begin to set (a small ladle is the right job for this). Then pour into the prepared loaf tin. Cover the mix with the excess clingfilm. Place the loaf tin in the bain marie and place in the oven for one hour and 10 minutes. To check whether it is cooked insert a skewer or thin knife into the centre. It should come out dry and clean. Remove from the oven and allow to cool in the bain marie. Refrigerate overnight and turn out when you need it. Slice with a hot knife. It should be pink in the centre.

This is the most silky smooth parfait I know. It can also be made with chicken livers with great success. It's very simple. It just needs a little forward planning and pre-ordering from your butcher. This amount makes a 450g/1lb loaf tin, enough for yourself and some friends. It will last three to four days in the fridge and is best made one or two days before you need it.

200 g / 7 oz duck livers (sinew removed)
60 ml / 2 fl oz ruby port
30 ml / 1 fl oz brandy
4 shallots, peeled and diced
1 clove garlic, sliced
1 sprig thyme
2 eggs
200 g / 7 oz melted butter
half teaspoon pepper
half teaspoon salt

This is lovely with the onion marmalade (see Onions) or gingered peach chutney (see Ginger).

## Confit of Duck – Master Recipe

**Serves 4**

Marinade

few sprigs thyme

3 bay leaves

12 black peppercorns

3 sprigs rosemary

3 cloves garlic thinly sliced

1 onion chopped

½" piece root ginger peeled and sliced

4 star anise

4 tablespoons soy sauce

1 pinch rock salt

peel of 1 orange

4 large duck legs

2 kg / 4½ lb goose fat, duck fat or beef dripping melted

4 teaspoons honey

This is perfect with the warm chorizo and butter bean salad. It is also a fantastic pairing with béarnaise sauce (see Eggs) and spinach.

Place the duck legs in a large bowl. Add the ingredients for the marinade and mix well. Cover with clingfilm and leave in the fridge overnight. Place the duck legs with all the marinade ingredients and enough fat to cover well in a saucepan. Simmer very gently for 2 hours until really tender. Leave to cool in the fat and chill until needed. Just before serving scrape off the fat. Pan fry the duck portions until golden and crispy. Pour off the excess fat from the pan (this you can keep until the next time along with the rest of the fat). Place the duck legs, skin side up, on a roasting tray. Spoon the honey over the top of each leg and place under a pre-heated grill until caramelised.

If you have the space, the more confit you prepare the better, as you can then just remove what you need from the fat, and heat them as required

## Roast Duck with Honey, All-spice and Black Pepper

Boil a kettle, then pour the water over the duckskin. Dry thoroughly, then preheat the oven on the hottest setting. Score the duck with a sharp knife at 1 cm spaces and place it on the roasting tray with some of the oil on the bottom. Then brush the bird completely with the honey. Sprinkle evenly with the salt, pepper and all-spice and place in the oven for up to 20 minutes until caramelised. Allow to rest in a warm oven for 20 minutes. This allows the bird to relax. The meat becomes tender and the flesh, a nice rosy pink.

You can also stuff the bird. The recipe for an easy stuffing follows.

**Serves 2**

This is the method I always use when roasting duck. I prefer to confit the legs separately and use them for lunch or as a starter.

Frequent basting is crucial here, otherwise the honey will burn on the tray rather than caramelise on the bird. Take out the bird when it is an amber colour. At this point it will not be cooked but a further 20 minutes resting in a warm place will give a succulent pink result.

1 duck crown approx 900 g / 2 lb

1 heaped tablespoon honey

1 generous pinch cracked black pepper

1 pinch rock salt

sprinkling of all-spice

3 tablespoons veg oil

## Almond and Raisin Stuffing with Sage and Onion

Cook the onion in the butter until soft and translucent. Mix with all the other ingredients gently. Season and stuff into the bird.

**For 1 duck**

110 g / 4 oz butter

1 large onion, finely diced

a handful pineapple sage or sage, chopped

a pinch green peppercorns (preferably in brine but if not soaked dried ones in hot water)

1 cup soaked raisins, blond if possible

50 g / 2 oz toasted almonds

350 g / 12 oz white breadcrumbs

salt and pepper

## Cream of Sweet Potato Soup with Smoked Duck

This is a richly delicious soup, one of my favourites. Of course you don't have to serve the smoked duck with it, it's quite OK on its own. The duck just adds an extra dimension. The cumin gives the sweet potato a little bit of character. The pool of yoghurt with the pink of the smoked duck on top is visually stunning.

Slowly sweat the vegetables in the butter until soft. Add the flour, potatoes, cumin and sage. Cook for 1–2 more minutes then add the stock, tomato purée and smoked paprika. Bring to the boil. Cook for about 10 minutes. Pick out the sage and liquidise. Season. Divide the soup into 4 bowls. Spoon the yoghurt on top, the shredded duck on top of that, and if you're feeling flash deep fry a sage leaf to put on top again.

**Serves 4**

1 medium onion, finely chopped

1 large carrot, finely chopped

2 sticks celery, finely chopped

75 g / 3 oz butter

1 pinch of flour

4 sweet potatoes (the orange variety), peeled and finely chopped

1 teaspoon cumin seeds

1 sprig sage

$1^{1}/_{2}$ l / $2^{1}/_{2}$ pints chicken stock

1 teaspoon tomato purée

1 teaspoon smoked paprika (optional)

1 heaped tablespoon natural yoghurt

$^{1}/_{2}$ smoked duck breast finely shredded

## ... aromatic duck with pancakes ... you get one good one and you're hooked. You will spend forever trying to get one as good again. It's like chasing the Holy Grail.

Imagine a cookery world without eggs. It just couldn't happen. We take them for granted, forgetting their omnipresence in our kitchens. No matter how healthily you try to eat there is always one morning you get up and really fancy a fry, the eggs cooked over easy so when you cut into them the yolk runs all over the plate to be hungrily mopped up with bread and butter.

I'm very fussy about my eggs. When you become aware of the conditions that chickens are commercially reared in, you buy free-range eggs as well as free-range chicken.

In wintertime I poach or fry eggs and serve them atop colcannon with black pudding and gammon, or poached like eggs benedict but using brioche, lentils and garlic sausage instead of the muffin and ham, the hollandaise just masking the egg. The yolk oozes over the brioche and lentils. A dash of warm sherry vinegar through the lentils cuts through the richness of the dish.

In the summer I really run rampant. Boiled eggs with everything. Drop the eggs into boiling water for 6 minutes, then refresh them under cold water. To cook an egg any more for me is sheer folly. The yolk becomes grainy and hard to digest. Peel, cut in half, season and admire the soft orange creaminess of a perfectly cooked egg, the centre just set, a sauce all on its own. These I serve with fish stews or a lovely summery dish of grilled sardines, roasted peppers and capers. Try them with slivers of bayonne ham and a rémoulade of celeriac. Or chopped with a poached fillet of salmon coated in a light cream sauce with paprika, spring onion and new potatoes. For the perfect sandwich, boiled egg, butterleaf lettuce, chopped tomato, spring onion and mayonnaise, plenty of salt in between slices of soft white bread, nothing new here. Just certain things that when made properly can be more satisfying than any amount of fancy meals.

One of my favourite ways to eat eggs is oeufs en meurette. This is eggs traditionally poached in Beaujolais on garlic toast with bacon and mushrooms, simmering in a red wine sauce. A very popular number in Burgundy bistros but also elevated to three star status by Marco Pierre White.

However, one of the greatest eggy treats in the Flynn household happens on Sunday mornings with the papers. Boiled egg and marmalade sandwiches. Take two slices of buttered toast, spread with orange marmalade. Boil some eggs (soft of course). Scoop out the eggs and spread generously over the toast. Sprinkle with salt, sandwich together and eat with plenty of napkins. This also works very well with thinly sliced brown bread. I have told many friends about this ritual and my penchant for boiled egg and marmalade sandwiches, and all of them without exception, tell me I am a sick puppy. I'm afraid I can't take the credit for this particular sandwich. That goes to Máire but I am hooked and I think you should know.

## Classic Oeufs en Meurette

I know that lashing a bottle of wine into a starter for 4 people is a tad excessive. I got this recipe from a book of French classical cooking so we may as well do it right but by all means cut down on the wine to be economical – maybe just drink a little bit more while you're eating it.

Reserve a quarter of the bottle of wine and put the rest in a saucepan with the beef stock, herbs and onion. Cook over a high heat until reduced by three quarters. Strain and return to the pan and thicken by adding the butter and flour mixture a little at a time and whisking constantly over a moderate heat. Season and allow to simmer.

Cut the bacon into small pieces and fry in the butter until golden. Remove the bacon and add the mushrooms and onions to the fat. Cook through. Set aside with the bacon.

Scrub the (fried) bread with the garlic and place it on 4 serving plates. Heat the vinegar with the wine that you kept back and poach the eggs in same. When cooked, lift out and place an egg on each bread portion. Garnish with the bacon, onions and mushrooms. Spoon over the red wine sauce and sprinkle with parsley.

**This is a perfect starter for 4 people**

1 bottle Beaujolais (or some light red wine)
275 ml / ½ pint beef stock
1 sprig thyme and 1 bay leaf
1 small onion, peeled and chopped finely
1 teaspoon butter and 1 teaspoon plain flour (mixed) for thickening
salt and pepper
4 rindless streaky bacon rashers
25 g / 1 oz butter
12 button mushrooms
12 button onions, peeled
8 bread slices fried in olive oil
1 clove garlic, peeled
1 tablespoon red wine vinegar
8 eggs
1 teaspoon chopped parsley

... one of the greatest eggy treats in the Flynn household happens on Sunday mornings with the papers. Boiled **egg** and marmalade sandwiches ...

AN IRISH ADVENTURE WITH FOOD

## Steamed Salmon with Curried Egg and Spring Onion Sauce

This is a twist on kedgeree without the smoky aspect. I also use this sauce for my smoked haddock balls (see Haddock). Otherwise it really goes well with the salmon.

**Serves 4**

The sauce
1 small onion, finely chopped
1 carrot, finely chopped
2 stalks celery, finely chopped
50 g / 2 oz butter
1 teaspoon curry powder
120 ml / 4 fl oz white wine or 4 fl oz unsweetened apple juice
120 ml / 4 fl oz chicken stock
2 bay leaves
1 pinch black peppercorns
350 ml / 12 fl oz cream

4 x 175 g / 6 oz pieces of salmon fillet
2 boiled eggs, placed into boiling water for 6 minutes then refreshed and roughly chopped
8 spring onions, finely chopped
50 g / 2 oz soaked raisins
pinch paprika
squeeze of 1 lemon
salt and pepper

Sweat the onion, carrot and celery in the butter until soft and translucent. Add the curry powder and cook for one more minute. Add the white wine or apple juice and the chicken stock, bay leaves and peppercorns and reduce by half, then add the cream. Cook gently until the sauce is at coating consistency.

Season and pass through a sieve, squeezing the vegetables as much as possible.

Meanwhile, season your salmon and steam for 4-5 minutes. Re-heat your sauce and add the egg, spring onion, raisins and a squeeze of lemon.

Place the salmon on the plates. Cover half of each piece of salmon with some sauce. Sprinkle with paprika and serve with boiled new potatoes, green beans or buttered spinach.

I'm very fussy about my eggs. When you become aware of the conditions that chickens are commercially reared in, you buy free-range eggs as well as free-range chicken.

steamed salmon with curried egg and spring onion sauce

# Bearnaise Sauce

**Serves 4–6**

225 g / 8 oz butter
4 shallots, finely chopped
1 teaspoon cracked black pepper
1 pinch fresh tarragon
90 ml / 3 fl oz dry white wine
90 ml / 3 fl oz white wine vinegar
6 egg yolks
1 pinch dried tarragon
salt
juice of ½ lemon

We serve this with all our grills. No other sauce for me could do the job. The method might be a little bit scary at first but once you've done it, it's simple.

Melt 200 g / 7 oz of the butter in a stainless steel pan. In another stainless steel pan fry the shallots in the remaining butter. Add the cracked pepper and dried tarragon and mix together. Add the wine and vinegar and reduce the lot to a syrup. Strain everything through a sieve, squeezing well to release all the juices. Place this in a stainless steel or pyrex bowl and add the egg yolks. Place the bowl over a pan of simmering water and start to whisk until thick and fluffy. After 2–3 minutes start to drizzle the melted butter onto the egg yolks amalgamating as you go along. When all the butter is in, add the fresh tarragon, salt and lemon juice and keep in a warm place. This is the best sauce for steak. It is ready to use straightaway but it will keep for a couple of hours.

# Coffee and Cardamon Crème Brûlée

This is a lovely combination derived from a coffee I had in a Moroccan restaurant some years back.
A nice touch with these is to serve them in cappuccino cups.

**Serves 4–6**

450 ml / 12 fl oz milk
450 ml / 12 fl oz cream
16 cardamom pods, crushed
rind of one orange
8 egg yolks
125 g / 4 1/2 oz sugar
half small cup of very strong coffee
2 tablespoons demerara sugar (for glazing)

Boil the milk, cream, cardamom pods and orange rind together. Cream the egg yolks and sugar. Whisk the boiling liquid into the eggs in a large bowl. Return to a medium heat and stir continuously stir until thickened. Pass through a sieve. Pour in the coffee. Allow to cool. Place in cups or ramekins and place them in a roasting tin half-filled with water in a preheated oven 160°C/Gas 2½ to bake for 45 minutes or until set. You will know they are set when there is just a slight wobble in the centre of the cup. Allow to cool and refrigerate for 2–3 hours. These are best served slightly chilled.
Spread the demerara sugar over the top of the cups and glaze with a blow torch or under the grill until caramelised.

# French Toast with Parma Ham and Marinated Cherry Tomatoes

This is a simple starter that is as good with ham as with Parma ham. It would be a perfect dish for brunch. The marinated cherry tomatoes elevate it to lunch status. The addition of rocket leaves or baby spinach dressed in olive oil and balsamic vinegar would enhance it even more.

Beat the eggs and pepper together. Melt some butter in a non-stick frying pan until foaming. Immerse the bread in the egg mixture and allow to absorb some of the egg, cooking in batches. Fry the bread in the butter on both sides until golden brown. Drain on kitchen paper and keep warm. Repeat the process with the rest of the bread and serve with the Parma ham and marinated tomatoes.

**Serves 4**

French toast
4 eggs
50 g / 2 oz grated Parmesan
60 ml / 2 fl oz milk
salt and pepper
all beaten together
75 g / 3 oz butter
white country bread cut into 8 slices, each 1 cm thick

8 slices parma ham
1 recipe marinated cherry tomatoes (see Tomatoes)

Jim Figerty came to town around 1969. I know this, having confirmed it with the accomplices to the crime, my sisters. For those of you not in the know, he's the man who put the figs into the fig rolls.

To celebrate the visit of this luminous dignitary, there was a fancy dress festival held on the back of a lorry in the middle of the Square. Now to the best of my knowledge, Jim was a Charlie Chaplinesque figure so they dressed me up as a mini Jim but dangled dozens of fig-rolls on strings around my body for a sort of Crocodile Dundee effect. The long and the short of it was that I won and I remember Jim Figerty hoisting me over his head to the tumultuous applause of the crowd. I like to think of it as one of my finest moments.

Well that did it for the family. I brought home the trophy and they were greedy for more. Another fancy dress competition was coming up. Around then, there was a famine in Biafra. There were collections, news flashes and sermons from the pulpit. The family planned the dastardly deed over hushed cups of tea in the kitchen, eyes darting over to me, their victim. I was only five but I knew their game. Then crubeens and cabbages arrived from Tommy Powers. I eyed them suspiciously. Dad and Kevin were the only ones that ate them but there was enough for ten. Either they had turned into savages or ...

My sisters grabbed me around one o'clock. I was helpless. It was an ambush and these were determined apaches. Mags, my tactful older sister, said I was 'a nice size' back then. Now between you and me, I was a mini meat loaf. I remember being made to wear a little stripy t-shirt that made my belly stick out over my shorts. I was whinging so then they stooped to bribery. 'If you shut up and stay still, we'll give you some chocolate'. That did the trick. My chronic addiction to chocolate had started in the days when my pram was left outside the shop, and people would coo coo at me (for naturally I was cute) and stuff

# Beautifully ripe figs need virtually nothing doing to them. I serve them with confit of duck. I simply drizzle honey and sprinkle all-spice over them and stick them under the grill. They caramelise beautifully.

my face with chocolate till my head was covered in it.

I saw one of the sisters stringing up the crubeens and cabbage. I took no notice because the chocolate had placated me. Then they started to tie them onto me. First the crubeens, then the cabbages. Then came the coup de grâce. They hung a sign from me that said in big bold letters FREEDOM FROM HUNGER. Jesus, the mortification of it.

It was only a few steps to the lorry as we lived on the Square. Straightaway the sisters knew they were on to a winner. The deafening giggles were a testament to their success. I was hoisted again (this time with some difficulty) onto the stage. I was a star once more. I have seen some pictures of me on that day but they certainly won't be pulled out and passed around. My sisters were like medal hungry Eastern European Athletic coaches, prepared to resort to anything to ensure the success of their charge. Time has passed and I have forgiven them. After all

they did give me chocolate.

Fig rolls were about all we knew about figs back then. 32 years on you still don't fight through trays of them to get at the carrots but they are around. Beautifully ripe figs need virtually nothing doing to them. I serve them with confit of duck. I simply drizzle honey and sprinkle all-spice over them and stick them under the grill. They caramelise beautifully. You can also serve them with some cinnamon ice-cream and mulled wine syrup. Figs are delicious soaked in a little dark rum and dipped in batter, deep-fried in clean oil until golden brown, then coated in a cinnamon caster sugar mixture like a doughnut. Then drizzle with honey and serve with lightly whipped cream. Of course, you probably know figs are a classical and perfect accompaniment to cured ham, be it Bayonne, Parma or San Danielle.

I am giving you two recipes for figs, one as a starter and one as a dessert. Please do not serve them at the one meal.

# Honeyed Figs with Crispy Goat's Cheese Sandwich

**Serves 4**

1 log of St Maure cut into eight rounds

1½ figs per person

8 deep fried wonton pastries

honey and all-spice

drizzle olive oil

This is extremely simple to do. Grill the figs as described and keep them in a warm place. I have a fondness for St Maure goat's cheese as it has no rind. It melts easily and has a rounded creamy texture, not as sharp as some goat's cheeses can be.

Filo pastry will work as a substitute if wonton pastries are not available. but this will need to be cut, buttered and baked. Try as best you can to keep the wontons square. Then sandwich two pieces of goats cheese between two pieces of pastry. Repeat three more times.

Preheat an oven to 160°C/Gas 2½ and pop the goat's cheese sandwiches in for five or six minutes or until the cheese has started to melt. Divide the figs among the plates and perch the sandwiches on them. Drizzle the olive oil around and serve. If you really want to impress your guests add some Parma or Bayonne ham to this dish. Place the ham on the plate, then the figs and sandwich as before.

# Rum and Raisin Pannacotta with Caramelised Figs

This is a fantastically easy dessert to make. With the figs, some caramel and, of course, the accompanying raisins, it's a dream to eat. You will need small pudding moulds or ramekins for this.

**Serves 4**

450 ml / 16 fl oz cream

2½ leaves of gelatine soaked until soft in cold water

50g / 2 oz caster sugar

dark rum to taste

Caramel sauce

110g / 4 oz caster

110 ml / 4 fl oz approximately water

50 g / 2 oz soaked blond raisins

4 ripe figs (quartered, leaving the skins on)

Bring half the cream to the boil, take off the heat and add the gelatine and the sugar. Whisk in thoroughly. When they are dissolved, add in the rest of the cream and the rum and pour into moulds and chill overnight. For the caramel sauce, dissolve the sugar with 80 ml of the water in a saucepan over heat and bring to the boil. Wash down the inside of the pan with a pastry brush dipped in cold water to prevent crystals from forming. Cook until the sugar turns a deep amber colour. Take off the heat and whisk in another 30 ml of water bit by bit. This will splash a little so be careful. Add in the raisins and the quartered figs. Allow to cool. To serve, dip the pannacotta moulds into hot water to loosen the pannacotta and overturn, tipping it out onto plates. Spoon the caramelised figs and raisins around the pannacotta and serve.

honeyed figs with crispy goat's cheese sandwich

I never developed a taste for caviar. I liked truffles but I could live without them, yet when it came to foie gras, I fell in love with its silky seductiveness. Highly prized and very, very expensive, only top restaurants that charge top prices can afford to put it on their menus. My sous chef at Chez Nico all those years ago used to feed us slivers of hot foie gras on rare occasions. We were like chicks being fed by their mother, all of us vying for the largest piece. The first time I ate it properly was in Hilaire in Old Brompton Road, glazed with apples and a madeira sauce. I formed a love hate relationship with it when I was put in charge of making the foie gras terrine under Nico's piercing gaze. This was his pride and joy and it almost became my nemesis, sometimes reducing me to a gibbering wreck. The making of the terrine was akin to surgery. Under controlled temperatures, it first entailed removing the outer membrane, followed by the sinews. If the liver was too cold, working with it was difficult and wasteful. Too warm, it would quickly be reduced to a greasy mush. Then the marination. Equal quantities of white port, Armagnac and Sauternes, a sprinkling of quatre épice and marinate for not more than 20 minutes. Have your terrine lined with clingfilm, and mind that you have no wrinkles in the film. Have your water bath ready at 65 degrees centigrade, your oven pre-heated to 110 degrees centigrade, then fill your terrine. The aim was to have one homogeneous block, layer by layer, carefully packing all the gaps with a spoon, forming a slight dome, rising above the terrine. Cover with the residual clingfilm, again no wrinkles, ensuring that the excess foie gras that will have turned to butter can be saved for our glorious sauce albufera. Place the terrine in the water bath. Let it sit for 12 minutes. Cook in the oven for another 12 minutes. Remove and place in a tray to come to room temperature. Drain off the excess foie gras butter, place in the fridge with a terrine press on top (a wooden board cut precisely to cover the terrine) and weighted with three 1 lb weights, and allow two days in the fridge to mature.

'Hey Oirish', we are going to turn out the terrine tomorrow. 'Yes, Nico', I would say meekly, not wanting tomorrow to come. To say I had butterflies the next day would be

# My sous chef at Chez Nico all those years ago used to feed us slivers of hot **foie gras** on rare occasions. We were like chicks being fed by their mother. All of us vying for the largest piece ...

an understatement. He would thunder into the kitchen, bristling with excitement. I would have a water bath hot and ready to submerge the terrine to enable us to turn it out. All the other chefs would be working furiously, their eyes darting over, knowing it could go either way. There would be silence while he assessed my work, taking off a slither and considering the appearance and flavour. I awaited his pronouncement. I have had my disasters in my time and his screams would rattle the windows at the other side of the building but if he was pleased, he would put his arm around me and say 'My God, Irish, this one is really special'. The ultimate compliment, our hearts lifted, our confidence soared. It was going to be a good day after all.

Nico held foie gras in such high esteem that in his early days, if there was a fault, he would throw it in the bin. This, he would say, was the difference between mediocrity and excellence. Oh, when it is excellent, there is no finer thing spread on toasted brioche with a crisp salad of French beans and artichokes, bathed in a truffle vingairette.

Foie gras is difficult to get and very expensive

– at the moment around €40 per kg so you have to be careful with it. You can buy cooked foie gras in tins from good delicatessens. For fresh, you may have to ask them to order it for you or if you are friendly with a local restaurateur, they should be able to get it easily enough from their wholesaler. A simple method of cooking it is to slice it into 1 cm slices. Heat a clean frying pan (no fat) until it is smoking. Be sure to turn your extractor on full blast and sear on both sides for 30 seconds until mahogany brown. Remove from the pan, season and eat with toasted brioche and some apple chutney or fried apple slices (have these ready beforehand). A good accompaniment to foie gras is Sauternes or Maderia.

This recipe comes by way of Marco Pierre White's *Canteen Cuisine*. I would not presume that I could provide you with a better recipe to start with. It's not worth making a terrine as luxurious as this in a small amount so this recipe yields about 15 slices.

## *Parfait of Foie Gras with Chicken Livers*

200 ml / 7 fl oz port

200 ml / 7 fl oz madeira

100 ml / 3-45 fl oz brandy

8 shallots, peeled and finely sliced

1 garlic clove, crushed

2 generous sprigs thyme

400 g / 14 oz fresh foie gras

400 g / 14 oz fresh chicken livers

sea salt

8 eggs at room temperature

800 g / 1³/₄ lb unsalted butter melted and just above blood heat

To finish and serve (this part is optional and purely for presentation purposes):

150 g / 5 oz unsalted butter

coarsely ground white pepper

Preheat the oven to 160°C/Gas 2¹/₂ and have ready a terrine or pâté mould (12 x 4 1/2" and 4" deep).

Place the port, madeira and brandy in a pan with the shallot, garlic and thyme and boil to reduce until almost dry. Remove the thyme.

Slice the foie gras and chop the chicken livers. Place in a pan and warm gently, covered with 1 level tablespoon of white sea salt.

Place the port mixture and the livers into a liquidiser and blend until fully liquidised. You may need to do this in batches. Add the eggs and mix well.

Add and mix in the warm melted butter, then working quickly, push through a sieve into a warm container. Transfer to the terrine and cover lightly with a piece of kitchen foil.

Place in a bain marie (a roasting tin half filled with water) and cook in the preheated oven for 1 hour 10 minutes. Remove from the bain marie, cool and then refrigerate for 24 hours.

To finish, melt a quarter of the butter and soften the remainder. Emulsify together by whisking – this lightens the butter.

Spread a thin layer of this light butter on top of the parfait, then chill to set. Run a hot knife around the edges and turn out onto a board. If it is difficult to get out, it may be sticking on the bottom. Put a tea towel over it and pour on some boiling water. This will loosen it.

To serve, slice the parfait with a hot knife and place a slice just below the centre of the plate. Sprinkle with a little sea salt and coarsley ground white pepper. I would serve this with onion marmalade or ginger and peach chutney. (See Onions or Ginger)

# There is a restaurant in San Francisco called the Stinking Rose which is totally devoted to **garlic**. It's in everything, even the desserts.

The secret with garlic really is to hide its presence by not using too much, unless, of course, you are feeding sworn garlic lovers. Then you can give them roast garlic mash, chicken with 40 cloves of garlic (a famous dish) or lamb smothered with a creamy garlic and rosemary sauce. If you wait for the elephant garlic to come into season you can roast it gently in its skin in olive oil, a little sugar and rosemary, splashed with sherry vinegar. When it's soft, squeeze the skins and out pops sweet mild garlicky purée. You can serve this as a starter with toasted country bread, brushed with some olive oil. It would be perfect with a light tomato salad (plum, vine or cherry beefsteak, not those greeny red ones that can be used for grenade practise). This is also a dinky little garnish for pan fried scallops with chopped parsley and a squeeze of orange juice, served with some peppery rocket.

The numero uno popular dish in Ireland using garlic is garlic mushrooms. It always amazes me that people who ordinarily would never touch garlic adore garlic mushrooms, even the most conservative eaters. Instead of the usual button mushrooms with the bullet proof crust which are often seriously lacking in flavour, why not top a flat cap or field mushroom with breadcrumbs turned in garlic butter, toasted pinenuts and crispy bacon. Bake in the oven until the top is crispy.

There is a restaurant in San Francisco called the Stinking Rose which is totally devoted to garlic. It's in everything, even the desserts. For me garlic is indispensable. Without it there often seems to be something missing. But discretion is the key.

# Nico's Light Garlic Cream Sauce

This sauce is emblazoned on my memory from my days with Nico in London, always served with roast rack of lamb.

large bunch of thyme

300 ml / ¹/₂ pint cream

3 tablespoons olive oil

4 peeled shallots

6 peeled cloves garlic

salt

squeeze lemon

¹/₂ chicken stock cube diluted in ¹/₂ cup boiling water

This is essentially slowly-roasted garlic and shallot that are mixed wit thyme-infused cream and chicken stock, and then blended.

Firstly, pre-heat the oven to 120°C/Gas 1.

Take a small roasting tray. Spread out a large sheet of tin foil and place the shallots, garlic and olice oil in the centre. Bring the foil together and seal. Cook for 1 hour or until soft and lightly golden. Meanwhile, bring the chicken stock, cream and thyme to the boil, leave to one side for 20 minutes to give time to infuse, and then pick it out. Add the garlic, shallots and olive oil mixture. Blend, season, add the lemon juice, pass through a sieve and reserve until needed.

# Garlic Butter Crumbs

Garlic butter

225 g / 8 oz butter

3 large cloves garlic, crushed

Garlic crumbs

110 g / 4 oz breadcrumbs

50 g / 2 oz garlic butter melted

pinch salt and pepper

For the garlic butter, mix the butter and garlic together, roll in clingfilm and refrigerate until needed Preheat the oven to 180°C/Gas 4.

Mix the breadcrumbs with the butter and place on a shallow roasting tray in the oven for 4 to 5 minutes. Toss once or twice during cooking to make sure they are evenly brown and crunchy.

We always have these to hand to sprinkle over pasta, or any otherwise soft-textured dishes.

## Roast Garlic and Potato Soup with Pan Fried Scallops

In a small pan bring the olive oil to a sizzle. Add the garlic and sugar and cook on a very low heat until soft and golden brown. Drain the oil into a larger pan, add the butter, throw in the onion and leek and cook gently with a lid until soft and translucent. Add the potato and stir until coated. Cook over moderate heat for two to three minutes, then add the chicken stock, browned garlic and rosemary. When the potatoes are cooked add the cream and cook for a further 2 minutes. Take out the rosemary. Liquidise and pass through a fine sieve.

Heat a non stick frying pan. Add a drizzle of olive oil. Fry the scallops for 1 minute on each side. Season and squeeze some lemon over them.

To serve, spoon the soup into a shallow bowl. Garnish with three lightly crusted caramelised scallops and shower the soup with the finely chopped chives.

This is a soup/starter. The roast garlic gives a lovely deep flavour to the soup. Garlic and scallops make a perfect marriage and the hint of rosemary, together with the olive oil, makes the taste more complex.

Serves 4

60 ml / 2 fl oz olive oil
8 large cloves of garlic, peeled
1 pinch sugar
75 g / 3 oz butter
half onion, finely diced
half white of leek, finely diced
4 large rooster potatoes, finely diced (other potatoes
    will suffice)
1.2 litres / 2 pints chicken stock
1 sprig rosemary
100 ml / 4 fl oz cream
12 scallops, cleaned
squeeze of lemon juice
handful chives, chopped finely

## Goat's Cheese Mousse

This is ever-present on our menus in the restaurant. We serve it in various guises: a filo cannelloni with red pepper relish and basil oil; as part of an antipasto platter, sexily piped onto a plate with olives, grilled aubergines and pequillo peppers, toasted ciabatta on the side; or as part of the cheese course with some sesame grissini for serious scooping. Of course, technically it's not a mousse but it's made light and fluffy by some whipping in the mixer.

Leave the cheeses at room temperature until soft. Whip with the K beater or paddle on the mixer this will incorporate air into the mixture. When aerated and thoroughly smooth, add the rest of the ingredients.

Serves 4 as a starter

1 small log goat's cheese (we use St Maure)
$1/3$ the (above) amount of a light cream cheese
1 teaspoon honey
1 small clove garlic, peeled and crushed
pinch of salt and ground white pepper

To serve this we pipe it with a plain nozzle to make life easy. You could also spoon it onto plates. Some finely chopped marjoram or chives would make a nice addition if you fancy but I do like the plain unadulterated whiteness of this.

## Aïoli

8 garlic cloves, blanched (cooked vigorously for three
     to four minutes in boiling water, then cooked for
     another three to four minutes in fresh water)

1 teaspoon English mustard

2 egg yolks plus one whole egg

2 teaspoon white wine vinegar

juice half a lemon

300 ml / ½ pint groundnut oil

60 ml / 2 fl oz extra virgin olive oil

2 tablespoons crème fraîche

Aïoli is essentially a posh garlic mayonnaise. The flavours are made more subtle and rounded by the blanching of the garlic. The addition of olive oil gives it authenticity and an extra dimension. We use this with any Mediterranean style dishes, ie, anything with olives, red peppers or basil.

To make the aïoli, whizz the garlic cloves, mustard and egg yolks and whole egg in a food processor until smooth. Add the vinegar and lemon juice and whizz briefly to combine. With the machine running, gradually trickle in the groundnut oil and then the olive oil to form a smooth rich mayonnaise. Fold in the créme fraîche, season and set aside.

## Adaptations of Aïoli:

Chilli aïoli – Make as above, but add chilli sauce to taste and a touch of tomato purée for colour.

Saffron aïoli – Infuse some saffron strands or powder in a few drops of boiling water for five minutes. Add this mixture to the aïoli.

Smoked paprika aïoli – If you ever come across little tins of smoked paprika powder, snap them up. Add a pinch to aïoli and you have a wonderful, smoky piquant flavour. If you add some into the saffron aïoli, you get a truly wonderful sauce.

Sauce bourride – This is a light version of aïoli. Simply make by heating some chicken stock and whisking the aïoli into it until a creamy, frothy consistency is attained. It must never be boiied or it will split. The same job can be done with any of the rest of the flavoured aïolis. Beautiful with seafood and poached chicken with crispy green vegetables.

## Sherry Cream Dressing

This is not an overly garlicky dressing but it is interesting. It's delicious if you want to dress French beans, asparagus or broccoli either for a salad or for a creamy element to a main course when there is otherwise no sauce, ie, grilled salmon with creamy French beans and new potatoes, nice for lunch during the summer.

Whisk everything together. This will keep in the fridge for up to a week. Just give a good shake to the container before draping it round your vegetables.

Makes 300ml / ½ pint

2 shallots, finely chopped
30 ml1 fl oz hazelnut or walnut oil
splash sherry vinegar
60 ml / 2 fl oz pale cream sherry (eg, Croft Original)
one clove garlic, peeled and crushed
150 ml / ¼ pint sunflower oil
55 ml / 2 fl oz cream
salt and black pepper

## Creamy Celeriac Purée with Garlic

This is half sauce, half purée. Decadently rich so use sparingly but bursting with flavour. We used to serve it with our pigs trotters with a lentil and garlic sausage salad. I would serve this with fillet of beef, breast of duck, rack of lamb. It's earthy and robust and goes with rich meats.

Place all the ingredients except the honey, salt, pepper and white truffle oil into a pot and simmer slowly until the celeriac is cooked. Strain through a sieve, pull out the thyme and keep the juice. Transfer the mixture to a food processor. Add as much of the reserved liquid as necessary to make a smooth cream. Add the salt and pepper and honey to taste and finish with a tiny splash of white truffle oil if you wish. You are going to have some liquid left over and this could be used to make a fabulous potato and celeriac soup.

You could also use this method to make a parsnip, sweet potato, turnip or carrot purée or indeed a mixture of any of these.

Serves 4–6

one head of celeriac peeled, diced and washed
300 ml / ½ pint cream
600 ml / 1 pint milk
three whole cloves garlic
one sprig thyme (tied in muslin)
half a chicken stock cube, crumbled
one teaspoon honey
salt and ground white pepper
splash white truffle oil (optional)

Did you know that the Chinese have been using ginger since 600BC both as a spice and as a medicinal food? In its latter role, ginger is believed to soothe the intestines, ward off the common cold and do wonders for the sexual appetite.

In the restaurant, pregnant ladies have often asked us to chop some ginger into hot water to alleviate the symptoms of morning or all day sickness. I am afraid I cannot attest to this either as the only sickness I suffer in the mornings is due to overindulgence rather than pregnancy.

We use four types of ginger in the kitchen. In order of popularity they are fresh, pickled, crystallised and powdered ginger. I pair fresh ginger mostly with fish, especially crab or lobster when I can get it at a good price. The Chinese combination of ginger, garlic and spring onions cannot be bettered, whether they are bound through a mayonnaise or cream sauce, butter or sesame oil and soy sauce. The addition of plump blond raisins sweetens the astringency of the ginger to give a better balance. Fresh ginger is better finely chopped or shredded and then blanched a couple of times. This softens it and mellows the flavour, allowing it to complement rather than dominate a dish. One of our most popular dishes is lemon sole fillets, stuffed with a salmon and crab mousse that has been given the ginger, garlic, spring onion and raisin treatment. These little rolls I poach in a light white wine cream, whereby the fish releases its flavour into the sauce. All this I pour over some warm fettucine and spinach, together with some chopped tomatoes and chives for colour and then a splash of curry oil to finish.

Pickled ginger is my next favourite. You can

# Fresh ginger is better finely chopped or shredded and then blanched a couple of times. This softens it and mellows the flavour, allowing it to complement rather than dominate a dish

buy this in Asian supermarkets. This is sliced ginger that has been lightly cooked in vinegar, sugar and salt. It is very useful to cut through a creamy dish. I use this in a crab crème brûlée we have on as a starter - see Crab. The creamy crab custard is given both acidity and flavour by the ginger. I would also use this through pasta or noodles if they have an oriental edge. By the way, the syrup from pickled ginger tastes fabulous and I always use it for something, either in our Asian noodle dressing or maybe in a sweet-corn chowder, again to give it that little bit of interesting acidity.

Crystallised ginger, or confit ginger, is intensely sweet and sugary. I use this finely chopped through the blinis that go with our deep fried duck with plum sauce and pickled cucumber – a sort of reworking of the crispy duck with pancakes that we all love when we go out to a Chinese restaurant. The sweet ginger blinis with slightly sour pickled cucumber complement the crispy duck and earthy plum sauce.

Now, powdered ginger. I confess I am not a great fan of this. I suppose I prefer it in pudding and biscuits where its coarseness can be controlled with sugar. I have had too many dishes where it's been used too liberally and it's like lots of little people in your mouth, all punching to get out at the same time. It is, however, a vital ingredient in my curry oil. Visually beautiful when it is drizzled over fish, pasta or chicken, it releases a wonderful aroma right under the customers' noses. They have no choice but to surrender and dive in. Those sneaky tricks we cooks will employ to seduce you!

## Salad of Cos with Crab and Creamy Ginger and Grapefruit Dressing

**Serves four as a generous starter**

juice of 1 lemon

50 g / 2 oz sugar

25 g / 1 oz very finely diced fresh ginger

30 ml / 1 fl oz sesame oil

120 ml / 4 fl oz crème fraîche

4 shredded spring onions

1 handful chopped coriander

10 g / ½ oz toasted sesame seeds

2 heads baby cos lettuce, picked and washed

450 g / 1 lb crab meat

1 pink grapefruit, segmented and diced

To make the ginger cream, boil the lemon juice, sugar and ginger, and allow to cool. Whisk in sesame oil and crème fraîche. If too sweet, add a little more lemon juice to taste. Then add in the spring onions, coriander and sesame seeds. Arrange the cos on four plates. Place the crab into a bowl, season and divide over the cos lettuce. Spoon the dressing over the crab and the cos, and scatter the pink grapefruit segments on top.

## Curry Oil

This is essential in my kitchen. Once made, it keeps for a month or so, well sealed in the fridge.

This recipe makes just over one litre. Use curry oil sparingly. A little goes a very long way.

1 teaspoon turmeric

1 teaspoon ground coriander

1 teaspoon ground cumin

1 teaspoon ground ginger

4 cinnamon sticks

10 cardamom pods (crushed)

peel of one orange

2 cloves garlic, crushed

basil or coriander stalks if you have them

1 tablespoon brown sugar

1 generous pinch salt

1.2 litres / 2 pints veg or sunflower oil or, even better,

It is very handy to store this in a squeezy bottle, rather like those old fashioned tomato ketchup squeezers you used to see in cafés.

You can also use it for cooking, for stir-fries, or pan frying chicken breasts or fish to give them a little extra flavour.

Pour enough oil into a heavy-bottomed saucepan to cover the bottom of the pan. Put all the ingredients in and mix. If the mixture looks too dry, add a little more oil and cook slowly over a low heat for 3 to 4 minutes to bring out the flavour of the spices. Add the remaining oil and bring it up to a gentle simmer.

Keep the mixture on the lowest setting of your cooker for 3 to 4 hours – the longer the better. Allow to cool and scrape everything into a container. While in the fridge, the solids will settle to the bottom allowing you to pour off the clear oil.

## Ginger and Cumin Butter

This is an adaptation of the classic beurre blanc. I serve it with mackerel or smoked haddock and poached chicken. You could also use it as a sauce for pasta to be served with fish or chicken.

Cook the shallots and ginger slowly in a knob of the butter so they are soft and translucent. Add the pepper, cumin, vinegar, white wine and chicken stock. Reduce to a syrup. Add cream. Bring to the boil quickly and add the butter bit by bit amalgamating with a whisk as you go along. When the butter is well incorporated, season, add the sugar and the lemon and pass through a sieve into another pot. If it's a little thick add a splash of milk.

**Makes roughly 600 ml / one pint**

6 small shallots, finely chopped
1 knob (2 cm piece) fresh ginger, peeled and finely diced
300 g / 11 oz butter, cut into slices
1 teaspoon cracked black pepper
one teaspoon ground cumin
75 ml / 3 fl oz white wine vinegar
150 ml / ¼ pint white wine
75 ml / 3 fl oz chicken stock
50 ml / 2 fl oz cream
salt
pinch of sugar
squeeze of lemon

## Ginger and Nectarine Relish

This will make three to four jam jars of relish. It keeps forever and it's delicious with pâtés and cold meats.

450 g / 1 lb nectarines, quartered
250 g / 9 oz sliced white onions
1 tablespoon chopped rosemary
60 ml / 2 fl oz sunflower oil
110 g / 4 oz raisins
2 teaspoons coriander seeds, crushed
4 teaspoons ground cinnamon
4 cardamom pods, crushed
4 cm knob ginger, peeled and finely diced
350 g / 12 oz caster sugar
3 bay leaves
200 ml / 7 fl oz cider vinegar

In a large pot, sweat the onion for 5 to 6 minutes. Add the rest of the ingredients. Bring to the boil and cook for one and half hours until thick and syrupy. Cool and place into sterilised jars.

# Haddock

It's winter and it's raining again, monsoon season in Dungarvan. Occasionally the sun returns to tease us, then retreats behind threatening clouds. With weather like this, my mind turns to comfort food. Soups, stews, puddings, lots of sauce, mopped up with crusty bread or sliced pan lashed with butter. The pubs have lit their fires, stout sales increase and everybody has pulled out their winter woollies. It's time for smoked haddock. Everyone has had smoked haddock at home in white sauce with onion and floury potatoes, the smoky flavour permeating through the sauce. It goes well with cream or butter sauces, needing the moisture it loses

during smoking. The smoked haddock we have become used to in shops and supermarkets with the lurid yellow tinge is not actually haddock at all but coley or pollock. This is not technically misrepresentation. It's always been that way. The real McCoy is almost twice the price and a white grey colour. The taste is milder and the flesh tends to break up less but hey, I'm not a snob. Some fabulous dishes can be made with both. The only thing the dyed haddock is not suitable for is grilling as it gets strong and tough. Make chowders and pies with it. Marry it with boiled eggs and curry powder. Remember kedgeree, the staple of the Raj. Curried rice

with flaked haddock, eggs and sultanas and eaten with mango chutney.

Poach the haddock in some stock, milk, a bay leaf and an onion. At home, it doesn't take much to make the haddock in cream sauce something special. Strain the juice, add a dash of cream and reduce by a third, then thicken with what we chefs call a beurre manié. That is softened butter, mixed with equal quantities of flour to make a paste, then whisked vigourously into your sauce to get a nice smooth creamy result. If you are feeling flush you could drop in some saffron and chopped tomato. Turn some cooked pasta through this and the haddock flakes. Garnish with some chopped dill or chives to enhance the flavour and make the colour more vibrant. You could also use some of the cooking liquid splashed with cream and set with eggs for a quiche filling or filo pastry tart. Courgettes, spinach, even peas are sublime served with smoked haddock. Gently poach a fillet, and set it atop some champ with some hollandaise. Go crazy and pair it with black pudding. It works, or flake it into scrambled eggs and chives. Serve on toast with bucks fizz for a special Sunday morning treat. Go on, go on, go on ...

# Gratin of Smoked Haddock

I love gratins of every kind. This one is a perfect winter dish, pungent with the smokiness of haddock. I would serve this simply with some buttered spinach and maybe a poached egg on top.

**Serves 4**

450 ml / ³/₄ pint milk

150 ml / ¹/₄ pint cream

pinch grated nutmeg

2 cloves garlic, crushed

25g / 1 oz butter

6 large potatoes, peeled and thinly sliced

350 g / 12 oz smoked haddock cut into ¹/₂ cm strips

110g / 4 oz grated cheddar cheese

Preheat the oven to 180°C/Gas 4.

Bring the milk and cream and nutmeg to the boil with the crushed garlic. Butter a 10" / 25 cm by 2" / 5 cm deep gratin dish. Layer the potatoes and strips of smoked haddock alternately in the dish, adding a little of the hot cream/milk mixture each time. Season with salt and pepper as you go. Finish off with a layer of potato making sure the liquid comes to the top. Press down with a fish slice to make sure all the potato is submerged. Sprinkle with the cheddar cheese and bake for 45 to 50 minutes until the potatoes are cooked through with a nice golden crust. If you feel the top is browning too quickly, turn down the oven.

# Smoked Haddock and Butterbean Chowder

**Serves 4**

600 ml / 1 pint milk

300 ml / ¹/₂ pint cream

300 ml / just over ¹/₂ pint chicken stock

1 medium onion, sliced

pinch white pepper

4 bay leaves

350 g / 12 oz smoked haddock

25 g / 1 oz soft butter

25 g / 1 oz flour mixed into a paste with the butter

1 teaspoon mustard

1 standard tin butterbeans, drained and rinsed

2 large potatoes, baked or steamed, then peeled and diced into 1 cm cubes

a few sprigs chervil, chopped

Everyone likes chowders. On a wintery day when you are cold and hungry few things can satisfy you more. Half soup, half stew, this one is simplicity itself. Just finish with some chopped chervil for colour and a gentle flavour.

Bring the milk, cream and stock to the boil and add the onions, pepper and bay leaves. Add the smoked haddock and poach for 4 to 5 minutes. The haddock should be covered by the liquid.

When cooked, drain the milk mixture into another pot and start to reduce a little. Whisk the flour and butter paste into the milk, bit by bit until it forms a creamy consistency. Add the mustard, then flake and add the haddock, butterbeans and potatoes. Heat for 2–3 minutes, without boiling. Season and place into warm bowls. Garnish with the chervil.

## Crispy Smoked Haddock Balls

Cook the haddock as for the chowder, and allow to cool.

Drain the haddock and flake into the mashed potato, avoiding skin and bone. Add salt, pepper and two of the eggs and mix well. Divide the mixture and shape into smallish balls (around 3 cm) on a floured tray.

Whisk the remaining eggs and add a splash of milk. Place the breadcrumbs in a bowl. Firstly flour the balls, then run them through the egg wash and finally coat thoroughly with the breadcrumbs. Repeat until all the batch is breadcrumbed.

### To cook

Preheat a deep fat fryer to 180°C. Drop the haddock balls into the oil and allow to cook for 3–4 minutes or until golden brown. Serve with the curried egg and spring onion sauce (see Eggs), French beans and a wedge of lemon. If you don't have time to make the sauce use some mayonnaise mixed with mango chutney and mild curry paste.

The beauty of these balls, if you pardon my expression, is their perfect roundness and crispiness. The filling itself is no mystery but combined with the sauce and served with some French beans, they are a super lunch dish or even a starter in the evening.

**Serves 4–6**

1 onion, finely sliced
4 bay leaves
600 ml / 1 pint milk
450 g / 1 lb smoked haddock, cut into chunks
6 large potatoes, peeled, boiled and mashed
salt and pepper
4 eggs
1 splash milk
200 g / 7 oz white bread crumbs
2 tablespoons flour

It's winter and it's raining again, monsoon season in Dungarvan ... The pubs have lit their fires, stout sales increase and everybody has pulled out their winter woollies. It's time for smoked haddock.

# ... I began to cook hefty steaks of hake with golden onions and mash, all gloriously rough.

The first time I cooked hake was from a recipe in Simon Hopkinson's book, *Roast Chicken and Other Stories*, which is still my favourite cookbook. At the time I was working diligently in Chez Nico, cooking well and doing exactly as I was told. We always used prime fish: prawns, turbot, scallops and sea bass. I imagined these fish to be the royalty of the sea, gazing scornfully at the others, knowing they were only good enough for pies or to be deep fried and served with vinegary chips after a night in the pub, while they were going out in style lathered in truffle butter sauces or Champagne sabayon. Oh, what a noble end.

But with the help of Mr Hopkinson I embraced simplicity and realised how little I actually knew. My cooking began to transform. Where before I cooked delicate, intricate dishes, now I began to cook hefty steaks of hake with golden onions and mash, all gloriously rough.

Hake remains my favourite fish and is an almost constant on my menus. The Spanish have the measure of it. Hake fetches extraordinary prices in Spain, almost as much as we would pay for turbot or sea bass. Still rarely seen on Irish restaurant menus, it is the same price as cod but much more interesting and sophisticated. As long as we can keep some from the Spanish, I expect it is only a matter of time before it becomes as ubiquitous as cod, and with the prices of prime fish remaining through the roof we should try to explore less well-known species. Hake is a pleasure to prepare having few bones. It's pink-tinged flesh requires a sharp knife and sure hands when filleting. Alternatively it excels when cut into steaks, dusted in flour and paprika and cooked in sizzling olive oil with diced chorizo. At the last minute squeeze on some orange juice and chopped herbs and a splash of white wine vinegar. Serve with pilaf rice flavoured with saffron.

# *Bouillabaisse of Hake and Mussels with Chorizo and Celery Cream*

Bouillabaisse can be made with virtually any flavour you like. I've got the crunchy freshness of chopped celery heart and leaves paired with saffron and chorizo. This is a soup come stew – the broth is meant to be eaten first, then tackle the fish. It's best served with plain boiled rice or plain boiled new potatoes.

To make the celery cream: heat the olive oil in a frying pan, add the butter and when it starts to foam tip in the shallots, celery, carrots and garlic. Cook for 5 to 6 minutes or until softened but not coloured, stirring occasionally. Add the white wine and chicken stock and reduce by half. Then add the cream, orange rind, rosemary and cardamom pods. Bring to a simmer, and cook for 15 minutes. Season well, then pass through a strainer into a large clean pan and return to a simmer, add the saffron, stirring occasionally. Add the mussels and cook until half opened. Then add the hake pieces for a few minutes until just tender. When almost cooked add the tomatoes, potatoes, shredded lettuce and reserved celery leaves. Fry the chorizo in a heated non-stick frying pan until crisp, then stir into the fish mixture with the chives. You can have these ready beforehand. Keep the oil to drizzle over the stew.

Ladle the hot soup into warm shallow serving bowls. Chop the hard-boiled egg white and egg yolk separately and use to garnish the soup with the croutons and spring onion before serving.

Serves 4

For the celery cream
60 ml / 2 fl oz olive oil
110 g / 4 oz unsalted butter
8 shallots, finely chopped
1 celery heart (reserve the leaves and add them, cut
    into 1 cm lengths, at the end), finely chopped
3 carrots, finely diced
3 garlic cloves, finely chopped
300 ml / 1/2 pint dry white wine
1 l / 1 3/4 pints chicken stock
300 ml / 1/2 pint cream
grated rind 1 orange
1 fresh rosemary sprig
10 cardamom pods, crushed
pinch saffron strands

For the fish
450 g / 1 lb mussels, scrubbed and beards removed
900 g / 2 lb hake cut into 4 cm cubes with the skin on

For the soup
1 punnet cherry tomatoes
12 new potatoes, boiled
1 head iceberg lettuce, shredded
110 g / 4 oz chorizo, finely diced
handful snipped fresh chives
4 hard-boiled eggs
garlic crumbs (see Garlic) and whole spring onions, to
    serve

grilled hake with spicy pepperonata, new potatoes and aïoli

# Grilled Hake with Spicy Pepperonata, New Potatoes and Aïoli

The creamy whiteness of the hake contrasts beautifully
with the ruddy pepperonata stew. This stew is a particularly good recipe to have in your arsenal. It goes
with virtually everything. Vegetarians love it and the
spices give it a little kick that ordinary pepperonata
does not have.

**To make the pepperonata sauce** heat the olive oil in
a frying pan, add the butter and when it starts to foam
sweat the peppers, onion, garlic and chilli for about 10
minutes or until softened. Add the spices and cook for
another 3 minutes. Stir in the tomatoes, stock and
beans and heat gently, stirring to combine and cook
for a further 15 minutes. Season and reserve.

Preheat the grill. Arrange the hake fillets (brushed
with garlic butter) on a tray and brush liberally with
crème fraîche. Season and sprinkle the remaining
garlic butter over the top of the fish. Cook for 3–4
minutes.

**To assemble:** spoon a pile of pepperonata sauce in the
centre of each warm serving plate. Place the hake on
top and scatter with the olives. I would normally serve
this with some aïoli (see Garlic) and basil oil (see Olive
oil), new boiled or saffron potatoes or pilaf rice.

Serves 4

olive oil, for frying
knob butter
3 red peppers, seeded and finely sliced
1 onion, finely sliced
2 garlic cloves, crushed
1 red chilli, seeded and finely chopped
pinch cumin powder
pinch paprika
pinch cayenne pepper
pinch curry powder
1 standard can plum tomatoes, puréed
120 ml / 4 fl oz strong chicken stock
200 g / 7 oz white cannellini (canned) beans, drained
    and rinsed
200 g / 7 oz kidney beans (canned), drained and rinsed
20 black olives
salt and freshly ground black pepper
4 x 150 g / 5 oz skinless fillets of hake
60 ml / 2 fl oz melted garlic butter (see Garlic)
1 tablespoon crème fraîche

Note: you can use all of one type of bean if you can't
get small tins.

# Lamb and daffodils mean it's spring again. Lamb's my favourite meat ... Roasted garlic, ratatouille, peppers, beans, Jerusalem artichokes, dauphinoise potatoes, basil mash – all of these things I have eaten with lamb.

Lamb and daffodils mean it's spring again. Lamb's my favourite meat. You will probably hear me say that about duck or beef as well. I'm not lying. It's just that as I am writing about a particular ingredient, my mind conjures up the beautiful flavours of each of them. Roasted garlic, ratatouille, peppers, beans, Jerusalem artichokes, dauphinoise potatoes, basil mash – all of these things I have eaten with lamb. Many more as well but these stick. Lamb stew, the rich brown variety or the classic white Irish version eaten with buttery brown bread and a pint of Guinness. The slightly mushy potatoes thickening the liquid are so hearty and totally satisfying. Rack of lamb, loin of lamb, lambs' kidneys with creamy mustard sauce over pilaf rice. Lamb chops with mushy peas; roast leg of lamb, studded with garlic and rosemary; lamb's liver and bacon, with sage and onion gravy. The now ubiquitous lamb shank never fails to impress with some couscous and tomato cumin cream. We have Moroccan spiced leg of lamb on our menu sometimes. Marinated in yoghurt and spices to tenderise it, roasted and served cold, thinly sliced with roasted peppers, baba ganoush (aubergine purée) and chick pea fries.

I think cumin has a particular affinity with lamb. Exotic and earthy in its tones, stewed with tomato, white beans and a tiny pinch of saffron, it begs to be eaten.

# Crispy Lamb Chops with Creamy Sweet and Sour Onions

Crisp, tasty lamb chops sitting on a bed of creamy onions: heaven. Ideally you would serve this with sautéed potatoes and some nice French beans.

**Serves 4**

75 g / 3 oz breadcrumbs

50 g / 2 oz parma or prosciutto ham, finely chopped

3 tablespoons freshly grated Parmesan cheese

salt and freshly ground black pepper

8 lamb cutlets, trimmed and batted out lightly with a
    meat hammer

2 eggs beaten

3 tablespoons olive oil

3 large garlic cloves, peeled

## Creamy Sweet and Sour Onions

**Serves 4**

50 g / 2 oz butter

2 large onions, thinly sliced

8 bay leaves

1 clove garlic, finely chopped

2 teaspoons brown sugar

2 tablespoons sherry vinegar or white wine vinegar

90 ml / 3 fl oz strong chicken stock

90 ml / 3 fl oz cream

salt and pepper

Mix together the breadcrumbs, Parma ham and Parmesan cheese then spread out on a large plate and set aside. Season the lamb and brush lightly with the beaten egg. Press the lamb into the breadcrumbs to coat evenly but lightly.

Heat the oil in a large non-stick frying pan, add the garlic cloves and heat gently until golden brown, then discard the garlic.

Fry the lamb in the garlic infused oil over a low to moderate heat for 3 to 4 minutes each side until deep golden brown and crispy.

Melt the butter and add the onions and bay leaves. Cover with a lid on a very low heat for 20 minutes, stirring occasionally. Don't allow to colour. Remove the lid and turn up the heat a little. Add the brown sugar and the sherry vinegar. When this has evaporated, add the stock and cream. Cook for another 10 minutes or until the cream has reached a coating consistency around the onions. Season and serve.

This is both a sauce and a vegetable and is very adaptable to different dishes. If you are using pork, use cider instead of vinegar and some grain mustard, or season with horseradish for beef.

# Grilled Lamb Steaks with Stuffed Beef Tomatoes and Feta Cheese

Lamb steaks are steaks cut from the leg of lamb. They need quick cooking as otherwise they may be tough. Marinating them overnight both adds flavour to and tenderises the meat. These would also be good with couscous, chickpea fritters or roasted provençale vegetables in olive oil. Mashed potatoes with some basil oil drizzled over the top together with the marinated cherry tomatoes would be good as well.

This marinade can be used for other meats, chicken, beef or duck.

Mix the marinade ingredients together, coat the lamb and marinate for 24 hours.

Preheat a grill, place the lamb steaks on the grill tray and cook for 3–4 mins on each side or in a frying pan for 2 to 3 minutes on each side. If they start to curl, make an incision in the edge of the steak and it should release the tension. Season and serve pink.

4 x 200 g / 7 oz leg of lamb chops

For the marinade
3 cloves garlic, crushed
2 sprigs rosemary
6 bay leaves
40 ml / 1$\frac{1}{2}$ fl oz olive oil
40 ml / 1$\frac{1}{2}$ fl oz vegetable oil
2 tablespoons balsamic vinegar
peel of one lemon
black pepper

## Stuffed Beef Tomatoes with Feta Cheese

Combine the feta, olives, spinach and garlic butter in a bowl. Stuff into the tomato cavity and sprinkle the pine kernels on top. Drizzle with some melted garlic butter and olive oil and place the lids on top. Drizzle the lids with a little bit more garlic butter and olive oil. Season and place in a roasting tray and place in a hot oven 180°C / Gas 4 for 10 minutes until the tomatoes are just soft to touch. During cooking, the skin will have cracked and partially come away from the tomatoes. Just pull off the remainder before serving them. Any cooking juices in the tray, pour over the tomatoes when you serve for a nice glossy shine.

Arrange the tomatoes beside the lamb and serve with some plain boiled rice and pitta bread and perhaps some cucumber raita (see Cucumber).

These stuffed beef tomatoes are a very handy dish to have up your sleeve. They can be used as a starter or a very tasty vegetarian dish.

110 g / 4 oz feta cheese crumbled
50 g / 2 oz black olives chopped
200 g / 7 oz (uncooked) young spinach
50 g / 2 oz garlic butter, melted (see Garlic)
4 beef tomatoes, hollowed and the tops reserved
50g / 2 oz pine kernels
60 ml / 2 fl oz good olive oil
salt and pepper

# Brochettes of Lamb's Kidneys with Potato Sauce and Sweet and Sour Roast Onions

You either like kidneys or not. If you do you will like this. The potato sauce is in a way derived from a meal that I had in Jamin, Joel Robouchon's Restaurant, at the end of the 1980s. His potato purée was so liquid and soft I thought just by adding some more milk and cream it would become a sauce.

**Serves 4 as a starter**

8 lambs kidneys, diced into 1 cm / ½" squares

16 fresh bay leaves, broken up

4 small onions

olive oil, for frying

15g / ½ oz sugar

2 teaspoons sherry vinegar

25 g / 1 oz garlic butter

175 g / 6 oz smooth mashed potatoes (roughly two decent sized spuds)

60 ml / 2 fl oz milk

50 g / 2 oz butter

60 ml / 2 fl oz cream

salt and freshly ground black pepper

Preheat the oven to 180°C/Gas 4.

Alternate kidney and bay leaf pieces on 8" x 5" / 12 cm wooden skewers soaked in water for 10 mins. Allow 2 skewers per portion and 1 kidney per skewer. Cut the onions in half through the middle (not through the root). Heat a little oil in a small frying pan and fry the onion cut-side down for about 2 minutes until golden brown. Turn them cut side up and sprinkle with salt, pepper, sugar and vinegar and then bake in the preheated oven for another five minutes. This can be done ahead of time.

Heat a separate frying pan, add a little of the oil, quickly fry the brochettes for 3 to 4 minutes, turning occasionally. Season and dot with garlic butter. Place the mashed potato in a small pan and cook over a medium heat with the milk, butter and cream, whisking to combine.

When the potatoes are at a sauce consistency (you may have to add a little more milk if they are stiff) divide onto four warm plates. Next add the roast onion, then the brochettes. Garnish with a sprig of parsley and serve.

## Braised Lamb Shanks with Cumin, Chick peas and Dates

Lamb shanks are my favourite cut of lamb, supremely flavourful and when cooked you can almost cut them with a spoon. This is a beautiful rich stewy dish with Morrocan overtones. Long, slow cooking is the secret to bring out all the flavour of the meat. Eat with rice or couscous or plain mashed potatoes.

Dust your lamb shanks in half the flour. Take half the oil and put it into a large frying pan. When hot, brown the shanks on all sides. While this is happening take a large pot, take the remaining oil and cook the onion gently for 3–4 mins. Add the cumin and garlic and cook some more. After 2–3 mins add the remaining flour and brown a little. Add the plum tomatoes and their juice, mashing them a little with the back of a wooden spoon. Scrape the bottom of the pan while amalgamating the ingredients. Add the lamb shanks, redcurrant jelly, chickpeas, rosemary and orange peel and cover with the chicken stock. If your shanks aren't completely covered just top up with a little water. Cover and cook for 2 to 2$\frac{1}{2}$ hours or until tender. After two hours, stir in the dates and leave the lid off for the remaining cooking time to allow the juice to evaporate and thicken. I would normally serve these with either saffron, plain or pilaff rice.

**Serves 4**

4 lamb shanks
2 tablespoons flour
120 ml / 4 fl oz olive oil
1 large Spanish onion (finely chopped)
1 tablespoon cumin seeds, dry roasted and ground
2 cloves garlic (finely chopped)
2 standard tins of plum tomatoes
1 tablespoon redcurrant jelly
1 standard tin of Chick peaswashed and drained
1 sprig rosemary
peel of an orange
2.4 l / 4 pints chicken stock
a handful of dried dates (halved)

# Lamb stew ... Rack of lamb, loin of lamb, lambs' kidneys ... Lamb chops... roast lamb ... lamb's liver ... lamb shank ... spiced leg of lamb ...

To bring out the best in a **leek**, the thing is to treat it gently. Discard the dark and bitter leaves, the white and light green are the best ... like Jekyll and Hyde, the same but yet so different.

The silent and reliable leek rarely stars – it is usually the understudy to much more brash partners. There are always leeks in our fridge. Ever present in our soups and sauce bases, the white giving sweetness which is the first sensation our palate looks for when deciding whether we like something or not. The leek is generally rendered down for flavour and then passed through a sieve, thereby remaining unseen and unappreciated except perhaps in the ubiquitous leek and potato soup – one of the most fabulous and simple soups you could make.

To bring out the best in a leek, the thing is to treat it gently. Discard the dark and bitter leaves, the white and light green are the best. Simmer gently in butter, with the lid on to start and then without to concentrate the juices. Add salt and pepper, taste and let your mind wander. The beauty of simplicity never ceases to amaze me. But cooked on too high a heat and neglected, they take on an altogether different character. Bitter and unsightly, like Jekyll and Hyde, the same but yet so different.

Into those golden leeks for a breast of chicken you could slosh some cream and chicken stock, reduce and when thickened add a little of a mustard of your choice. Here's a hint – never add mustard until the end when making a sauce. Mustard becomes bitter when cooked. This is just as nice with beef, pork or even lamb.

For salmon swap the mustard for some horseradish; with mussels, a little curry powder; prawns and crab, some tomato; or softly gratinated with potatoes and cod for a winter lunch.

Alternatively, chop them into rounds, and cook in boiling salted water for two to three minutes. Cool quickly in cold water, give them a gentle squeeze and dress with vinaigrette. Serve with cold baked ham and grated hard boiled egg and warm crusty bread.

Getting back to that classic, leek and potato soup. When served cold on a hot day it becomes the classy Vichyssoise. But to take Vichyssoise further, whisk in some good olive oil and crème fraîche. Use this as a dressing to drizzle around some poached lobster or salmon. Serve with a zesty tomato salad and good old-fashioned chips and drink plenty of Chablis. Humble and unassuming, now a star – but then the Welsh have always known that.

## Smoked Salmon with Buttered Leeks and Poached Egg

This is a nice lunch or brunch dish

**Serves 4**

4 eggs

4 thick slices of toasted wholemeal bread

25 g / 1 oz butter

1 quantity leeks in horseradish cream (see recipe later)

225 g / 8 oz smoked salmon

Poach four eggs making sure to keep them runny. Arrange the toast on four plates and butter it. Spoon the leeks in horseradish cream on each slice of toast. Divide the smoked salmon into four and drape it over the top of the leeks. Finish each with a poached egg, salt and milled black pepper.

## Leek, Gabriel Cheese and Black Trumpet Tart

**Serves 6-8**

This is to all intents and purposes a quiche but with a delicious intense filling. The trumpets are optional but add a nutty flavour and contrasting colour. Gabriel cheese is from west Cork, intense and special. If you can't find it, substitute another strong cheese, i.e., Parmesan.

small handful of black trumpet mushrooms

1 tablespoon garlic butter (see Garlic)

50 g / 2 oz butter, cubed

110 g / 4 oz flour

1 egg yolk

pinch salt

4 leeks, washed, diced, blanched and refreshed

150 g / 5 oz Gabriel cheese diced into 1 cm cubes

4 eggs

300 ml / ½ pint milk

300 ml / ½ pint cream

salt and pepper

I also do a version of this tart with bacon and cabbage which I serve with a butterbean and lemon salad.

Preheat the oven to 180°C/Gas 4.

To soak the mushrooms, pour some boiling water over them to cover and allow to sit for 1 to 1½ hours. Remove from the water and wash thoroughly to remove grit. The liquid can be strained and frozen to make a mushroom sauce at a later date. Trim the tough stalks from the mushroom and cut into 1 cm pieces. Sweat these in the garlic butter.

Rub the butter into the flour. Add the egg yolk and salt and a little water to form a dough. Chill for 30 minutes. Roll out and line a 20½cm tart or flan tin and bake blind for 10–15 minutes or until the pastry is golden and crisp. Reduce the heat of the oven to 160°C / Gas 2½ to bake the tart.

Squeeze the leeks of all excess water and scatter them with the mushrooms and Gabriel cheese on the base of the tart. Mix the eggs, milk, cream and seasoning together and pour over the leeks. Place in the oven for 20–25 minutes until set. Serve warm with some new potatoes.

## Leeks in Horseradish Cream

These creamed leeks are extremely versatile. You can use them with most fish, chicken, even duck. I also substitute the leeks for creamed peas and bacon when I fancy.

**Serves 4**

Melt the butter over a low heat and add in the flour. Stir with a wooden spoon for 2 to 3 minutes and gradually add in the milk little by little, whisking continually to make sure there are no lumps. Take your time with this. The slower, the better. After 10 minutes, add the stock, cream and bay leaves. Cook out carefully for another 10 minutes and then add the horseradish, salt and pepper to season. If you do have some lumps, strain the sauce.

### For the leeks

4 large leeks cut into 2 cm dice, excluding the very green bits. Wash and blanch until soft. Refresh under cold water. Squeeze out the excess water and add the leeks to the horseradish béchamel (above). This does need to be used on the same day as the leeks discolour.

### Horseradish béchamel

A béchamel is an old fashioned sauce that is perfectly good and very versatile as long as it's made with a light hand. Technically, to get a bit cheffy on you, mine is a cross between a béchamel and a velouté (made with stock) as if I have some bacon stock handy I add it. This keeps the sauce nice and light and enhances the flavour.

25 g / 1 oz butter
25 g / 1 oz flour
300 ml / ½ pint milk
60 ml / 2 fl oz bacon or chicken stock (optional – you can just use more milk instead)
60 ml / 2 fl oz cream
1 bay leaf
1 tablespoon commercial creamed horseradish

A little tip: if your sauce seems a little thin, hold off on your stock and just crumble a cube in. It will give depth of flavour without making it runny.

Simmer gently in butter, with the lid on to start and then without to concentrate the juices. Add salt and pepper, taste and let your mind wander. The beauty of simplicity never ceases to amaze me.

... No celery, no problem – a little celery salt or celeriac. No fennel – fennel seeds or a dash of Pernod will be a good substitute. No herbs for garnish, OK – deep fry some spinach instead, but if we run out of lemons, we are in trouble ...

In our kitchen here, I can think of lots of ingredients that we could do without if we ran out and the shops had closed. No celery, no problem – a little celery salt or celeriac. No fennel – fennel seeds or a dash of Pernod will be a good substitute. No herbs for garnish, OK – deep fry some spinach instead, but if we run out of lemons, we are in trouble. OK smarty pants, if you have limes fine, but if they are not a regular item on your shopping list you are snookered.

Lemon syrup forms the basis for some of my sauces or dressings including the lemon hummus cream in the chapter on chickpeas. Cream or oil based sauces need some acid to cut through them to make them palatable. Now, that acid can be wine, vinegar or citrus. In mayonnaises, which we are all familiar with, I like to use lemon in conjunction with the vinegar sometimes. The danger here is that they can be too sharp so to avoid this I add a little sugar for balance. This is brought together with some water cooked a little to make a syrup. I make this in large quantities to add to things when I think they need them.

One of my favourite desserts is a well-made lemon tart. This classic even appeals to people that don't have a sweet tooth as the citrussy bite detracts from the sugar content. Lemon curd is another must have, either spread on scones with some jam to be totally decadent, sandwiched between a fluffy sponge or simply a dollop over a crunchy meringue with some berries and cream when they are in season. It's a sure winner. Make some and it will keep in a sealed container in the fridge for three to four weeks.

## Lemon and Rosemary Dressing

This is a delicious perky dressing. I use it with warm cannellini beans or some French beans to serve with ham, duck or chicken or alternatively we use it as a dressing with cos lettuce to serve with poached smoked salmon.

Bring the lemon juice, vinegar and caster sugar to the boil. Add the rosemary, coriander seeds and cream and cook gently over a low heat until it starts to thicken. Allow to cool and strain. This will keep in the fridge for 2 to 3 days.

juice of 2 lemons
30 ml / 1 fl oz white wine vinegar
75 g / 3 oz caster sugar
1 sprig rosemary
1 pinch crushed coriander seeds
300 ml / 1/2 pint cream

## Gremolata

1 large bunch flat leaf parsley, chopped
grated zest of one lemon
half teaspoon rock salt
1 green chilli, very finely chopped
1 shallot, very finely chopped

This is lovely stuff. Serve with veal, fish or chicken to give a fresh zingy flavour. It is particularly nice with scallops or prawns (pan fried and served with a fresh salad).

Mix together with enough olive oil to make a loose paste. Leave in the fridge for a few hours before serving if possible to allow the flavours to develop.

## Lemon and Lime Posset

**Serves 6**

900 ml / 1 1/2 pints cream
250 g / 9 oz caster sugar
2 lemons juiced
2 limes juiced

Bring the cream and caster sugar to the boil and cook for two to three minutes. Add the lemon juice. Allow to cool slightly. Pour into glasses and allow to set in the fridge.

Lemon curd
200 g / 7 oz butter
250 g / 9 oz sugar
juice of 5–6 lemons
10 eggs

This is the easiest dessert to make in the world. OK, it is laden with cream but the acidity of the lemon cuts through it. Eat this with your favourite biscuits, that's all it needs.

Take a stainless steel or Pyrex bowl, place it over a pot of simmering water and melt the butter in the bowl. Add the sugar and lemon juice. When they have dissolved, add the eggs and cook over a low heat for approximately 1 hour or until the mixture has thickened, stirring frequently. This will keep in the fridge for 3 to 4 weeks.

# Lemon and Basil Tartare Cream

I find that sometimes traditional tartare sauce is a bit cloying. This is lighter, fresher tasting and the addition of crème fraîche at the end gives it a lovely consistency. I use this with any amount of fish, particularly deep-fried or breadcrumbed dishes, i.e., calamari, sole or cod.

Place the raw eggs in a food processor or electric mixer and add the mustard and white wine vinegar. Throw in a pinch of salt and start the machine. Add the oil very slowly until it's all in, thick and creamy. Then add the olive oil and lemon syrup and turn the mixture out into a bowl. At this point, add the crème fraîche, basil oil, capers, gherkins, eggs and shallots. Season. If it's too thick, add a dash of warm water. If too sweet, a squeeze of lemon juice or vinegar.

**Makes about 600 ml / 1 pint**

3 whole eggs (this makes for a lighter mayonnaise than just egg yolks)
half tablespoon Dijon mustard
2 tablespoons white wine vinegar
300 ml / ½ pint sunflower oil or peanut oil
60 ml / 2 fl oz light olive oil
juice of ½ lemon and 25 g / 2 oz caster sugar made into a syrup
1 tablespoon crème fraîche
3 tablespoons of basil oil (if you don't happen to have this, shredded fresh basil will do)
25 g / 1 oz capers
25 g /1 oz gherkins finely chopped
1 hard boiled egg, chopped
1 shallot finely chopped
salt and pepper

# Polenta, Almond and Lemon Cake

My friend Tim gave me this recipe. This is a beautiful moist cake. It will keep for ages in a tin and is just the thing with a cup of tea. We serve it warm with plum ice-cream and lemon syrup for Sunday lunch. It's beautiful simply with some whipped cream.

Preheat the oven to 160°C/Gas 2½.
Line a deep baking tray or 2 lb loaf tin with some parchment or greaseproof paper.
Beat butter and sugar until light and pale. Add almonds and vanilla extract. Beat in eggs, gradually. Fold in lemon zest and juice, polenta and baking powder and finally the salt.
Bake for 45 to 50 minutes.

**Serves 4**

175 g / 6 oz unsalted butter
175 g / 6 oz caster sugar
175 g / 6 oz ground almonds
1 teaspoon vanilla extract
3 eggs
zest of one lemon
juice of half lemon
75 g / 3 oz polenta flour
½ teaspoon baking powder
¼ teaspoon salt

Passion, oh what a word. Overused, bandied about and attributed to all sorts of people and their endeavours. Artists, fashion designers and the usual array of crafty people.

I'm almost suspicious of people who announce that they are very passionate about something. I think it is far more dignified to have this said about you. Then you can mumble something about being graciously flattered while maintaining the 'I just love what I do' angle, eliciting protests and indignation at one's modesty.

I loved two things, let's say, obsessively, food and girls. I became aware of the latter a few years prior to the former. I remember being thirteen and leaning out of my bedroom window praying for a naked woman to appear in my bedroom. Lord only knows what I would ever do with her if she turned up. Nevertheless, this carry on lasted nearly a week, only to be stopped by a chest cold from leaning out of the window, thereby allowing God to hear me better.

These days my enthusiasm for girls is curtailed by the presence of my wife so I am left with food. I can't stop thinking about it. There is no doubt that this obsession has been very helpful in my career but I am cursed with drifting off into my own gastro world during conversations with friends. Constantly condemned to gazing at other people's plates, silently assessing their dinner. Sure I can enjoy myself with the best of them, but if my head was a scratch card, underneath would be bearnaise sauce, ravioli, soufflé, rosemary and chicken. Match three and you get a dish.

Holidays, hah. Máire and I have been on holidays where the food was bad, leaving me in a sulk for the duration, longing for my foodie fix. While changing at Heathrow on the way home, I would plead, 'we can dash into London, grab lunch at the River Café and leg it back in time for the connection'. For prospective holidays, I fumble

# I'm as happy as the next guy in a beach hut but there's got to be decent calamari, or wok fried prawns with garlic and ginger to go with my beer.

through the *Time Out* or Fodors guide assessing the country's or city's merits based on the quality of its restaurants. They don't even have to be posh. I'm as happy as the next guy in a beach hut but there's got to be decent calamari, or wok fried prawns with garlic and ginger to go with my beer. As you may have guessed, I'm not the type to go rubbing factor nothing all over me, tubes don't come that big.

Chill I hear you say. Yes, I need a hobby. Straightaway I invent a new sport, perfect for me. Cooking for girls. What could be better? My two favourite things. But seriously so many things are ruled out. I would perhaps have the physique for darts, shot putt or the hammer but these sports are really lacking in glamour. Skiing is out because of some bad experiences in the local roller disco in the early 1980s that left me mentally scarred for life. I have settled for fishing, the sport of gentlemen. I've got the wellies and the wax jacket and the lovely Blackwater. My father's old cloth cap beckons me from the dresser. The only thing I don't have is a clue. Mind you, I'm rodless as well but that can be rectified. My friend David has offered to help. He has got the land, the knowledge and all the kit. Who knows, maybe the sight of me striding through the dewey grass, laden with trout and salmon may arouse some Catherine Cookson-esque passion with my girl. Now, there's a thought. However, until I organise that, there's a small matter of new menus, new veg in season, a proliferation of game. How would my customers like that cooked? Should I try some hare with chocolate á la Pierre Koffman, or beautiful mallard with pears braised in red wine, crispy savoy cabbage and pommes anna. For lunch special bangers and mash with onion gravy. Real comfort food, they'd like that or ... there I go again.

When it comes to luxury ingredients, lobster has to be in the top five, along with caviar, truffle, foie gras and morels. This roll call of élite ingredients is almost prohibitively expensive but when you do fork out the cash, you want to make sure that nothing will go wrong. I confess to rarely having lobster on my menu. I think it's the fact that I'm really not wild about it. What? I hear you say. Blasphemy! It's true. If Mr Crab and Mr Lobster were having a fight, I would be shouting for Mr Crab. When I do have it I like to make tortellini or ravioli, slightly undercooking the lobster and mixing it with salmon mousse, tarragon and brandy to be served with a citrus sauce. Otherwise I precook the lobster and warm it though the oven with garlic, ginger and chilli butter before serving. The warm lobster soaks up the butter, and emits a heady perfume. I never got the attraction of lobster thermidor. Cheese and lobster just doesn't do it for me, although somebody might blow my socks off with a fabulous one some day.

Cooking lobster really is a simple affair. Get a decent sized lobster – 400 g to 600 g. Bring a large pot of salted water to a fast boil. The kindest way for the lobster is to dispatch them quickly by inserting a knife into the brain. Between the head and the rest of the body two lines meet to form a cross. This is where you should insert the knife quickly and the lobster will die instantly. Naturally this is not for the squeamish so you may need to find a burly heartless man. That shouldn't be too hard. Plunge the lobster into the boiling water making sure it is totally immersed. Take the pan off the heat immediately and allow the lobster to cool in the water. If the lobsters are small, take them out of the water after 20 minutes.

Then you can begin to prepare the lobster. Tear off the legs and set aside. Sit the lobster on a chopping board with its tail extended and take a heavy sharp knife. Insert it in the original incision and very quickly and firmly cut it in half. A tea-towel may be helpful to hold the lobster in place. Extract the meat and remove any coral or membrane. Discard the other material from the head. If you are ambitious, you could freeze this for a sauce or soup. Rinse the head and body. Cut the tail into bite-sized pieces and reassemble in the shell. At this point, attack the claws. You have to have patience for this. Each claw will be broken into three pieces. The claw will separate easily enough. The arm joint will have to be cut with a heavy knife. If you have special equipment for this job, lucky you! If not, take a hammer to the claw. A gentle tap once or twice should do it, then try to extract the claw in one piece and do the same with the knuckle. The arm is a little trickier. A small vegetable knife will prize out the meat for you. When all the meat has been removed, arrange it attractively in the head. Season and slice the garlic, ginger and chilli butter generously on top. Refrigerate until needed, then warm through a moderate oven for 5 to 6 minutes.

## Baked Lobster with Roasted Beef Tomatoes and Creamy Butterleaf Salad

Cook the lobster according to the method given. You can either use the garlic, ginger and chilli butter (see Crab) or plain garlic butter with some chives or chervil going through it. Whatever butter you are using, before placing the lobster in the oven, place thin slices of solid butter along the length of the lobster which will melt while it's heating and keep it from drying out.

Place the tomatoes, cut side up, on a roasting tray. Drizzle with the oil. Scatter over the salt, pepper, thyme and garlic and place in a preheated oven 140°C / Gas 1 for 20 minutes. Remove from the tray and allow to cool.

### Lettuce

Take the hearts of two lettuces. Wash and dry them carefully. Mix the cream and the vinegar with salt and pepper and turn the leaves in the dressing. Distribute them on plates beside the tomato. You should serve this simply with some new potatoes.

This salad would also be a lovely base for poached salmon or sautéed scallops or prawns.

This is a simple accompaniment to lobster.

### Serves 2

1 large lobster
2 beef tomatoes, cut in half
2 tablespoons olive oil
rock salt
cracked black pepper
pinch chopped thyme
1 clove chopped garlic
2 butterleaf lettuces

### For the dressing

4 tablespoons cream
1 tablespoons red wine vinegar
salt and pepper

Sit the lobster on a chopping board with its tail extended and take a heavy sharp knife. Insert it in the original incision and very quickly and firmly cut it in half. A tea-towel may be helpful to hold the lobster in place. Extract the meat and remove any coral or membrane.

# *Ragout of Lobster with Spring Vegetables and Mild Garlic Cream Sauce*

**Serves 4**

Technically this is not a ragout at all but a compilation of carefully cooked ingredients, cooked separately, then put together in your fanciest serving dish (just make sure it's oven to table), glistening with colour and bursting with freshness. This is how we would prepare this in the resaurant. We use shallow copper pans for serving and by doing it this way, I know that everthing will be just as it is intended when it gets to the customer. It is prepared in three stages.

• The lobster

• The sauce

• The vegetables

All of these can be cooked earlier in the day to be reheated in a matter of minutes when needed.

2 large lobsters (prepared as above, out of the shell – you can discard the shell)

1 recipe mild garlic cream (see Garlic)

4 young carrots, peeled and cut into 1cm slices

1 handful French beans, topped and tailed

1 handful peas (frozen is fine)

1 bunch asparagus, trimmed and peeled

2 small leeks, washed, trimmed and left whole

12 to 15 new potatoes, depending on size

1 handful roughly chopped celery leaves

1 bunch chervil

For this you need a large pot of boiling salted water, a large basin of iced water, patience and a large slotted spoon or small sieve to scoop out the vegetables.

You are going to cook each vegetable separately as each vegetable has a different cooking time and in order to keep them perfectly crunchy you have to do this.

Start with the leeks. Cook these whole (so they don't fall apart) for 4 to 5 minutes until just soft, then remove and place into the iced water. Next in go the carrots for two minutes and remove and place into the iced water. Then add the beans for two minutes, and place into the iced water. Next the asparagus – depending on size you will have to use your own judgement for this. Just don't overcook them as the tips will disintegrate. The peas will only take one minute. While you are doing all this, have your new potatoes cooking away in another pot.

Drain all the vegetables into a colander. Remove the leeks, squeeze dry and cut into 1 cm slices at an angle. Arrange the vegetables and the lobster meat attractively in a serving dish. When you are ready to serve, pre-heat the oven to 180°C/Gas 4. Heat the sauce separately. If it's not quite coating consistency, reduce it a little. Pour the sauce over the lobster and vegetables and place in the oven for 10 minutes. Remove, scatter with the celery leaves and chervil, and serve.

Other suggestions with lobster.

Guacamole cream (see Avacado) and marinated cherry tomatoes

Brown butter and citrus cream (see scallops with turnip, brown butter and citrus vinaigrette in chapter on Turnip)

Sauce bourride with saffron (see Garlic under adaptation of aïoli)

ragout of lobster with spring vegetables and mild garlic cream sauce

I used to hate mackerel – for two reasons that have got nothing to do with the taste of it. There used to be an old lady who sold mackerel once or twice a week on the corner of the square. She would sit on a stool with a glistening box of mackerel in front of her, swatting flies and chatting to the odd passer by. Accompanying her was a big mangy dog, her companion, her pet! I was about eight years old and stupidly I patted the dog whereby it took a chunk out of my chin. Bloody Paul, bloody dog, bloody mackerel. A couple of years later, one evening, the boats came in laden with even more mackerel than usual. On occasions like this it was not unheard of for the fisherman to give the surplus away to whoever was around – mackerel and pollock being flung onto the quayside, my mother was ready with her plastic bag. I had the job of gutting. Lucky me. My father liked nothing better than fried mackerel and new potatoes. I could never even look at a mackerel without thinking of that dog and the mark he left me with. So reluctantly I sat down to eat one, grumbled something and took a bite. My throat seized up. Panic set in. I had swallowed a bone. I thrashed round the place and my father had to stick his fingers down my throat to prise it out. Bloody mackerel! Of course, as the years went by, the size of the bone grew to something resembling a lamb shank. Now I always serve mackerel in season and the customers love it. I'm a big boy now but I carefully pin bone my fish to eliminate the prospects of that happening to myself or my customers.

If the fish are small, I gut them and take the heads of, trim the gills and dredge them in paprika-laced flour, place them into a pan of foaming butter for 2 to 3 minutes on each side and serve them with pickled red onions,

# Smoked **mackerel** is one of my all-time favourite foods. Its densely textured, almost buttery flesh is brilliant summer food.

new potatoes and butterleaf lettuce, dressed in home-made salad cream. Summery, fresh and perfect with some good brown bread and crisp white wine. Now that I have finally mastered the barbeque at home, I know they work really well stuffed with herbs and garlic, coriander seeds and drizzled with olive oil. A tomato salad and baked potatoes complete the dish. This I have found is the ideal way to cook mackerel because the smell doesn't linger around the house for days. Our cat Delia has a field day but has decided against venturing too near the barbeque from a previous nasty experience.

If the fish is too big I fillet and pin bone it, quickly fry and serve with oriental spiced cabbage (see Cabbage).

Being an oily fish, acid is a key ingredient to give balance. So whether it's in a complex sauce such as a beurre blanc or simply a squeeze of lemon or drizzle of red wine or cider vinegar, it must be present. Chinese pickled ginger makes a fine simple accompaniment enhanced with spring onion, soy sauce and crispy garlic on a bed of buttered noodles.

Smoked mackerel is one of my all-time favourite foods. Its densely textured, almost buttery flesh is brilliant summer food. Sometimes we serve this as a whole warm fillet on some linguini with a roasted aubergine, fennel and orange butter sauce. Just use the recipe following, adding finely diced roasted aubergines. Swap the lemon for orange and throw in some finely chopped fennel or dill at the end. As a starter it's fab with roasted beetroot, horseradish cream and the best leaves you can find. A nice sharp dressing will cut through the richness of the fish. When buying smoked fish, look for mackerel that tastes of more than smoke. A delicate rounded flavour is what you want.

# Roast Mackerel with New Potatoes, Beetroot, Ginger and Cumin Butter

Serves 4 as a main course

Makes 600 ml / 1 pint
6 small shallots finely chopped
300 g / 11 oz butter cut into slices
1 teaspoon cracked black pepper
75 ml / 3 fl oz white wine vinegar
150 ml / 1/4 pint white wine
55 ml / 2 fl oz cream
75 ml / 3 fl oz chicken stock
pinch cumin powder
25 g / 1 oz pickled ginger, finely chopped
salt
pinch of sugar
squeeze of lemon

4 x 200 g / 7 oz mackerel (heads off and gutted)
flour
4 medium sized beetroot wrapped in foil and roasted
    in a slow oven until they are soft
20 cooked new potatoes (less if they are large)
2 heads baby cos lettuce (little gems)
2 small red onions, finely sliced

For the sauce

Cook the shallots slowly in one knob of the butter so they are soft and translucent. Add the pepper, vinegar, white wine, chicken stock and cumin. Reduce to a syrup. Add cream. Bring to the boil quickly and add the rest of the butter bit by bit, amalgamating with a whisk as you go along. When the butter is well incorporated, season, add the sugar and the lemon and pass through a sieve into another pot. Add the chopped ginger and keep warm. If it's a little thick add a splash of milk but remember this sauce must not boil.

Flour the mackerel, dusting off excess flour and seal in a hot pan. Place in a preheated oven for about 5 minutes, turning once. Slice the beetroot and assemble with potatoes on a warm plate. Place the cos lettuce on top. Scatter the red onions on top of the cos and the mackerel on top of that. Spoon the sauce all around.

# Smoked Mackerel Pâté

50 g / 2 oz softened butter
110 g / 4 oz light creamed cheese
250 g / 9 oz of smoked mackerel (skin and bones removed)
2 tablespoons sour cream
1 squeeze lemon juice
a few drops chilli sauce
tablespoon of commercial creamed horseradish
salt and pepper

Serves 6-8

This is a very tasty and simple, lovely for a light lunch. I would serve this with a pickled cucumber (See Cucumber) or the Marinaded Cherry Tomato Salad (see Tomato) or the Tomato and Avocado Salsa (see Avocado).
Cream the butter and the cream cheese together. Mash the fish with a fork to break up and gently mix the fish, sour cream, lemon juice, chilli sauce, horseradish and seasoning into the cheese mixture. Press into a bowl and serve lightly chilled.

# Mushrooms

I spent half a drizzly day last September picking bags full of wild mushrooms in the wood above our home. I put them in the cold room at work and searched to no avail through my books to see if any would help me in identifying them. I told the lads not to go near them while I figured out my treasure. I hadn't much time.

After work, I transferred my research to the pub where I met David, a neighbour and an authority on anything that swims, waddles, flies or shoots through the ground. Get rid of them, he told me urgently, before someone uses them by mistake. He then told me of a man who had had kidney failure after consuming a particularly poisonous variety. That was enough for me. Abandoning my pint (that's how serious it was) I raced back to the restaurant and binned them.

Another neighbour recently dropped in three puffball mushrooms the size of small footballs which I duly sliced, sautéed and served with garlic bread and rocket leaves. These puffballs are amazing things indeed. They grow overnight and if they aren't picked will rot within two days to grow back faithfully again the following year. So if you are lucky enough to find one, memorise where, so you can come back again for a snack. There is no mistaking these babies: their sheer size and creamy whiteness are like beacons in green fields.

My favourite wild mushrooms are girolles. Alongside cépes and morels they reign supreme, outclassed only by the truffle. They are expensive so not often found in restaurants outside the Michelin variety. Scottish girolles are of exceptional quality, all to do with the rainfall in natural wooded areas where they have a symbiotic relationship with the oaks, elms, beeches and horsechestnuts. Trashy conifers won't do: they are the nouveaux riches of woodlands. As most of our hardwood forests were cut down in more tumultuous times except in small pockets around the country, we have to search harder for our wild mushrooms. I don't know enough about them to mess around with them. Foraging can be fun but only when you know what you are doing. From now on, I'll buy strictly from my suppliers.

The great thing about the different varieties of mushroom is how each one has its own flavour. Sometimes that flavour is an acquired taste: the smoky meatiness of the morel, the nuttiness of the girolle, the distinctiveness of the cépe. Once you develop a taste for them, they are utterly addictive. Some cooks have such a love of them, their menus abound with mushroomy twists and turns. It's important never to wash mushrooms as they just absorb the water through their pores. It's best to wipe them with a damp cloth or brush and although tedious, the result is worthwhile.

Other notable wild mushrooms are chanterelles, pied de mouton, and trompette de la mort or black trumpet. Around 1,000 varieties grow in this country but only 30or so are edible. All these mushrooms are available in dried form and are really handy to have around., sold in good delis or again use your contact in a local restaurant to get you some from his supplier. They simply need reconstituting by pouring gently boiling water over them. After an hour, lift out the mushrooms and strain the juice through a cloth, taking care not to disturb the sediment at the bottom. This juice makes a fabulous sauce when reduced with a little white wine or vermouth, a touch of garlic and some cream added in at the end. Sauté the mushrooms in a little garlic butter and add some chopped shallots. Mix the lot with your favourite pasta, sprinkle with Parmesan and you have a dish to die for. Pure essence of mushroom.

Cépes also come frozen, either whole or in pieces. I am using these at the moment through a mousseline of chicken which I serve with a French onion and chestnut broth. The whole dish is meaty, yet without any meat.

# Roast Chicken, Potato and Wild Mushroom Soup

Heat the garlic butter in a pan. When foaming, add the mushrooms. Cook for 2 to 3 minutes over a high heat until all the juices have evaporated. Season and reserve.

Take a large pot. Melt the butter and add in the flour. Cook on a low heat until you get a sandy colour and whisk in the hot stock little by little to get a smooth paste. Keep adding until all the stock has been incorporated and you have a smooth liquid. Add the milk and cream and cook gently for 15 minutes. Season with salt and pepper. If you have lumps at this stage you can pass the soup through a sieve into another pot. Divide the potato, wild mushrooms, chicken and lovage between four bowls and ladle over the soup. Then scatter the marjoram on top. If you really want to push the boat out, you could add a drizzle of white truffle oil to each bowl.

Serves 4

Chicken and mushrooms as we all know have a natural affinity. The potatoes give a chunky chowder-like effect to the dish. Marjoram gives a lovely fresh flavour.

25 g / 1 oz garlic butter (see Garlic)
handful wild or not so wild mushrooms cleaned and
    sliced
50 g / 2 oz butter
25 g / 1 oz flour
725 ml / 1¼ pints chicken stock, heated to boiling
    point
150 ml / ¼ pint milk
90 ml / 2 fl oz cream
2 medium potatoes, cooked and diced
110 g / 4 oz of roast chicken meat, diced
pinch lovage or marjoram finely shredded will do
(if you can't get this, finely chopped celery leaves
    will do)

# Oriental Pickled Mushrooms

**Serves 4 as a main course for light lunch**

60 ml / 2 fl oz sesame oil

2 handfuls of assorted wild mushrooms wiped clean
    and left as chunky as possible

2 large shallots, finely chopped

2 cloves garlic finely chopped

1 green chilli finely diced

30 ml / 1 fl oz sherry vinegar

120 ml / 4 fl oz light soy sauce

25g / 1 oz chopped pickled ginger

handful chopped coriander

1 teaspoon honey

Wild mushrooms have long had medicinal qualities in the Orient. Here I am pickling wild mushrooms with oriental flavours. This can be served warm with noodles or boiled rice, or mixed with little gem lettuce as a salad.

Heat the oil in the pan and wait until almost smoking. Carefully put the mushrooms in, stirring now and again for about three minutes or until the moisture has evaporated. Season, add the shallots, garlic and chilli and cook for one more minute. Tip the mushrooms into a bowl and add the sherry vinegar, soy sauce, pickled ginger, coriander and honey. This will last three or four days in the fridge.

# Mushroom Risotto with Black Pudding

You may have guessed by now that I love risottos and use them a lot. This one is a very earthy, strong flavoured risotto, and the black pudding gives a lovely meaty dimension which goes really well with the mushrooms.

1 black pudding (standard size) cut into 1 cm dice

2 tablespoons sunflower oil

50 g / 2 oz butter

1 onion finely chopped

1.2 litres / 2 pints chicken stock

110 g / 4 oz flat cap mushrooms cut into 1 cm dice

400 g / 14 oz arborio rice

1–2 tablespoons freshly grated Parmesan

salt and black pepper

Parmesan flakes

tablespoon chopped sage

Quickly fry the black pudding in a pan until crispy. Drain on a kitchen towel and keep warm.

Melt the butter in a large pan. Add the chopped onion and cook without colouring for 2–3 minutes. Meanwhile, bring the stock to the boil. Add the diced mushrooms to the onions, increasing the heat of the pan. Allow the mushrooms to cook for 2–3 minutes. Add the rice and continue to cook over a medium heat for a further minute. Add the hot stock a ladle at a time, allowing it to become absorbed by the rice before adding another ladle. Continue this process, stirring almot continuously to keep cooking even. This will take 15–20 minutes. Add the sage.

Once the risotto is cooked, add the grated Parmesan and check the consistency is of a rich creamy texture. If the risotto needs a little more liquid, use some water. Season with salt and pepper and spoon onto a plate or into bowls. Sprinkle with Parmesan flakes and warm, crispy black pudding.

Note: Some black puddings have a tendency to break up. You need to find a densely textured one without too much oatmeal or barley visible.

# Wild Mushroom Butter Sauce

This is an adaptation of the classic beurre blanc. Less vinegar is used so the subtle mushroom flavour is allowed to come through.

This is fabulous with fish or chicken but again you must remember once it's made never to boil it as it will split. Unsalted butter is best for this but at a push use salted and don't season too much.

Melt a knob of the butter in a pan and add the shallots. Fry until transparent and add the dried mushrooms and pepper. Cook gently for 1-2 minutes and add the white wine, sherry vinegar, chicken stock and rosemary. Reduce by two thirds, almost until the mixture is syrupy. Add the cream and bring to a gentle boil. Chop the remainder of the butter and whisk it in, little by little until it's completely amalgamated. Take off the heat and check for seasoning. Allow to stand for 15 minutes and pass through a muslin cloth. Keep standing in a warm place until you need it. If you like, chop some chives and add them just before serving. This is even better with dried cépes or girolles. The forest mix is the cheaper, more readily available variety.

**Serves 4**

175 g / 6 oz butter
2 tablespoons finely chopped shallots
50 g / 2 oz of dried forest mushroom mix
half teaspoon cracked black pepper
90 ml / 3 fl oz dry white wine
60 ml / 2 fl oz sherry vinegar
150 ml / ¼ pint chicken stock
1 sprig rosemary
90 ml / 3 fl oz cream
60 ml / 2 fl oz sherry vinegar
squeeze lemon juice
splash of milk to thin the sauce if it is too thick

# Field Mushroom Soup with Gorgonzola, Crispy Bacon and Garlic Crumbs

Serves 4

50 g / 2 oz butter

30 ml / 1 fl oz olive oil

2 cloves garlic, crushed

4–6 large field mushrooms, finely chopped or
    processed

1 sprig rosemary

1 teaspoon tomato purée

1.2 litres / 2 pints chicken or ham stock

60 ml / 2 fl oz milk

splash sherry vinegar

100 g / 4 oz gorgonzola cheese, cut into cubes

4 rashers streaky bacon, diced and cooked until crispy

50 g / 2 oz breadcrumbs, cooked in garlic butter until
crunchy and golden

handful chopped parsley

I just love this soup. Field or breakfast mushrooms, call them what you like, are packed with flavour and I think are even better if you use seconds. You'll get them cheap from your veg man after 2 or 3 days. Around this time, their flavour seems to mature and becomes more intense. The gorgonzola gives a piquant creaminess to the soup, the bacon and garlic crumbs add crunch and even more flavour.

Melt the butter and olive oil and sweat the onions and garlic in it. Add the finely chopped mushrooms. Cook for 4 or 5 more minutes until the juices come out and disappear again. Add the tomato purée, rosemary and then the stock. Bring to the boil and cook for 10 minutes. Then add the milk. Bring back to the boil. Season, add the sherry vinegar, salt and pepper. Remove the rosemary. Liquidise and pass through a sieve into a clean pot. It might need to be reheated. To serve divide into bowls and garnish with the gorgonzola, crispy bacon, garlic crumbs and parsley.

# Grilled Flatcap Mushrooms with Rocket, White Truffle Oil and Parmesan

This is one of my favourite simple, earthy salads. It serves four as a starter or two as a supper dish served with lovely wholesome bread.

30 ml / 1 fl oz olive oil

50 g / 2 oz butter

8 medium field mushrooms (stems trimmed)

2 cloves garlic, crushed

splash balsamic vinegar

two good handfuls rocket

75 g / 3 oz grated fresh Parmesan cheese

25 g / 1 oz toasted pine nuts (or flaked almonds)

drizzle white truffle oil (optional)

salt and pepper

Melt the olive oil and butter and pan fry the mushrooms for 1-2 minutes on each side. Add the garlic and cook a little longer. Then add a dash of balsamic vinegar. Season and place the mushrooms in a bowl in a warm place for 15 minutes. The mushrooms will secrete their juices to mingle with the garlic butter, olive oil and balsamic vinegar. This is the dressing. Serve the mushrooms on top of some rocket leaves, spoon over the dressing that's left in the bowl and sprinkle the Parmesan and pine nuts on top. Just before serving, drizzle a little white truffle oil over each.

grilled flatcap mushrooms with rocket, white truffle oil and parmesan

# Mussels

I certainly wasn't brought up in a culinary hot house. My earliest experiments involved fry-ups for the lads upon our return from the disco in Kill village on the Honda 50s. Sausage curry was a famous part of my repertoire on these occasions. It was truly disgusting but we lads were hungry after our exertions 'hunting women' as we referred to it.

With my less than glowing Leaving Cert, perhaps I thought the approval for my late night feasts might lead me on a path to culinary glory so I found myself in a local bar/restaurant doing the peeling and chopping. It was an informal place – lovely people and an inspirational chef called Paul McCluskey. I got the bug. I will never forget one day deep in winter, the regulars were watching a rugby match. They were hungry after their feed of pints and the chef put big bowls of moules mariniéres on the bar, with baskets of warm bread, and everyone got stuck in, ordered more Guinness and stayed late in great form. What a day.

It was my first taste of mussels and I have loved them ever since. I still think you cannot beat cooking them with white wine, shallots, garlic and some bay leaves. Steaming them open and scooping out the mussels into big bowls, adding a dash of cream to the juice and thickening with what we chefs call beurre manié (equal measure of butter and flour), throwing in some chopped parsley before smothering the mussels and sending them out to the customer. These days, I suppose I try to be a clever clogs and add cider, curry powder or coconut milk to the pot, depending on what accent I want to give them but it's still the best way to eat them bar none. However, when they are baked to a crisp with garlic breadcrumbs and loads of butter, they do come a close second. I add them into seafood stews, their bluey black lustre giving another dimension to the array of prawns, salmon, gurnard or monkfish. They are also in my fridge munching away on porridge. I kid you not. Mussels are alive until they are cooked so by washing them, de-bearding them and keeping them for up to three days in water in the fridge, they can still eat. A handful of porridge oats in the water will make them plumper. These babies started me on the road so I look after them.

## Mussels with Angel Hair Pasta and Saffron

Cook the pasta in a large pan of boiling salted water until al dente. Be careful, as it doesn't take very long. Heat the butter and olive oil in a heavy-based pan, add the onions and cook gently for 10 minutes or until softened. Add the garlic, saffron and curry powder and cook for 1 minute.

Increase the heat, add the mussels and wine, cover with a tight-fitting lid and cook for 3 to 4 minutes or until the shells have opened. Discard any that remain closed. Add the crème fraîche and stir to heat through.

Drain the pasta and add to the mussel and cream mixture. Toss together and season to taste. Add the tomatoes and serve garnished with chopped chives.

**Serves 4**

The combination of pasta, saffron and mussels is very rarely bettered. I love angel hair but you must be careful cooking it. If it's overcooked it just becomes mushy. If you are nervous, use spaghetti.

350 g / 12 oz angel hair pasta
25 g / 1 oz butter
1 tablespoon olive oil
2 onions, peeled and finely diced
3 cloves garlic peeled and chopped
pinch of saffron threads
teaspoon of curry powder
900 g / 2 lb fresh mussels in shells, cleaned and
    de-bearded
120 ml / 4 fl oz white wine
120 ml / 4 fl oz crème fraîche
salt and pepper
2 plum tomatoes, quartered, de-seeded and diced
chives to garnish

## Big pot of Mussels with Red Pepper, Basil and Garlic Broth

Put everything into the pot bar the basil oil. Cover with a lid and steam for 10 minutes, shaking every now and again until all the mussels have opened. Add the basil oil, season, stir and divide evenly into four bowls.

**Serves 4**

2 kg / 4 lb washed and de-bearded mussels
100 ml / 4 fl oz white wine
4 tablespoons red pepper relish
4 gloves garlic, peeled and crushed
120 ml / 4 fl oz cream
1/2 tablespoon of cracked black pepper
pinch of salt
4 tablespoons basil oil

These are two examples of a mussel dish we have in the restaurant. They are lovely, light and fresh. They are easy to put together if you have all the ingredients readily at hand. Easy for me to say, I know, but I'm going to presume you have a batch of red pepper relish and basil oil in your fridge (cheeky boy that I am!). This is real one-pot cooking, transfer the pot to the table and ladle the mussels out followed by the juice which is eaten like a soup with loads of crusty bread. You will need a big pot with a tight fitting lid for these ones.

# Mussel, Leek and Bacon Risotto

**Serves 4**

This is a very popular risotto dish, unpretentious and satisfying.

450 g / 1 lb washed mussels
1 splash white wine
1 clove crushed garlic

Place the mussels in a large pot with a tight-fitting lid and add the wine and garlic. Cook over a high heat for 8–10 minutes until all the mussels have completely opened. Drain through a colander. When cool, pick the mussels, discard the shells and strain the juice, omitting the sediment at the bottom.

The risotto
1.5 litres / 2¹/₂ pints chicken stock
1 sprig rosemary
1 tablespoon olive oil
110 g / 4 oz diced streaky bacon
75 g / 3 oz butter
2 leeks, halved, finely sliced and washed
400 g / 14 oz arborio rice
50 g / 2 oz Parmesan cheese
1 tablespoon garlic crumbs (see Garlic)
1 tablespoon toasted almonds
1 tablespoon mascarpone cheese or crème fraîche

Heat the stock with the rosemary to just below simmering point. In a large saucepan heat the olive oil over medium heat. Cook the bacon until brown and crispy and remove from the pan. Turn down the heat, add in the butter and add the leeks. Cook for 2–3 minutes until soft. Add the rice and stir to make sure all is coated with butter. Add the mussel juice into the rice, then start to add the hot stock one ladle at a time, stirring constantly and making sure the liquid has been absorbed before adding more, the whole process will take about 15–20 mins. The risotto is done when the grains are tender yet firm to the bite. Add the Parmesan, mussels, bacon and mascarpone. Serve with a sprinkling of the garlic breadcrumbs and toasted almonds.

## Mussel Soup with Saffron

My years at Chez Nico are the foundation of the way I cook now. I learned so many things in my time there, the single and most important of which was how to taste. Flavour was of paramount importance and the cultivated palate was the cook's best asset. The flavours of his food were intense, sharp and clear. This soup cannot be bettered. Along with his Mediterranean fish soup, it is the most outstanding fish soup I have ever tasted.

**Serves 4 to 6**

110 g / 4 oz butter

2 tablespoons olive oil

half onion, finely diced

1 carrot, finely diced

half leek, finely diced

1 small bunch fresh parsley

4 gloves garlic, finely chopped

1 tablespoon dried tarragon

2 sprigs fresh tarragon

salt and pepper

700 g / 1½ lb mussels

½ bottle dry white wine

400 ml double cream

1 pinch saffron

1 tablespoon freshly chopped chives

Melt the butter with the olive oil in a large frying pan and sauté the diced vegetables until soft. Add the parsley, garlic and tarragon with a little salt and plenty of pepper, and cook for a further couple of minutes, stirring well. Remove from the heat. Scrape the mussels well and make sure they are very clean. Pour the wine into a large saucepan and throw in the mussels. Cook until they open, then leave to cool. When cool, strain, reserving the liquid, and remove the mussels from their shells. Pass the liquid through several layers of muslin, making sure all the sediment is discarded. Pick out some of the best mussels and set aside. Place the remaining mussels in the pan containing the vegetables. Pour in the strained wine and simmer for 20 minutes. Tip the contents into a strainer and press well to extract all the juices. Return the liquid to a clean saucepan, add the cream, bring to the boil and add the saffron. Simmer for a few minutes, stirring well, and skim off any scum which may rise to the surface. To garnish, add the reserved mussels and sprinkle with the chives.

Note: If you take care when cutting your vegetables I don't see any reason why they can't stay in the soup, with the result that you have a delicate little chowder.

## Big Pot of Steamed Mussels with Apple and Ginger Broth

**Serves 4**

Put all ingredients except chives into a pot. Steam on high heat, shaking every so often until all the shells are open. Divide evenly into bowls and sprinkle with chives.

2 kg / 4 ½ lb washed and de-bearded mussels

150 ml / ¼ pint Crinnaghtaun apple juice (or the best apple juice you can find)

150 ml / ¼ pint cream

½ teaspoon ground ginger

½ teaspoon curry powder

squeeze lemon juice

chopped chives to garnish

1 onion, finely sliced

½ tablespoon cracked black pepper

pinch of salt

# ... olive oil is synonymous with summer ... when the boats are back in the water, the people are more cheerful and the cheeky sun is playing hide and seek with us, out comes the olive oil.

Here's the thing. I don't use buckets of olive oil. I'm more a butter and cream man myself but I always keep two types of olive oil in the kitchen. Blended and extra-virgin. I often read in food magazines and cookbooks that one should try and find certain types of olive oil from a little village in Tuscany or Liguria, invariably pressed in November after the harvest. But if you can locate this fabulous nectar, are you prepared to shell out the money for the pleasure of having this Tuscan granny hand pressing the olives in an ancient and traditional manner? My advice would be to try the different oils available to you, find your favourite and stick to it.

Figures from the olive oil information bureau state that in Ireland we now consume 220% more olive oil than we did in 1991. That's great but I bet if somebody compared similar fast food statistics the increase would be bigger again so let's not proclaim ourselves a nation of gourmets just yet. I didn't have to think very long to come up with my favourite way to use olive oil – nothing flash, just an understanding of the ingredients involved, which to me is the basis of all good cooking. Beautifully ripe tomatoes, sliced red onions, olives, feta cheese with olive oil and balsamic vinegar with lots of black pepper and a little salt. Add cucumber if you like. There is simply no point in doing this with inferior tomatoes. Toss the tomatoes, onions and olives together. Season, scatter the feta then drizzle over plenty of olive oil and a splash of good balsamic vinegar. Let it sit for 15 minutes or so

at room temperature, then serve with crusty bread. The oil forms a sauce with the juice of the tomatoes to be mopped up with the bread. This Greek salad is at the heart of Mediterranean cooking. It tastes even better if you are dining al fresco and it will evoke memories of holidays past.

For me, olive oil is synonymous with summer. I can't bring myself to use it on dark wintry days. Cuisine of the sun doesn't seem right when you are reluctantly crawling from your bed on winter mornings but when the boats are back in the water, the people are more cheerful and the cheeky sun is playing hide and seek with us, out comes the olive oil. Summer is the time to have big salads at lunchtime, perhaps with roasted peppers and aubergines with crumbled goat's cheese and

crunchy toasted breadcrumbs for texture. Maybe some ratatouille with grilled hake and a frothy aïoli or a brandade of cod with tapenade and buttered toast, olives and basil oil, a veritable kaleidoscope of flavours and colours.

Olive oil is indispensable in pestos and salsa, bursting with goodness and vibrant healthiness. It's come a long way from the days in my father's chemist where it lurked in corners, only to be taken for medicinal purposes. Up to 8 oz per day for constipation (can you believe that?). It was also used for ulcers, for application around stiff joints and as a very attractive hair pomade for men. Ooooh, sexy!

## Basil Oil

1 very large handful fresh basil leaves
150 ml / ½ pint extra virgin olive oil
1 clove garlic, finely chopped
a few leaves of fresh mint (optional)
salt and pepper

This is a very handy staple to have in your kitchen. It makes sense to get basil in and make this as when you buy a bunch of basil you may not use it all and it just goes off in your fridge. This preserves the basil, allowing you to use a little at a time with no waste.

To make the basil oil; place the basil, mint, olive oil and some seasoning in a food processor and whizz until blended. Chill until needed. The mint gives a little zippiness and an extra dimension to the flavour.

## Feta Cheese Marinaded in Olive Oil

450 g /1 lb feta cheese, cut into cubes
600 ml / 1 pint extra virgin olive oil
1 pinch black peppercorns
1 red chilli, de-seeded and sliced
4 peeled garlic cloves
4 bay leaves
4 sprigs of marjoram or rosemary
juice of 1 lemon
50 g / 2 oz caster sugar

These make lovely presents if presented in nice jars with lots of colourful things inside them. The oil preserves and enhances the cheese which could be used on salads with pasta, over the roast provençale vegetables that follows or even as a little cheese course.

Bring the lemon juice and caster sugar to the boil to make a syrup and allow to cool. Place the cheese in the clean kilner jars taking care not to smudge the sides. Blanche the peppercorns, chilli, garlic, bay leaves, marjoram or rosemary, in boiling water for 1 minute, then add to the jars. Pour over, cover and leave for at least two days before using. These should keep for up to a month in the fridge.

... indispensable in pestos and salsa, bursting with goodness and vibrant healthiness. It's come a long way from the days in my father's chemist where it lurked in corners, only to be taken for medicinal purposes ... for ulcers, for application around stiff joints and as a very attractive hair pomade ... !

## Olive, Lemon and Caper Purée (Tapenade)

Tapenade can be quite an intense affair, strong and overpowering, a definite off putter for people who are only so-so about olives. I'm putting a little lemon syrup through it to lighten and sweeten it, making it that more palatable, and a little bit of honey at the end gives richness and depth of flavour. I use this to smear on crostini to serve with tomato or pepper soup. It's good as a pizza base or with goat's cheese. It keeps for ages in the fridge.

Put all the ingredients including the lemon syrup into a food processor until you get a fine paste. Remove and chill.

**Makes 450g / 1 lb purée**

juice of 1 lemon
50 g / 2 oz caster sugar
bring the lemon juice and caster sugar to the boil to make a syrup and allow to cool
250 g / 9 oz stoned black olives
75 g / 3 oz capers
90 ml / 3 fl oz light olive oil
2 cloves garlic, peeled and crushed
1 tablespoon honey

## Roasted Provençale Vegetables with Olive Oil, Garlic & Balsamic Vinegar

First you need to skin the peppers. Heat a non-stick frying pan with a little of the olive oil over a high heat and sear the peppers until brown and crispy on all sides. Place them into a bowl and cover tightly with clingfilm. You can also put them in a plastic bag and tie it. This will trap the steam. In the same pan on a lower heat throw in the red onions and fry for 3–4 minutes. If there is not enough oil, add a little more. Tip these into a roasting tray, oil included. With some fresh oil start to brown the aubergines and courgettes. You may have to do these in batches. When they are almost done, add the garlic, cook for a short time with the vegetables and tip these into a roasting tray with the onions. Next peel the peppers, de-seed and cut each into 8, and add to the roasting tray with the other vegetables. You can do all this a couple of hours in advance and all you need to do is to run the tray through a pre-heated oven 180°C/Gas 4 turning once or twice to re-heat. Add the balsamic vinegar, salt and pepper. Mix well and serve with a dollop of basil oil.

I serve this with various main courses in summertime. Sometimes I add Chick peasto the mix. You could also eat these with the marinaded feta cheese or with some plain couscous and a dollop of lemon hummus cream.

**Serves 4**

2 large red peppers
120 ml / 4 fl oz olive oil
4 red onions, peeled and quartered
1 small aubergine, sliced like the courgettes
2 courgettes, washed, sliced into 1 cm slices
2 cloves of garlic
60 ml / 2 fl oz balsamic vinegar
2 tablespoons basil oil

Hard fry, soft fry. I say that a lot in my kitchen. These two methods of cooking onions will produce two totally different flavours. To soft fry, cook some finely chopped onions gently in butter with a lid on for a prolonged period to produce a soft translucent base with a gentle sweetness. This is what I do if I want a mild creamy soup or sauce which will not overpower fish or meat. Add sugar, sherry vinegar, lots of bay leaves and rosemary and reduce until thick and you have sweet and sour onions to go with roast beef or lamb. For a beautiful onion soup, use more onions, add some diced potato, some chicken stock or perhaps ham stock if you have it. Cook, finish with cream and a touch of horseradish, and purée. Garnish with some leftover ham or chicken and herb of your choice.

Hard fry: This means to caramelise the sugars that come out of the onions to a mahogany brown, giving a more robust earthy flavour. The secret here is to keep scraping the bottom of the pan with a wooden spoon. When they have turned the desired colour you can do as you please. Add red wine and a shop bought gravy, no-one will ever know the difference. Perfect with sausages, the posher the better and a creamy parsnip mash. You can make a classic French onion soup by adding a good stock, white wine or cider and garlic and finish with a splash of cognac. Cook slowly for 40 minutes, put into bowls, cover with crunchy slices of toasted croutons and gruyère cheese and grill until the cheese is bubbling.

Onions are one of the few ingredients that no chef could do without, essential in everything from soups to sauces. Of course, we know that but for me it is a vegetable in

**Onions** are one of the few ingredients that no chef could do without, essential in everything from soups to sauces ... but for me it is a vegetable in its own right.

its own right. I use its structure to give an intricacy to a simple dish. Peel and cut across the grain making sure not to take too much off either end, thereby exposing the individual rings, then carefully place cut side down into a pan with hot oil until brown. Turn over and sprinkle with sugar, sherry or balsamic vinegar. Dot with a knob of butter and some chopped thyme and put in a slow oven until soft, making sure they retain their shape. You will end up with a caramelised onion, each ring standing out individually. This is a simple process that elevates steak and onions into restaurant status. If you want to use this onion with a pan-fried breast of chicken, use the same principle with the biggest onion you can find. Cut into 1cm rings, more care is needed here so they don't break up. When cooked the onion will look amazing with the chicken on top, perhaps with a wedge of camembert melted on top of the onion and served with crispy bacon.

Crispy onion rings will never go out of fashion. Again using really big onions adds a sense of drama. At home I would have no hesitation in serving them when some friends come round. Lace the batter with some curry powder and serve with your favourite dip.

There are a lot of unusual recommendations on how to peel an onion without crying. The most recent one I have heard is the placing of a wooden spoon lengthways in your mouth. I'm not joking! I heard it on the radio. The wood absorbs some of the fumes (allyl sulphide) and the spoon end is supposed to disperse the remaining fumes away from your eyes. Some people!

If you really don't want to cry place the onion in a freezer for 10 minutes before peeling.

# Gorgonzola Fritters with Red Onion Relish

**Serves 4**

50 g / 2 oz flour

1 beaten egg

2 tablespoons milk mixed with the egg

50 g / 2 oz breadcrumbs

225 g / 8 oz piece of gorgonzola, cut into eight

9 red onions finely sliced

50 g /2 oz butter

120 ml / 4 fl oz red wine

2 tablespoons redcurrant jelly

crushed juniper berries (optional)

1 pinch all-spice

salt and pepper

toasted walnuts

Everybody loves deep fried brie. This is just a twist on that, the blue cheese isn't too strong, melts really well and goes with the onions.

Flour, egg and breadcrumb the cheese wedges and keep in fridge until required. Soft fry the red onions in the butter for 3 minutes, add the red wine and redcurrant jelly, juniper and all-spice. Cook on a medium heat until fully reduced and syrupy. Reserve and keep warm.

Deep fry the gorgonzola at 180°C. Drain on a kitchen towel and place on top of the relish and scatter with as many toasted walnuts as you like. The red onion relish is also particularly good with duck and game.

# Onion Marmalade

This goes with all our pâtés, with our confit of duck, fillet of beef, any strong flavoured meat you care to imagine. It is easy and well worth making. My mother even puts it on toast (ahem).

1.5 kg / 3 lb finely sliced onions

2 tablespoons salt

1.2 kg / 2 ¼ lb sugar

600 ml / 1 pint white wine vinegar

1 teaspoon cloves, wrapped in muslin

2 tablespoons caraway seeds wrapped in muslin

Place the onions in a bowl with the salt. Cover and leave for a minimum of one hour in a cool place. Rinse and drain. Simmer the sugar with the vinegar and cloves for five minutes. Add the onion and caraway seeds. Return to the boil and simmer carefully for 2 to 2½ hours. When the syrup is thick and the onions translucent, pour into sterilised jars.

We discovered in our house that this onion marmalade is delicious in toasted cheese sandwiches.

# Roasted Red Onion with Feta Cheese and Baby Spinach

Sweat the onions lightly in the olive oil and garlic butter. Add the sugar, salt, pepper and thyme leaves and cook for 1 to 2 minutes over a medium heat. Splash in the vinegar. Remove the pot or pan from the heat and cover with clingfilm. Allow to come to room temperature. The juices will emerge to make a dressing. Then fold in the baby spinach making sure everything is nicely coated. Divide between four plates and place the feta cheese on top. Any excess juice, pour around the plate. Sprinkle the garlic crumbs on top.

The sweet roasted red onions contrast beautifully with the sharp feta cheese in this simple starter.

**Serves 4**

6 red onions, peeled and quartered
30 ml / 1 fl oz olive oil
25 g / 1 oz garlic butter (see Garlic)
1 teaspoon sugar
salt and pepper
1 sprig thyme, leaves picked off
30 ml / 1 fl oz white wine vinegar
1 large handful baby spinach
225 g / 8 oz feta cheese, cut into half inch cubes
50 g / 2 oz garlic crumbs (see Garlic)

# Cream of Onion Soup with Cheddar and Spring Onions

This is a white French onion soup, more like a creamy broth than a heavy purée. The apple juice gives a really fresh sweetness and the vinegar helps cut through the cream.

In a heavy bottomed pan melt the butter. When it starts to foam, add the onions, bay leaves and rashers. Give it a good stir. Put the lid on and cook on a medium heat for 10 minutes without any colour, stirring frequently.

Remove the lid and turn up the heat a little to get a light golden colour. Add the sugar and the vinegar and evaporate. Next add the stock, sage and cream. Cook for a further five minutes before adding the apple juice. Remove the sage and the rashers. Season, divide into bowls and sprinkle the cheddar and spring onions on top.

**Serves 4**

75 g / 3 oz butter
2 large Spanish onions, finely sliced
4 bay leaves
2 smoked rashers bacon (optional)
25 g / 1 oz caster sugar
1 splash white wine vinegar
600 ml / 1 pint chicken or ham stock
2 sprigs sage
150 ml / ¼ pint cream
150 ml / ¼ pint Crinnaghtaun apple juice (or best apple juice you can get)
75 g / 3 oz grated cheddar cheese
2 finely chopped spring onions

# Seared Beef Salad with Pickled Red Onions and Abbey Blue Fritters

**Serves 4**

For the pickled onions

60 ml / 2 fl oz red wine vinegar

1 tablespoon redcurrant jelly

2 cloves garlic

1 bay leaf

pinch cinnamon

60 ml / 2 fl oz water

2 red onions (peeled and sliced into half cm slices)

1 tablespoon sunflower oil

2 x beef fillet tails (around 150 g–175 g / 5–6 oz) each

salt and pepper

250 g / 9 oz ripe Abbey Blue brie

1 tablespoon flour

1 egg beaten with some milk

110 g / 4 oz white breadcrumbs

1 head butterleaf lettuce

For the dressing

60 ml / 2 fl oz walnut or hazelnut oil (olive oil will do)

1 drizzle honey

1 teaspoon wholegrain mustard

salt and pepper

1 splash warm water

This is a combination of two things that I love: Carpaccio of beef and deep fried brie. Abbey Blue is an Irish blue Brie so if you can't find it, use something similar. The onions in the middle bring the beef and the brie together and the mustard dressed butterleaf lettuce goes well with both. The tails of fillet beef are usually a very difficult piece of meat to do something with: too small and awkward in shape to serve as a steak. Here I sear the outside leaving the inside rare to blue and slice finely.

First of all pickle the onions by bringing the red wine vinegar, redcurrant jelly, garlic, bay leaves and cinnamon to the boil with the water. Drop the onions into the liquid and cook them over a low heat turning from time to time for three to four minutes. Remove from the heat and allow to cool in the pickling liquor.

Heat up the oil in a frying pan and sear the outside of the fillet tails all round till they are brown and crispy. This should take 3 to 4 minutes. Remove from the pan, season generously and set aside to cool.

Cut the cheese into wedges and dredge each piece through the flour, then the egg, then the breadcrumbs, making sure each piece is coated fully. Pre-heat the deep-fat fryer to 170°C / Gas 3.

Wash your lettuce. For the dressing whisk all the ingredients together.

To serve, slice the beef thinly and arrange on four plates. The meat will be cooked to different degrees as it tapers along to the tail so you can give the people who aren't so keen on very rare beef the more cooked slices. Dress the lettuce in the dressing and arrange beside the beef. Deep fry the cheese until brown and crispy, drain on a kitchen towel and divide between the plates. Lastly, divide some pickled onions between the plates.

# Red Wine and Redcurrant Onions

I always have lots of these in the fridge as they are so versatile and I use them so much, particularly in brown sauces, over meat and game, to give depth of flavour to the dish. I also use them in salad dressings, both creamy and oil based. For the home cook, they can be added into gravies or pan juices and spooned over the meat at the last minute.

Place all the ingredients into a pot and reduce over a low heat until the wine is completely evaporated and the onions have attained a jammy consistency. Allow to cool and place into jars. This will keep for up to a month.

Makes 2 x 450g / 1 lb jars

10 red onions, peeled and finely diced
half bottle red wine
3 tablespoons redcurrant jelly
2 cinnamon sticks or a good pinch cinnamon
4 bay leaves
8 juniper berries, finely crushed

# Red Wine Onion Dressing

This is a lovely salad dressing.

Mix everything together and dress your leaves.

Makes around 150 ml / ¼ pint

1 heaped tablespoon red wine and red currant onions
120 ml / 4 fl oz olive oil
30 ml / 1 fl oz red wine vinegar
salt and pepper

# Blue Cheese and Walnut Dressing

This again is based on red wine and redcurrant onions using blue cheese and walnuts. Lovely and creamy, it's good on its own like a Caesar dressing with some cos leaves but if you add smoked chicken or turkey, or even some leftover cold beef and grate some fresh apple or pear on top you have a delicious salad. The best leaves to use along with cos are baby spinach, rocket, mizuna or watercress.
Blend the cheese, stock and crème fraîche in the food processor or with a hand blender. Then fold in the walnuts and onions, salt and pepper. Refrigerate. If it's too thick, thin down with a little apple juice or warm water.

Makes about 280 ml / around ½ pint

50 g / 2 oz blue cheese
60 ml / 2 fl oz warm chicken stock
1 tablespoon crème fraîche
12 toasted walnuts, roughly chopped
1 tablespoon red wine and redcurrant onions
salt and pepper
1 splash apple juice, optional

(For another onion recipe, see Lamb – Crispy Lamb Chops with Creamy Sweet and Sour Onions)

# A vital part of the enjoyment of Parma's salty succulence is the slicing. Ideally you should be able to see your fingers through the ham for it to be tender enough to enjoy properly.

Stuck in with the rest of my New Year's resolutions is the usual promise to make my food simpler, eschewing the cheffy trickery that can sometimes overwhelm a dish. I read last year with great interest the final review by Jonathan Meades, the English *Times'* much-respected food critic. He awarded an unheard of 11 out of 10 to a restaurant in Bordeaux called La Tupina. This, he proclaimed, was his favourite restaurant anywhere and after fifteen years of reviewing the gamut of establishments, his opinion is well considered and to be valued. This place sounds right up my street. Regional Bordelaise specialities, stews, spit roasts, obscure local ingredients simply served: the chef's devotion to his region complete and consummate. I'm planning a trip to Bordeaux to try and capture some of Monsieur Xiradakis magic. If I don't, I would regard this as a great gastro opportunity missed. His personality shines through his restaurant, making it a unique experience, a very notable asset in these days of mass production where so many restaurants look the same and menus sound the same.

Good food starts with what you purchase. That goes for the domestic cook as well as the professional one. There are some ingredients that need nothing at all doing to them to make a fine meal, even for the crankiest of food critics. One such ingredient is prosciutto. This is almost generically called Parma ham in these parts, although fine hams also come from Bayonne, Normandy and Westphalia and undoubtedly the producers from Serrano in Spain would argue vehemently on the superiority of their produce over the Parma powerhouse.

I use either Parma or Bayonne myself. It's expensive. An average ham costs around 95 but it goes a long way and keeps for ages in the fridge. A vital part of the enjoyment of Parma's salty succulence is the slicing. Ideally you should be able to see your fingers through the ham for it to be tender enough to enjoy properly. Those rough, tough pre-sliced packets, although handy, are not representative of the pleasures of eating the properly cut stuff. If you know a deli that will cut it in front of your eyes, that is a far better option.

The eating of it can be as simple an affair as you like. Melon we all know about and there is no need to look down on something just because it's common. Make sure the melon is as ripe as can be and you're on the pig's back. My preferred choice of melon is Charentais – beautifully perfumed, it makes an ideal partner for Parma ham. Other partners are figs – again make sure they are ripe, either au naturel or drizzled with some honey and cinnamon and lightly grilled. At a recent dinner up in our house, I parboiled, then roasted Jerusalem artichokes in olive oil, thyme and garlic, then glazed them with a little brown sugar and a splash of balsamic vinegar (sherry vinegar might even have been better). I allowed them to cool and wrapped each one in a slice of Parma ham as an antipasto. Simple to do and absolutely no hassle to serve.

Try wrapping ham around verdant crisp asparagus when in season, drizzle with olive oil and lemon for a very elegant starter. In winter I pair Parma with celeriac. Some of my discoveries are made during the course of the munchies after a couple of pints. Our fridge here can be deeply frustrating when in this condition as everything we do is cooked to order and who wants to do that when there's an urgent need to slap something between two slices of bread. All I could see one night were some leftover dauphinoise potatoes and some Parma ham. Why not? Well, it was a revelation. Salty versus creamy. This little bit of tummy rumbling gave rise to my tart of dauphinoise potatoes with Parma ham on the à la carte menu. Creamy garlicky potatoes in a crisp pastry case. The spuds are baked in cream, thinned with a little milk and a couple of eggs to help it set. This means I don't have to reduce the cream which would make it overly heavy. I'll place a little rosette of Parma ham on top of the tart and then put a couple of leaves on top for colour and extra texture. Rocket, mizuna or baby spinach, depending on what I can get.

I like a mild goat's cheese with Parma. I'm going to give you a recipe that's simple and gorgeous. You do need a deep fryer for this and you will get the wonton skins in a Chinese supermarket if you are lucky enough to live near one.

## Crispy Goat's Cheese Fritters with Parma Ham

**Serves 4**

For the raviolis

1 log of white St Maure goat's cheese

16 wonton skins

1 beaten egg

2 slices of Parma ham per person

Pull the plastic centrepiece from the cheese and cut into 8 slices. Place 8 wonton skins on a clean surface and brush with a beaten egg. Brush one side of the remaining skins and cover the cheese pressing down on the edges firmly. Chill for 2-3 hours.

When ready to serve, deep fry until golden brown and crispy. Drain off any excess fat and serve with the slices of Parma ham.

## Lemon Risotto with Asparagus and Parma Ham

**Serves 6**

juice and zest of one lemon

1½ l / 2½ pints chicken stock

1.5 litres / 4 oz butter

1 tablespoon sunflower oil

1 onion, finely chopped

400 g / 14 oz Arborio rice

120 ml / 4 fl oz white wine

75 g / 3 oz grated fresh Parmesan cheese

salt and freshly ground pepper

16 spears of asparagus, peeled, trimmed and blanched

4 generous slices parma ham, cut into strips

Remove the zest of the lemon. Squeeze the juice of the lemon and reserve to one side.

Heat the stock to just below simmering point. In a large pan, melt half the butter with the oil over a medium heat. Add the onion and cook until tender and transparent. Add the rice and stir making sure it is evenly coated with the butter and oil.

Add the wine and cook until absorbed. Add the lemon juice and stock a little at a time, stirring constantly. Make sure the liquid has been absorbed before adding more. When all the liquid has been added the rice should be tender but have some bite. Stir in the lemon zest, remaining butter and the cheese and check for seasoning.

Warm the asparagus through in a little butter. Divide the risotto between four warm plates. Place the parma ham on top and garnish with the asparagus. If you fancy a little extra cheese scatter it on top.

# Parma Ham with Rémoulade of Celeriac

Celeriac is a delicious, underrated and underused vegetable. It tastes like a sweet and nutty celery. The crunchy texture is perfect with the softness of cured ham. This recipe is nothing new, but I just love it!

Place the egg yolks, mustard and vinegar in a bowl and mix together. Add the oil in drops at first, whisking in so the yolks can absorb the oil. When about half the oil has been added you can start adding in larger amounts just making sure the oil is incorporated as you go along. Whisk until all the oil has been absorbed and the sauce is thick and creamy and reserve.

Peel the celeriac with a serrated carving knife. Slice into 1/2 cm slices as best you can and cut the slices into thin strips. Alternatively you can grate the celeriac in a food processor or on the largest side of the grater. Pour over the lemon juice. Mix the celeriac with the mayonnaise, grain mustard and truffle oil. Arrange on four plates in a little mound and drape the Parma ham around. Give a twist of black pepper and serve. To make this a little more elegant in the restaurant we encase the celeriac in spring roll pastry, deep fry and serve with some rocket leaves and a roasted tomato.

**I also like to serve Parma ham with the following:**
Parmesan Fritters (see Parmesan)
Tomato and Avocado Salsa (see Avocados)
Marinated Cherry Tomatoes (see Tomatoes)
Goat's Cheese Mousse (see Garlic)
Canellini Beans in Lemon and Rosemary Dressing
    (see Lemons)

**Serves 4**

Mayonnaise
2 egg yolks plus 1 egg
1 teaspoon Dijon mustard
2 tablespoons white wine vinegar
1 teaspoon salt
500 ml / 17 fl oz of sunflower oil
1 head of celeriac
juice of 1 lemon
1 teaspoon wholegrain mustard
3 drops truffle oil (optional)
8 slices of Parma ham

... real Parmesan is expensive but it just transforms dishes as simple as linguini with butter. Try it. It's simplicity itself, pungent and heavenly.

There is no comparison between fresh Parmiagiano Reggiano and the powdered stuff that comes in tins. It stinks and gives the real McCoy a bad name.

I know real Parmesan is expensive but it just transforms dishes as simple as linguini with butter. Try it. It's simplicity itself, pungent and heavenly. Add a little bit of spinach and Parma ham. Immediately it is elevated to restaurant status. Of course you can have too much of a good thing. Lashing too much Parmesan on say, a risotto can overpower the other flavours so it's important to be judicious.

One of the best gadgets ever are those little hand held graters that you twirl a handle on to get just the right amount. Parmesan loses its flavour quickly and takes on a dry texture if grated too far in advance so try and pick up one of these things.

I once ate a fabulous pear and Parmesan risotto in the River Café in London. As simple as you can get. Not a fleck of colour, not in the least bit cheffy but the taste ... A simpler version of this coupling for afficionados is a wedge of Parmesan with a really ripe pear and I am told that this with a fine pinot gris or sherry would be heaven itself.

In 1994 I found a recipe for Parmesan fritters in Simon Hopkinson's book. These fabulous little babies have rarely been off my menu since. Gooey, delicious and undoubtedly bad for you. Serve them with Parma ham and my ubiquitous tomato and avocado salsa for lunch. Transform a tomato or pepper salad by popping on a few of these. Hot and cold will tantalise your palate even more. They are even great finger food with a mild chilli dip. Slosh them around with some good olive oil and balsamic vinegar with a rocket salad or tender baby spinach to make you feel you are eating something healthy. Try them with gammon and spinach, any type of ham, French beans or asparagus. They will be firm favourites forever.

I received some courgette flowers this morning so I am trying out a Parmesan custard: eggs, cream, Parmesan and nutmeg maybe, with some chopped oregano. I'll deep fry the courgette flowers in a light batter and serve with some crispy strips of bacon, the idea being to use the custard as a dip – crispy and creamy. I like to encourage people to be tactile with food. Break off some courgette, dip it in the custard, eat it with your fingers if you like, take a piece of bacon, dip again and pass it round to others. My greatest pleasure is when I hear that people are swapping food. I know it may not be to some people's taste but for a cook it's a sure sign of enjoyment.

# Parmesan Custard with Crispy Bacon and Deep Fried Courgette Flowers

I love savoury custards. I have an addiction to Marks & Spencers quiche lorraine and this is a little homage to it, the courgette flowers are a fancy twist, crisp green beans or little florets of broccoli will do the same without the batter to make your life easier. Crisp strips of bacon complete the flavours giving added texture.

Sometimes I make these custards with Gabriel cheese which is a fabulous cheese from West Cork. I'm not going to put much salt into the custard as the cheese is quite salty and coupled with the Parmesan it might be a salt overload.

**Custard**: Pre heat your oven to 160°C /Gas 2½. Warm a bain marie water bath on the top of the stove. Whisk the eggs, cream, 75 g / 3 oz of the cheese together. Add chives, a little salt, pepper and garlic and ladle into 4 buttered ramekins. Place these carefully into the bain marie. The water should come halfway up the ramekins. Place in the oven for 40 minutes. When cooked they should wobble slightly in the centre. This is the very same procedure as the crab crème brûlée. Remove from the waterbath and allow to cool.

**Batter**: Whisk all the ingredients except the egg whites together and leave in a warm place. Pre-heat the deep fat fryer to 180°C/Gas 4 then whisk up the egg whites and fold into the batter mix. Dust the courgette flowers with some flour and drop into the batter.

**Serves 4**

**To serve**: Pre-heat the grill. Dust the custards with the remaining Parmesan cheese and glaze under the grill. Deep-fry the courgette flowers until golden and crispy. Drain on kitchen paper and season. Bake the bacon until it is very crisp and rigid. Divide on 4 plates with the custards, bacon and garnish with a wedge of lemon

1 egg plus 2 egg yolks
450 ml / 16 fl oz cream
110 g / 4 oz grated Parmesan cheese
a handful chopped chives
salt and pepper
1 small clove garlic crushed
8 slices of thinly sliced rindless streaky bacon

The batter
110 g / 4 oz sieved flour
150 ml / ¼ pint beer
1 egg separated
60 ml / 2 fl oz water
salt and pepper
4 courgette flowers (when in season)

# Grape and Parmesan Risotto

This is as simple and unadorned as food gets; perfect for a light lunch with a crisp green salad and some toasted walnuts.

**Serves 4 to 6**

1.5 litres / 2½ pints chicken stock

3 tablespoons butter

1 tablespoon olive oil

1 onion, finely chopped

400 g / 14 oz Arborio rice

175 ml / 6 fl oz dry white wine

30 mixed seedless grapes, cut in half

salt and freshly ground black pepper

50 g / 2 oz Parmesan cheese, grated

Heat the stock to just below simmering point. In a large saucepan melt 2 tablespoons of the butter with the oil over a medium heat. Add the onion and cook until tender, about 5 minutes. Add the rice and stir for 2 minutes, until it is heated and coated with butter. Add the wine and cook, stirring until it is absorbed. Add the hot stock, 125 ml / 4 oz at a time, stirring constantly and making sure the liquid has been absorbed before adding more. After about 10 minutes stir in the grapes, salt and pepper. If more liquid is required use some hot water. The risotto is ready when the rice grains are tender yet still firm to the bite. Remove the pan from the heat, stir in the remaining butter and cheese and serve.

# Parmesan Fritters

110 g / 4 oz butter

110 g / 4 oz plain flour

450 ml / 16 fl oz hot milk

6 tablespoons freshly grated Parmesan

pinch nutmeg

10 fresh sage leaves chopped

2 egg yolks

salt

quarter teaspoon cayenne pepper

½ fresh mozzarella ball, chopped into small cubes

oil for deep frying

plain flour for coating

2 eggs beaten

fresh breadcrumbs for coating

I love this Simon Hopkinson recipe. Melt the butter in a saucepan. Stir in the flour and make a roux. Add the milk, stirring constantly to make a smooth thick sauce. The sauce must be very, very thick. Stir in the Parmesan, nutmeg and sage. Remove from the heat. Allow to cool for 10 minutes and then stir in the egg yolks and seasoning. Stir in the mozzarella carefully to avoid breaking up the cubes. Spread the mixture in a greased baking tin. Cover with clingfilm and leave overnight in the fridge.

Heat the oil to 190°C / Gas 5. Sprinkle some plain flour on a plate. Put the beaten egg in a shallow dish and spread the breadcrumbs on another plate. Remove the clingfilm and cut the cheese mixture into 2.5 cm squares and then fashion them into little balls. Dip them first into the flour, then into the egg and finally into the breadcrumbs. When they have all been coated, fry them in batches in the hot oil. They should take about a minute or so each – golden brown on the outside and creamy-cheesy on the inside.

# Green Summer Salad with Parma Ham, Quails Eggs and Parmesan Fritters

Sometimes I think it takes a different talent altogether to make nice salads. This is one that bursts with flavour and oozes with textures. You don't have to grill the Parma ham. I am doing so to give texture and extra flavour to the dish. If you can't get quail's eggs, use soft-boiled hens eggs and if you don't want to use parma ham, you can use streaky bacon rashers, grilled until crisp. This is a main course summer salad.

Bring a pan of water to the boil. Drop in the beans and cook for 6 minutes or until tender. Drain. Cool under the cold tap then pat dry and put into a bowl. Pre-heat the grill to its highest setting.

Bring a pot of water to the boil. Carefully drop in the quail eggs and simmer for 2½ minutes. Then refresh under cold water. Grill the ham until crisp and set aside.

Whisk together the mustard, garlic, vinegar and olive oil. Season to taste. Dress the beans, then gently fold in the salad leaves and arrange on 4 plates. Break the grilled ham into large-ish pieces and place on each plate. Halve the eggs and distribute between the plates. Place four fritters on each plate. Serve immediately.

**Serves 4**

225 g / 8 oz  green beans, trimmed
8 quails eggs
12 slices Parma ham
1 teaspoon Dijon mustard
2 cloves garlic, crushed
2 tablespoons white wine vinegar
5 tablespoons extra virgin olive oil
salt and freshly ground black pepper
110 g / 4 oz mixed salad leaves
12 Parmesan fritters

173

I feel it is only now that I am really learning to understand food. I suppose that's a funny statement considering that I have been cooking professionally for eighteen years. Maybe I am a slow learner but the older I get, the more I realise I have a lot to learn. The truly great cooks don't do much to their food but they rely on the best ingredients cooked with care and understanding. In my kitchen, I encourage my chefs to think about what they are doing, that recipes are only guidelines and that the whats, wheres and hows are all important. All five senses are used when cooking. Smells should be forever imprinted on their memory. When something is right and to get it wrong is alright as long as they learn from their mistakes. The subtlety of colour is as important as the silky sheen of a sauce and above all taste, taste, taste.

I'm a lot closer to nature than I ever was before having moved to the country. We are now surrounded by blackberry bushes, mushrooms and animals of all sorts and a plethora of people that all bake me under the table, turning out jams and chutneys of a stunning quality for the local country market every Friday morning. I recently went to the Country Market, totally unprepared for the serious business this was as I was elbowed out of the way constantly by agitated septuagenarian ladies intent on getting their favourite treat and nothing would get in their way. Home made cakes, quiches and buns and a couple of jam stalls, vying for the same customers, eyeing each other up suspiciously.

Freshly cut flowers nurtured with love to grace someone's living room and craggy mud covered carrots and parsnips waiting to be scrubbed, boiled and mashed with tons of butter. Fudge slices, caramel slices, fairy cakes, biscuits and jellies.

This sort of gathering happens religiously in towns and villages all over Ireland. These are indeed women to be cherished in the ever growing fast food no time to cook lifestyle which we now live. Both adults working to fund a mortgage, arriving home at 7.30 to tired to do anything but pop a pizza in the oven and eat in front of the telly.

The food at the country market may not

# ... just made that morning and packaged in margarine boxes or whatever is handy. We ate ours with piping hot tea, looking out at rainlashed Dungarvan bay and I wouldn't have been anywhere else.

look as good as professional pattissiers it is sold in tip top condition just made that morning and packaged in margarine boxes or whatever is handy. We ate ours with piping hot tea, looking out at rainlashed Dungarvan bay and I wouldn't have been anywhere else. Maire my wife tells me I am taking this country living a bit too seriously. She answered the door to me a few weeks ago to see me me standing there, dripping wet in the full country regalia. My favourite item of clothing at the moment is a wax jacket which she bought me some years ago and I swore I would never wear. I have also taken to wearing my late father's tweed cap so along with my green wellies and a stick with our young dog and cat, Olive (black, get it) and Delia (Smith of course) in tow she nearly fell down laughing. After picking her up off the floor highly indignant with her laughter I was offered the ultimate compliment. 'You look like Daddy'. Right I said, and vowed never to wear that particular ensemble in public again.

For the restaurant, I try to buy as much as I can locally. A veg man that grows anything for me to order gets up at 6am to pick his produce and it arrives on the restaurant doorstep at 10 am. You cant but understand the produce more when you have such a relationship with it. Comments like how big would you like your carrots are common. He has now bought his seeds for next year to ensure an even bigger variety of salads which are sold to our local veg shop who then sells them on to an even more knowledgeable and demanding public.

We now feel privileged to live in West Waterford. It is a secretly beautiful place, undeniably one of Ireland's hidden havens. We recently attended a friends wedding in Kilworth and gave some English friends a lift back to the reception in Dungarvan along the breathtaking Blackwater Valley route. We thanked our lucky stars that the sun was shining and they could see it at its best. Our visitors were astounded by the beauty of Cappoquin and Lismore castle and spent the evening telling us how lucky we were to live here. They had to return to London the following day and West Wateford would be just a memory. We on the other hand can enjoy it every day of the year.

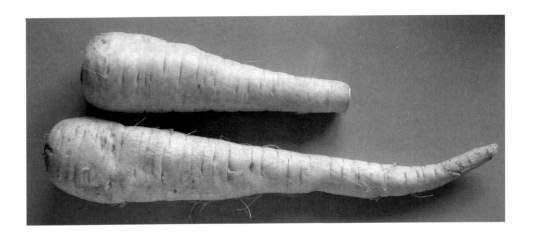

Parsnips are fantastic. I like the way they lie in greengrocers, ugly and muddy, crying out to be scrubbed and peeled to reveal their creamy flesh. I can cope with winter and being enveloped by the dark and rainy nights as long as I have parsnips to keep me company.

I can't wait to bake them with Parmesan, make soup with curry, apples and a swirl of crème fraîche. They are delicious mashed with spuds and served with an unctuous oxtail or lamb stew. What could be nicer than a creamy garlicky dauphinoise with a honey and ginger glazed grilled duck breast. (See Potato and Parsnip Gratin in Potato chapter.)

Alternatively, slice them thinly on a mandolin (a very cheffy piece of equipment – if you don't have one, a peeler will do nicely). Deep fry and serve as finger food with pickled ginger and coriander mayonnaise.

Parsnips are delicious cooked with onions, garlic and cream, puréed to be used as a filling for a filo or short pastry tart. This you could top with slices of smoked turkey, roast chicken or sautéed lamb's liver or kidneys. The list is endless and only curtailed by your imagination.

(By the way, Dutch seventeenth-century paintings depicting root vegetables spread around the housewife's feet do not signify untidiness but the fact that the tiled floor of the kitchen was the coolest place to store vegetables. So remember, think twice before giving out to your missus for not putting the shopping away.)

# Parsnips are fantastic. I like the way they lie in greengrocers, ugly and muddy, crying out to be scrubbed and peeled to reveal their creamy flesh.

## *Curried Parsnip and Apple Soup*

Begin by heating a small frying pan and dry-roasting the coriander, cumin and cardamom seeds – to toast them and draw out their flavour. After 2 minutes they will change colour and start to jump in the pan. Then crush them finely with a pestle and mortar. If you want to speed up the proceedings, use ready-ground spices and just toast them in the pan.

Next heat the butter and oil in a saucepan until the butter begins to foam. Add the onion and gently soften for about 5 minutes. Let the onion cook for another two minutes, then add all the crushed spices along with the turmeric and ginger, stir and let it all continue to cook gently for a few more minutes. Add the parsnips and the apple to the saucepan, stirring well, then pour in the stock, add some seasoning and let the soup simmer as gently as possible for half an hour.

Remove it from the heat, then liquidise and strain through a sieve crushing the parsnips well to extract the juice. Re-heat the soup, and taste to check the seasoning. Serve in hot soup bowls, garnished with crème fraîche and chopped chives.

This is a really nice winter soup. The touch of spice just gives it that extra something.

**Serves 4**

pinch coriander and cumin seeds
3 whole cardamom pods
50 g / 2 oz butter
1 tablespoon groundnut oil
1 medium onion, chopped
pinch turmeric
pinch powdered ginger
350 g / 12 oz parsnips, peeled, chopped into 2 cm / 1"
    dice
1 large cooking apple, peeled, cored and diced
725 ml / 1¼ pints chicken stock
salt and freshly milled black pepper
2 tablespoons crème fraîche to garnish
handful chopped chives to garnish

# Creamy Parsnip, Onion and Beef Broth

**Serves 4**

1 large onion, sliced

50 g / 2 oz butter

2 parsnips in small chunks

120 ml / 4 fl oz Crinnaghtaun apple juice (or a good
    quality apple juice)

230 ml / 8 fl oz beef stock

230 ml / 8 fl oz light chicken stock

120 ml / 4 fl oz cream

good pinch chopped marjoram

salt and black pepper

50 g / 2 oz flaked almonds

The success of this dish depends on the quality of the stock. I know being in a professional kitchen has its advantages in this regard. I usually use the stock from my daubes of beef. If you can't get good beef stock, use all chicken stock. I do not purée this soup as I mean it to be a chunky broth. It's important to take care when chopping the vegetables to have them uniform in size. To save you time, you may be come across vacuum-packed prepared parsnips. These would make the operation much easier.

In a large pan cook the onion gently in the butter (until translucent with the lid on). When soft add the parsnips and continue to cook for a further 3 minutes, add all the liquid and bring to the boil. Simmer until the parsnips are cooked. Add cream and cook for a further two minutes, then add the chopped marjoram. Season and serve garnished with flaked almonds.

# Crispy Parsnip Strips

These are good as an appetiser or as a dramatic and tasty garnish with meat dishes. You will need a deep fat fryer for this.

50 g / 2 oz flour

1 pinch ground ginger

1 pinch smoked paprika (optional)

2 medium parsnips

Mix the dry ingredients together. Peel the parsnips, then either with a mandolin or a vegetable peeler take long shavings from the parsnips. Toss in the flour, shaking off the excess and deep fry for 2 to 3 minutes at 180°C. Drain on kitchen paper. Season and serve at room temperature.

# Honey and Ginger Roasted Parsnips

Cook your parsnips in boiling salted water until they are three-quarters cooked. Remove from the water and allow to cool. You can take your parsnips to this stage beforehand. Pre-heat your oven to 180°C / Gas 4. Heat the oil in a roasting tray on the hob and add the parsnips. Turn round in the oil for a couple of minutes then place in the oven for 10 minutes, turning once or twice. They should be starting to get brown and crispy. Drain off any excess oil then add the butter, honey and ground ginger, salt and pepper. Put back in the oven for 5 more minutes taking care the honey doesn't burn by shaking the tray and rolling the parsnips round every so often until they get a nice amber colour. Remove from the oven, put into a serving dish and sprinkle with the toasted almonds.

These are essential Sunday lunch grub, golden, crispy and glistening.

**Serves 4**

8 small parsnips (peeled and with the tops cut off)
3 tablespoons sunflower oil
50 g / 2 oz butter
1 good tablespoon of honey
1 pinch of ground ginger
1 tablespoon toasted almonds

# Parsnip Hash Browns

These are dinky little things. As well as being a suitable potato based garnish, they can be used as croûtons on winter salads. Or fold some left-over corned beef through the mix to make a more substantial supper dish to be served with a fried egg. I primarily use these with duck although they are just as good with beef, venison or even lamb.

Peel the potatoes and grate them on the largest side of the grater. Then grate the parsnips. Add the egg, salt, pepper and nutmeg. Combine thoroughly to form the mix into rough 3 cm balls by flouring your hands and rolling between your palms. Set aside on a tray. Take a fresh tray and roll the balls in flour shaking off the excess. Pre-heat the fryer to 180ºC and immerse the hash brown for 3 to 4 minutes until golden brown.

**Serves 4**

You will need a deep-fryer for this
4 medium baked potatoes
2 large parboiled parsnips
2 eggs
salt and pepper
pinch nutmeg
75 g / 3 oz flour

To a chef, one of the most endearing qualities peas have is that seasonality is never an issue. Peas are one of the few vegetables that lend themselves to freezing. You can use frozen peas to make fabulous dishes. I use them all the time.

Their versatility cannot be ignored. They go with fish and meat equally, their magic enhanced when paired with a few spices. My brother is a vegetarian. I cooked him a potato, pea and cashew nut korma once. It went down a storm. Whenever I have trouble getting vegetables, I always turn to peas. They are usually knocking around on our daily specials.

I like having staples in the kitchen that can be used for numerous things, adapted for fish and meat starters and mains and even used hot or cold. Pea purée is one of those things. I know that this attitude has limitations in a domestic kitchen but my advice to any keen cook with freezer space is to always have them handy.

The simplest method to make a pea purée (mushy peas!) with frozen garden peas is as follows: sweat some chopped onion in butter. When soft and translucent add frozen peas and a little concentrated chicken bouillon. Cook for 10 minutes and place in a food processor with some mint and creamed horseradish. Season and keep in the fridge. The best way to reheat this is in the microwave. We use this purée to garnish lots of dishes. Lambs kidneys and liver, fillet steak with crispy onions and roast potatoes, grilled or poached salmon, roast chicken and crispy bacon or you could add a little cream to the purée and serve with some macaroni and some melted cambazola cheese.

# one of the most endearing qualities **peas** have is that seasonality is never an issue. Peas are one of the few vegetables that lend themselves to freezing

## *Cream of Pea Soup with Crispy Calamari and Bacon*

Crisp, clear flavours; crunchy textures and pure colours are all here. This soup is light and broth like. The calamari and bacon complement it perfectly.

Melt the butter in a pan. Add the onion and sauté for 5 minutes until softened. Stir in the peas, mint and stock and bring to the boil. Cook for 10 minutes as quickly as you can. Liquidise and season and strain through a sieve into a clean pan.

Dust the squid in the cornflour, then deep fry for about 30 seconds until crisp but not coloured. Drain and season well, then sprinkle with lemon juice.

Reheat the soup, stirring occasionally and then ladle into shallow serving bowls. Dollop some of the crème fraîche on the surface of the soup, garnish with mint and the crispy bacon and sprinkle on the calamari just before serving with the lemon wedges.

Serves 4

knob unsalted butter
1 small onion, finely chopped
350 g / 12 oz frozen garden peas
fresh mint, leaving a sprig to garnish
1.2 litres / 2 pints chicken stock
110 g / 4 oz fresh squid, cleaned, halved and cut into thin strips
50 g / 2 oz cornflour
vegetable oil, for deep-frying
juice of quarter lemon
100 g / 4 oz crème fraîche
4 streaky bacon rashers, grilled until crispy
1 lemon, cut into wedges
salt and freshly ground black pepper

## Pea and Onion Bhajis, Cucumber Raita

Just a small change to traditional onion bhajis, these I usually serve with lamb that has got a bit of spice, along with cucumber raita and maybe some couscous. It is a lovely spring/summer dish.

Place the flour, spices, chilli, fresh coriander and enough water to make a smooth, thick paste. Add the onion and the peas. Mix well and then form into 12 rough balls. Heat the oil to 170°C/ Gas 3 in a deep fat fryer and deep fry the bhajis for 4–5 minutes until deep golden and crispy. Drain on kitchen paper.

**Serves 4**

For the bhajis
75 g / 3 oz gram flour (chick pea flour - available in health food shops)
 pinch ground cumin
 pinch cayenne pepper
 pinch garam masala
 pinch ground turmeric
1 mild green chilli, chopped
1 tablespoon chopped fresh coriander
1 large onion, finely chopped
1 handful frozen garden peas, thawed

sunflower oil, for deep frying

Cucumber Raita (see cumcumbers)

## Curried Risotto of Peas

I use this with some grilled salmon and my yoghurt, chilli and coriander dressing. It would be pretty good with most fish and light meats i.e. chicken or rabbit. It is especially good with ginger marinaded chicken (see Ginger).

**Serves 4–6**

1.5 l / 2½ pints chicken stock
3 tablespoons butter
1 tablespoon seasame oil
½ tablespoon mild curry powder
peel of half an orange
one onion, finely chopped
120 ml / 4 fl oz apple juice
400 g / 14 oz arborio rice
175 g / 6 oz frozen petit pois

Heat the stock to just below simmering point. Add the curry powder and orange peel. In a large saucepan, melt the butter with the sesame oil. Add the onion and cook for 2-3 minutes over a low heat until soft and translucent. Add the rice and stir for 2 minutes. Then add the stock, bit by bit, making sure all the liquid is absorbed before adding more. After 10 minutes add the peas and the apple juice and cook for 5 more minutes until the rice is tender yet firm to the bite. If the rice is not yet cooked but all the liquid gone add a little hot water. Season and serve.

## Creamed Peas and Bacon

This sauce/vegetable I serve an awful lot with chicken, monkfish and sometimes scallops. Take the horseradish béchamel from the chapter on Leeks and add some blanched peas and sautéed bacon strips and just warm everything together.

## Pea and Ham Soup with Crackling, Chip Buttie and Y.R. Sauce

This soup is thicker and more substantial than the other. Frozen peas make a fabulous soup. If they are cooked in ham stock all the better. We never waste anything that has flavour, i.e., ham or chicken stock, duck jelly or bacon fat. Freeze them if you don't need them for they are certain to come in handy sooner or later. Mint and

horseradish give a lovely flavour to this. I honey-glaze the ham for some extra flavour then sprinkle the lot with a whisper of whipped cream and some crunchy crackling.

This is really a lunch. The chip buttie is an unpretentious nod to the type of food that I really like.

Sweat the onion in the butter until soft and translucent. Add the peas and the stock and cook rapidly for 10 minutes. Season, liquidise and pass through a sieve. Reserve until needed.

Whip the cream into soft peaks, fold in the horseradish and set aside.

Preheat your oven to 180°C / Gas 4. Mix the ham with the honey, butter and all-spice. Place on a tray and glaze in the oven until golden and crispy.

For the crackling
Remove the fat from the ham hock and cut into little strips. Fry in a pan or bake through the oven until crispy and golden.

To serve the soup
Re-heat the soup. Place some of the glazed ham hock in the bottom of four soup bowls. Ladle over the soup. Drizzle with the horseradish cream and top with crackling and some mint or sage. Serve with a chip buttie, spread with a little Y.R. sauce.

### Serves 4

1 medium onion (finely chopped)
50 g / 2 oz butter
500 g / 1.1 lb of frozen peas
1.2 litres / 2 pints of ham or chicken stock
60 ml / 2 fl oz cream
half tablespoon commercial creamed horseradish
200 g / 7 oz of cooked ham hock trimmed of fat and chopped into 1 cm pieces
1 drizzle of honey
25 g / 1 oz butter
pinch of all-spice
a pinch of chopped mint or sage

As a chef, if you want to progress and keep coming up with new dishes it's important to eat out a lot, not only for pleasure but for garnering new ideas. I recently ate peaches in a great restaurant, Chapter One, on Parnell Square in Dublin. These peaches were the most delicious peaches I ever tasted and I ate them with smoked chicken and lobster. Now I could be racking my tiny mind forever and I would never come up with such a combination but the lobster and peaches put me into gastro fantasy land and now I confess, peaches are my new thing. For me, it's a pleasure when a meal is so good, not only am I satisfied, but also catapulted in an entirely new direction. It must be borne in mind that experimentation can be a total disaster in the wrong hands. Understanding the ingredients is the key. Restraint is of paramount importance.

So what do I do with peaches? Well up to that meal I would have poached them very lightly in a vanilla and cinnamon syrup, peeled them carefully and served them with a smooth chocolate sorbet and whipped cream. Or even with raspberries and vanilla ice-cream to recreate that classic peach melba. A bellini parfait was a hit here last summer. Snatched from that famous cocktail of peach juice and champagne invented in Harry's Bar in Venice, the champagne gives an opulence to the smooth peach cream. But now ... new doors have been opened for me. Poached peaches go fantastically well with Caesar salad. Not so strange really as Parmesan cheese eats really well with peaches. I only put a hint of anchovy in the dressing though to prevent any conflict. I don't see that peaches wouldn't go with prawns if they go with lobster. I'll just make sure there is no garlic knocking around. Perhaps I'll poach them lightly in some white wine, herbs and vegetables. I've got some baby fennel in the fridge and I might braise that and put all three together. Something new to try. Poached prawns with baby fennel and peaches. I can make a little dressing with the poaching liquid, mixed with some olive oil. The birth of a new dish and I await my customers' reactions.

# It must be borne in mind that experimentation can be a total disaster in the wrong hands. Understanding the ingredients is the key. Restraint is of paramount importance. So what do I do with peaches?

## Poached Peaches

This is just a base recipe from which you can put dishes together, i.e., the gratin and the risotto. Of course you can use tinned peaches to save time, just don't let the gastro police catch you. If you can find white peaches for this, all the better. You need them just on the underripe side.

We use the poaching liquid over and over again. Each time it improves in colour and flavour and after a while we put a little drizzle of this nectar in the bottom of a champagne flute, not quite a Bellini but it is pretty good all the same.

Bring all the ingredients except the peaches to the boil. Drop in the peaches. If there isn't enough water to cover, add a little more. Cover the peaches with greaseproof paper and allow to simmer gently for 15–20 minutes. Remove the greaseproof paper and allow the peaches to cool in the liquid and use when needed. These will keep for up to 2 weeks. The flavour will get better all the time. If you want to bottle them, sterilise your jars and they will keep a lot longer than.

225 g / 8 oz sugar

1 vanilla pod (split lengthways and seeds scraped into the pot)

peel of half an orange

4 bay leaves

2 cinnamon sticks or a pinch of cinnamon powder

4 cloves

1.5 litres / 2½ pints water

90 ml / 3 fl oz of Peach Schnapps (optional)

12 peaches

risotto of baby courgettes, crayfish and peaches

## Risotto of Baby Courgettes, Crayfish and Peaches

This is a combination that resulted from my meal at Chapter One. You could substitute lobster or prawns for the crayfish for this delicious risotto.

Remove the zest of the lemon. Squeeze the juice of the lemon and reserve to one side.

Heat the stock to just below simmering point. In a large pan, melt half the butter with the oil over a medium heat. Add the onion and cook until tender and transparent. Add the rice and stir making sure it is evenly coated with the butter and oil.

Add the wine and cook until absorbed. Add the lemon juice and stock a little at a time, stirring constantly. Make sure the liquid has been absorbed before adding more. About 15 minutes into the cooking, add the courgettes and cook with the rice for 3–4 minutes. When all the liquid has been added the rice should be tender but have some bite. Stir in the crayfish, peaches, lemon zest, remaining butter and the cheese and check for seasoning.

**Serves 4**

one lemon
1.5 litres / 2½ pints chicken stock
110 g / 4 oz butter
1 tablespoon sunflower oil
1 onion, finely chopped
350 g / 12 oz Arborio rice
125 ml / 4 fl oz white wine
4 baby courgettes sliced into thin rings or 1 large
    courgette
175 g / 6 oz crayfish
2 peaches, peeled, stoned and diced into 1 cm cubes
75 g / 3 oz grated fresh Parmesan cheese
salt and freshly ground pepper

Note: There is a thought that Parmesan cheese and shellfish don't go together. I agree with this to a point but I do like a touch of Parmesan through any risotto so I use a little less when I use fish.

## Gratin of Peaches with Strawberries and Amaretto

This is a light summery dish. The Amaretto is optional but it does go really well with the fruit. An alternative would be Cointreau but it will be fine if you omit alcohol altogether.

Place the egg yolks and caster sugar in a bowl over a pan of hot water and beat until very thick and creamy. Halfway through add the apple juice or wine and Amaretto. Continue to beat until the mixture holds its shape.

Preheat a grill, divide the fruit onto four plates and spoon the sauce over the top of the fruit. Grill until golden brown and serve.

4 peaches halved and stoned and cut into chunks
1 punnet of strawberries (washed and halved)

This sauce should be made no more than half an hour before serving or it will start to collapse.

To make the sabayon
4 egg yolks
2 tablespoons caster sugar
150 ml / ¼ pint apple juice or white wine
2 tablespoons Amaretto

# Choose your fruit carefully. Eye them up well. Telltale brown spots foretell their suitability. Hover over the box for that distinctive smell. If you dare in this non-tactile shopping environment, give them a gentle squeeze to be sure ... **Pears**

The good thing about pears is their versatility. A ripe pear is a taste sensation, but one of the most frustratingly disappointing experiences is an unripe pear. Choose your fruit carefully. Eye them up well. Tell-tale brown spots foretell their suitability. Hover over the box for that distinctive smell. If you dare in this non-tactile shopping environment, give them a gentle squeeze to be sure.

I hardly ever use pears in the raw state. If I do, it might be diced through the pear and Parmesan risotto, or thinly sliced with some smoked chicken, baby spinach and creamy cambazola cheese (possibly my favourite cheese of the moment), dressed in a little walnut oil. Batons of celery thrown into the mix would give you a perfect winter salad.

I seem to be a sucker for cooked pears though. The champion of them all is pears poached in mulled wine, immersed in the liquid for up to a week or more. I serve these babies at room temperature on my cheese board – ruddy and regal, oozing with temptation, loftily perched above the Ardrahan, Gubbeen and Cashel Blue. Some simple oatmeal biscuits is about all you would ever want to eat with this. If you wanted to serve these warm, do so with some cinnamon ice-cream and maybe some brandy snap biscuits. One of the most delicious tarts you will ever taste is a tart bourdaloue: poached pears, cooked in a light almond cream (frangipane to those in the know) in a crumbly pastry base. Classically French, we used to do this in Chez Nico a thousand years ago and it is better than you-know-what!? A little trick if you like and you are handy in the pastry section is to put some pastry cream through the frangipane to give a custardy effect. To push the boat out altogether, add a splash of Poire William to the mix.

I'm sure you all know that pears and chocolate are a God-given combination. I would serve a quenelle of chocolate mousse with a white wine poached pear. I may also cut the pear in half, take out the core, turn on the flat side, sprinkle on the demerara sugar and either glaze under the grill or if you got a blow-torch for Christmas, glaze to your hearts content. The combination, chocolate pears and caramel – ooh sexy.

## Poached Pears in Mulled Wine

This is the base recipe for a lot of dishes I do. I know a bottle of wine for 8 pears seems a little excessive. But you can use the liquid over and over again or reduce it to make a syrup. If you skimp on the wine the colour and flavour of the pears will be insipid.

8 almost ripe pears peeled carefully to keep the shape Place all the ingredients in a deep pan. Cover with a layer of greaseproof paper, then poach gently for 20 to 25 minutes until they are soft but not mushy. Leave to cool and refrigerate in the liquid.

The liquid can be reduced a little if you wish to form a syrup. This can be used to pour over ice-cream or add some red wine vinegar and olive oil as a dressing for salad. If you are feeling particularly adventurous you could turn it into a sorbet. Whatever you do, do not waste it. You could always freeze it to use at a later date for another batch of pears.

**Serves 8 but 16 in salads**

1 bottle red wine

2 tablespoons redcurrant jelly

2 cinnamon sticks

4 cloves

2 bay leaves

300 ml / $^{1}/_{2}$ pint water

juice and peel of one orange

110 g / 4 oz demerara sugar

pinch black peppercorns

## Croustade of Crozier Blue with Poached Pears, Walnuts & Baby Spinach

Cream the two cheeses in the food processor. Roll the slices of bread with a rolling pin to flatten and spread them a little. Divide the cheese mix amongst four slices of bread, forming a little mound in the centre of each slice. Brush the edges with egg wash. Gently place the other slice over the cheese and press the bread together to form a seal around the edges. Take a large round cutter. Place it over the mound in the middle and cut the bread discarding the edges. Pre-heat the oven to 180°C / Gas 4. Transfer your croustades onto a buttered tray and dab the bread liberally with the melted butter. Scatter over the poppy seeds and place in the oven for around 15 minutes until golden and crispy. Take four plates and place three of the pear quarters on each to form a triangle. Toss the baby spinach in the walnut oil and put a little pile in the centre of the pears. Scatter over the walnuts and place one croustade on each plate on top of the spinach. Drizzle a little reduced pear juice around the plate and serve.

This is a crispy, creamy and pungent starter which you could also serve as a cheese course. Crozier blue is a sheep's cheese with a mild touch of blue that is really gorgeous. I add some cream cheese to it to make it even creamier still. The pears add a fruity richness and the spinach some crisp colour. If you can't find Crozier blue use Cambazola or Gorgonzola.

**Serves 4**

225 g / 8 oz Crozier Blue cheese

110 g / 4 oz of light cream cheese

8 slices semi-stale white bread with crusts removed

1 egg beaten with a little milk

110 g / 4 oz melted butter

1 pinch poppy seeds

3 mulled wine poached pears, quartered

2 handfuls of baby spinach (washed)

1 drizzle of walnut oil

20 toasted walnuts

salt and pepper

## Classical Tarte Bourdaloue

For the pastry

(this makes 350 g / 12 oz sweet pastry – you can freeze what you don't use for another time)

225 g / 8 oz plain flour

150 g / 5 oz butter

75 g / 3 oz icing sugar

1 whole egg

1 egg yolk

pinch salt

5 pears peeled, cored and cooked in the white wine recipe above

For the filling

250 g / 9 oz butter

250 g / 9 oz caster sugar

250 g / 9 oz ground almonds

3 eggs

50 g / 2 oz flour (sifted)

apricot jam to glaze

Sift the flour and salt together in a bowl. Rub in the butter until you reach the crumb stage. Stir in the sugar, then bind with the egg and egg yolk. Allow to rest for at least 30 minutes before using.

Preheat your oven to 175°C / Gas 3$^{1}/_{2}$.

Roll out the pastry to fit a 20 cm flan tin. Bake blind for 15 minutes or until the pastry is crisp and golden. Slice the cooked pears lengthways and remove the core.

Place the butter, sugar and almonds in a mixer and beat until they form a paste. Add the eggs, little by little. Then fold in the flour.

Pour the mixture into the pastry case. Arrange the pears flat side down on the mixture. Bake for 30 to 40 minutes.

Glaze the top of the tart with the apricot jam before serving warm with softly whipped cream.

## Poached Pears in White Wine

I use this for different types of desserts such as the tart below.

8 almost ripe pears (peeled carefully)

1 bottle white wine

2 cinnamon sticks

2 vanilla pods (1 teaspoon vanilla extract, not essence, can be substituted here)

2 cloves

300 ml / $^{1}/_{2}$ pint water

110 g / 4 oz caster sugar

peel of 1 lemon

pinch black peppercorns

**Serves 8 but 16 in salads**

Cook as for the mulled wine pears above, refrigerate and use when needed. For economic purposes you don't necessarily have to use a full bottle of wine. It's acceptable to use half the amount of wine if you increase the water and sugar levels. As long as the liquid is covering the pears you should be OK. In this case, if you reduce to a syrup afterwards, you could use it in the same ways as above. A little makes a delicious addition to Champagne or sparkling wine. It's also a very good base for cocktails. Try a little over ice with a shot of vodka and topped up with soda.

# Maple Glazed Pears with Cinnamon Sugar Biscuits & Mascarpone Cream

These biscuits are really great. I also serve them with the lemon posset (see Lemons) and cookie plate with other assorted biscuits.

Beat the butter and demerara sugar to a cream. Add the egg and vanilla, then stir in the flour and cinnamon until it forms a dough. Wrap in clingfilm in a sausage shape and chill for one hour at least before use.

Preheat the oven to 180°C/Gas 4. Remove the clingfilm and slice the cookie dough into $1/2$ cm slices. Place on a buttered baking tray. Sprinkle with the caster sugar and bake for 10 to 12 minutes. Remove from the tray and allow to cool on a wire rack.

**Serves 4**

4 pears poached in white wine
For 18 to 20 biscuits
110 g / 4 oz butter
110 g / 4 oz demerara sugar
1 egg
1 teaspoon vanilla extract
150 g / 5 oz flour
1 teaspoon cinnamon powder
50 g / 2 oz caster sugar

## Mascarpone cream

Fold all the ingredients together making sure the mascarpone is amalgamated and there are no lumps. To serve take four pears poached in white wine. Pop them into a hot oven for three to four minutes. Divide onto four plates. Drizzle over the maple syrup. Give two or three cookies per portion and a dollop of the mascarpone cream.

75 g / 3 oz softened mascarpone cheese
50 g / 2 oz icing sugar
120 ml / 4 fl oz lightly whipped cream
$1/2$ teaspoon vanilla extract
2 tablespoons maple syrup

# Pheasant

Pheasant is my favourite game bird. I am thrilled whenever I see one in the wild. I am equally thrilled to be cooking them.

There are a few things you should know about pheasant. The cock pheasant is the more handsome but the hen, although slighter and less gloriously plumaged, is often the plumper and juicier bird. A hen makes a perfect meal for two. A large cock pheasant can almost feed four. Younger birds (until Christmas) are ideal for roasting, older ones need a more considered approach, slow braising with lots of bacon, wine, onions and thyme or perhaps cider, cream and apples.

When roasting pheasant, you have to be careful it doesn't dry out. It has little fat content, which is good from the weight-watching point of view, but fat is a natural lubricant in roasting, melting in the cooking process and thereby basting the meat internally so a few rashers of smoked bacon are ideal for draping across the crown to prevent drying out. This season, I intend to try and roast pheasant that's been cut in half along the back bone and severed at the breast to form two equal portions. Put these on a plinth of sliced onion and strips of streaky bacon (smoked if you like). Sprinkle the lot with thyme, rock salt, cracked black pepper and juniper and a bit of orange peel, all-spice and duck fat. Now this is where I have the advantage I suppose. – always having a bucket of highly flavoured duck fat to flavour things like this. Vegetable oil will just about do. Put a drop of water or stock into the pan, cover tightly with the tinfoil and bake at 180°C / Gas 4 for 15 to 20 minutes. Then take the foil off, turn up the oven to 200°C and add two large tablespoons of redcurrant jelly into the tray. Allow it to melt and baste the bird. Pop it back into the oven and baste as often as you can for 10 to 15 minutes until the pheasant has a lovely glaze. This in effect is a Cumberland sauce that's clinging to the bird. The steaming initially should ensure a moist flesh with a lightly caramelised skin. Easy peasy. It should fall off the bone. Be careful of the tendons in the drum stick. They can be a right old pain. Now a word on chestnuts if you are stuffing the pheasant. Cooked and vacuum-packed, the chestnuts are really easy to use. You don't even need a knife, just crumble them if you like. Pheasant is not and should not be perceived as the food of crusty old country squires that have bagged a brace before bridge. They are easily affordable. As for obtainable? I can't tell you where to get them. I know it's easy for me because I can get this stuff delivered to my door.

If you are roasting pheasant, try it with the creamed cabbage (see Cabbage) or the sweet and sour creamed onions (see Onions). For a sauce, use the caramelised onion, chestnut and cider sauce (see Chestnuts). The stuffing in the duck chapter would be lovely with pheasant. Possibly the best of all would be the Creamy Celeriac Purée with Garlic (see Garlic).

# Stout Black Pheasant

Having always stocked run-of-the-mill beer, it struck me as madness that we paid most attention to the wine list (and of course the food) but were happy to tread water with the beer. I am now getting beer from the Carlow Brewing Company. I believe it's available in good off-licences and selected supermarkets. If you are a stout drinker, the O'Hara's is to die for.

This is sort of a pot roast so you need a deep heavy pan with a lid or a ceramic casserole. The pheasants will not be immersed in the liquid, just diligently basted.

The main ingredients here, stout and blackcurrant, are perfectly logical. I am just going to add red onions and chestnuts for an intensely satisfying dish. Then all you need is creamy celeriac mash.

Preheat the oven to 180°C / Gas 4. Then coat the jointed pheasant in half the flour. If you are using a metal casserole, e.g., Le Creuset, heat the walnut oil in it and brown the pheasant on all sides. You may have to do this in batches. If you have a ceramic casserole, do this in a frying pan and transfer to the casserole.

Remove the pheasants and add the quartered onions and bacon. Brown a little, then add the remainder of the flour and juniper. Cook the mix over a gentle heat, constantly scraping the base of the casserole to make sure it doesn't burn. Then bit by bit, add the stout, then blackcurrant, making sure there are no lumps. When it comes to a simmer, crumble in the stock cube. Then place the pheasant in the liquid with the bay leaves. Put the lid on and cook in the oven for 40 to 50 minutes, taking time to baste the birds as much as possible. When cooked the pheasant should be falling off the bone. Check the consistency of the liquid. If it's too thick, add a little water. If it's too thin, take out the pheasant, reduce the sauce down a little and replace the pheasant. At this point, add the chestnuts whole, season and serve with the celeriac mash.

**Serves 4**

2 hen pheasants, jointed
75 g / 3 oz flour
60 ml / 2 fl oz walnut oil (vegetable oil will do)
6 red onions, cut into quarters
2 rashers smoked streaky bacon
10 finely crushed juniper berries
500 ml / 17 fl oz O'Haras stout (or another brand of stout)
230 ml / 8 fl oz blackcurrant cordial
1 chicken stock cube
6 bay leaves
1 packet of cooked chestnuts

# Celeriac Mash

**Serves 4**

6 large potatoes, peeled, washed and diced
1 small head celeriac, peeled with a serrated knife and diced
2 cloves garlic
1 sprig thyme
60 ml / 2 fl oz cream
50 g / 2 oz butter
splash of milk if it's too dry
1 pinch freshly grated nutmeg
salt and pepper

Boil the potatoes, celeriac, garlic and thyme until soft, (approximately 20 minutes). Strain and remove the thyme. Add the rest of the ingredients and mash until smooth. Season.

I love pork and bacon, in particular the underdog cuts of the pork and bacon world. There's nothing better than a lusciously glazed belly of pork with colcannon or collar of bacon and cabbage – still my favourite dish. Crubeens, boiled, the sinuous meat taken off the bone ...

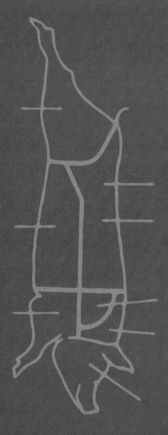

I love pork and bacon, in particular the underdog cuts of the pork and bacon world. There's nothing better than a lusciously glazed belly of pork with colcannon or collar of bacon and cabbage – still my favourite dish. Crubeens, boiled, the sinuous meat taken off the bone, pressed, refrigerated, dredged in egg and breadcrumbs and served with tartare sauce or vinaigrette and a creamy pint of Guinness, hubba, hubba! Robust, beautiful ham hock, infinitely more flavourful than any other cut of bacon. The dark gelatinous meat explodes in your mouth when boiled and honey glazed with cinnamon and cloves like a small Christmas ham. The leftovers served for tea with new potatoes, scallions and English mustard. Lots of bread and butter or lathered with a cheesy white sauce, coupled with a simple tomato and onion salad. Hot and cold, that's the trick, tease all the senses, no inhibitions, pick, slurp and savour.

Waterford city has a great tradition of pork and bacon. My father-in-law tells a story of how years ago after the dances they would frequent a take-away van which specialised in crubeens and pigs tails. One of the gang would ask the lady behind the counter 'Hey Missus, would ya have a pig's tail?' 'Yes,' she would say, whereupon he would roar, 'Well, how do you pull your knickers up then?', and everyone would fall about laughing.

# Roast Belly of Pork with Crubeen Samosas

I love belly of pork. There is nothing worse than dry stringy meat. You need a bit of fat for lubrication. The fat melts during cooking internally basting the meat. What could be better?

Preheat the oven to 160°C / Gas 2¹/₂. Place the onion in a single layer in the base of a roasting tin. Sprinkle with the garlic and half the sage, then pour in the stock. Sit the pork belly on top then splash with the cider. Sprinkle with the remaining sage, spices and seasoning, then cover with foil. Cook in the oven for 3 hours, basting occasionally, until the pork is very soft. Remove the pork belly from the oven, take away the foil and sprinkle the sugar on top. Increase oven to 200°C / Gas 6 and return the pork to the oven for 20 minutes or until glazed and golden. Remove pork to a warm plate and set aside.

Meanwhile, make the samosas; put the crubeens into a pan and cover with cold water. Bring to the boil, skim off any froth, then cover and simmer very gently for at least 3 hours or until the meat is very tender and falling from the bone. Drain well. When cool enough to handle, remove the meat, discard any sinew and bone. Put into a food processor and mix briefly to combine. Add the mustard and pepper and mix briefly again. Season well.

Brush the edge of each spring roll sheet with egg white. Divide the filling between them then fold over into triangles, brushing the edges with egg white to seal. Arrange on a tray and cover with clingfilm. Chill for at least 30 minutes to rest.

Preheat the oil to 190°C in a deep-fat fryer and deep-fry the samosas for 4–5 minutes until golden brown. Drain on kitchen paper.

I would serve this pork and samosas with colcannon, apple cinnamon butter (see Apples) and to be flash, maybe some crispy black pudding.

**Serves 4**

**For the pork**
1 large onion, sliced into rings
4 garlic cloves, chopped
1 bunch fresh sage, chopped
600 ml / 1 pint chicken stock
1.5 kg / 3¹/₂ lb pork belly, rind removed
150 ml / ¹/₄ pint dry cider
8 whole cloves
pinch ground all-spice
pinch ground cinnamon
pinch cracked black pepper
pinch rock salt
75 g / 3 oz demerara sugar

**For the samosas**
4 crubeens (pig's trotters)
1 tablespoon prepared English mustard
about 12 spring roll wrappers, thawed if frozen
1 egg white
vegetable oil, for deep frying

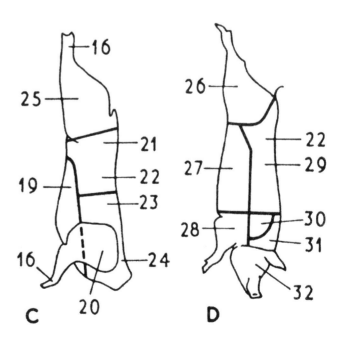

# Boiled Bacon with Black Pudding, Colcannon and Parsley Sauce

This is my favourite thing to eat in the whole world. It is a classic Irish dish, utterly delicious when done right. I hate waste so I make crackling with the fat and give it a little surprising seasoning in the form of Cajun spices. This gives a lovely texture to an otherwise soft textured dish. If you didn't fancy the idea or the calories, use some pancetta or streaky bacon. Bake it till crispy. Leave it whole and stab it into the colcannon for drama.

The quality of the black pudding is crucial. So many puddings you can buy are terrible but when they are right, the flavour is fabulous, bursting with cloves and cinnamon.

The quality of the colcannon depends on the potatoes. Fluffy not waxy is the rule so that they can absorb lashings of butter and milk and don't become gluey. King Edwards are my favourite.

1 collar of bacon

For the parsley sauce
bacon stock
$1/2$ chicken stock cube
2 bay leaves
90 ml / 3 fl oz cream
$1/2$ teaspoon of English mustard
plenty of chopped parsley

For the butter paste
25 g / 1 oz butter at room temperature
25 g / 1 oz flour
bind these together until you get a smooth paste

1 black pudding - optional. Use your favourite brand once it does not break easily.

Boil the potatoes and mash them quite roughly. Fold in the milk and butter, then the cabbage and spring onions. Season and grate a little nutmeg over them.

Boil the bacon for 2 to $2^1/2$ hours. When you insert a knife and it meets no resistance, then it's ready. Remove from the pot and allow to cool for 4 to 5 minutes and remove the excess fat. Put this fat in the freezer to firm up for 15 minutes. Cover the bacon in clingfilm and keep in a warm place.

Remove some of the cooking liquor, about 300 ml / $1^1/2$ pint. If you like you could reduce the remainder by half to make a stock for a soup which you can freeze to use at a later date.

Start to reduce the bacon stock and crumble in a little chicken stock cube. Add the bay leaves and start to add your butter paste. Mix in, whisking vigorously over a low heat. After about 10 minutes remove the bay leaf, add in the cream, mustard and parsley. Keep warm.

**For the crackling**: Remove the fat from the freezer and press out any excess water. Slice it into thin strips, this you can deep fry or bake. To bake it will take 10 to 15 minutes in a hot oven, taking care to separate the strips with a wooden spoon. When they are crispy drain on a kitchen towel. Sprinkle with salt and cajun spices.

To deep fry, drop into a hot fryer (one with a lid is best for this), taking care to separate the strips. Lift up the basket every 30 seconds or so to separate the crackling. This will take two to three minutes in total. Drain, season and sprinkle with cajun spices. This is the most effective method but please be careful, it will spit a lot.

Cut the black pudding into slices, brush with a little butter and bake for 5 to 6 minutes in a moderate oven.

**To assemble**: Slice the bacon into $1/2$cm slices, 2 per person and arrange on warm plates. Heap the colcannon haphazardly beside the bacon. Spoon over as much sauce as you like and a couple of slices of black pudding per plate and scatter the crackling over the colcannon.

boiled bacon with black pudding, colcannon and parsley sauce

# *Caramelised Ballotine of Turkey and Ham*

**Serves 8**

For the chicken mousse
500 g / 1.1 lb chicken breasts (raw) diced
2 egg whites
salt and pepper to season
500 ml / 17 fl oz cream
(All the ingredients should be straight from the fridge
and you need to work quickly. The cream needs to be
incorporated as fast as possible as the heat generated
by the machine could split the mixture.)

1 ham hock
1 large onion, chopped
50 g / 2 oz butter
1 handful chopped fresh sage
75 g / 3 oz soaked raisins
30 g / 1$^1$/$_2$ oz green peppercorns in brine (optional)
handful peeled pistachio nuts (optional)
2 kg / 4$^1$/$_2$ lb turkey breast
16 rashers of back bacon
75 g / 3 oz demerara sugar
25 g / 1 oz flour
120 ml / 4 fl oz red wine
1 tablespoon redcurrant jelly

This will not suit the traditionalists who take pleasure in a golden bird, plump with stuffing sitting on the table. However, it is a twist on the original that once made takes all the mess out of carving. The turkey breast is cut into escalopes and laid on top of rashers of back bacon, then rolled around a stuffing made from chicken mousse, ham hock, sage and onion and a few pistachio nuts. This is rolled in clingfilm, steamed, removed from the wrapping and fried in a pan to crisp the bacon. At the last minute, add some demerara sugar which caramelises into a golden sweet crispy crust. When done, the ballotines can be kept warm in the oven and sliced on the bias when needed. I would serve them with the Brussels Sprout and Cheddar purée (see Brussels Sprouts) and Colcannon (see Potatoes).

If you wish, you could use your own traditional stuffing in these. Just make sure that it is not too dry. Add a little more butter than usual and an egg to hold it together, just to be on the safe side.

Place all the ingredients except the cream into a food processor. Blitz until smooth. Then add the cream. Blitz again until the cream is evenly distributed. Return to the fridge and keep chilled until needed.

Boil the ham hock until cooked (1$^1$/$_2$ hours approximately). Allow to cool and dice into 1 cm cubes. Sweat the onions in the butter until golden and soft. Add the sage and cook for one more minute. Add the raisins, and green peppercorns and pistachio nuts and allow to cool. Fold this into the chicken mousse and keep refrigerated.

For the turkey you will need eight escalopes 8 cm wide by 12 cm long (approx) and about a half cm thick. Your butcher should prepare these for you no bother but if he will not, cut the turkey breast with a very thin sharp knife at a 45° angle into slices around 1/2 cm thick. Then bat them out with a rolling pin. Be careful – you don't want any holes but you do want them stretched to the required size. If there are some holes, don't worry. Patch them up with a few pieces of turkey here and there. It will all be wrapped in bacon anyway.

To assemble you need a chopping board and a good heavy roll of clingfilm. Lay the cling open side down on the chopping board and pull the cling a good 30 cm towards you. Lay the rashers top to tail to form a rectangle and give these a little bat to flatten and amalgamate. Then lay the turkey over the bacon, leaving an edge of bacon all around. Sprinkle with pepper (no salt, the bacon is salty enough) and spoon 2 tablespoons of the mouse on one end of the turkey. With the help of clingfilm, roll the meat around the mousse working away from you. Try to form the shape of a pillow. Use plenty of cling to secure it really tightly, then tuck the edges underneath. Repeat this for the rest of them and refrigerate. These can be made the day before.

To cook the ballotines, heat a steamer and cook the turkey on full steam for 15 to 20 minutes. They will puff up and get firm. You may have to do this in batches, depending on the size of your steamer. This can be done one hour before serving. 20 minutes before serving, snip open the clingfilm, straining the copious juices into a pot and pat the turkey dry with a kitchen towel. Heat the frying pan as I said before and crisp up the turkeys all round. Then sprinkle with the sugar, taking care to turn down the flame once the sugar goes in to prevent burning. Turn frequently and transfer to a warm oven. If you are doing this in batches, you will have to rinse out the pan in between to remove the caramelised sugar.
The steaming can be pre-done. Simply caramelise and transfer to a clean tray to be heated later.

The sauce
When you remove the last batch of turkey, stir the flour into the pan with a balloon whisk taking care the sugar in the pan doesn't go too far. After one minute whisk in the red wine, and redcurrant jelly and reserved juices. Cook for 1 more minute. Strain into a jug and keep warm.

# ... years ago after the dances they would frequent a take-away van which specialised in crubeens and pigs tails.

# Potato

'They're nice today, Mam', 'Yes, lovely and floury', she would say. 'Now take it easy on the butter, you'll kill yourself with that, Dad', or he would say 'They're a bit waxy today, Mam, where did you get them?' A name would be supplied to which he would reply, 'that's unusual, his spuds are usually good', the disappointment evident. So goes a normal Sunday lunch discourse in my in-laws' household.

There is nothing better than peeling a freshly steamed potato, lathering it in butter and salt and savouring every mouthful with lamb or pork chops or chicken or steak and onions. This indeed is one of the pleasures in life. Another is chips. Everyone loves them. Everyone has an opinion on them. Thin and crispy are a little more sophisticated and belong in the environs of a restaurant where they may be haughtily called pommes frites or shoestring potatoes. The thick and soggy ones have to be eaten on the way home after a few pints.

In my teens I had an illustrious career in a chip van for a couple of summers. Those were heady days on the road to the various festivals in the locality where Gina, Dale Haze and the Champions, Dickie Rock or The Indians or the more youthful Chips were playing. I used to fancy the arse off the girls from Chips and before the rush on the chip van, I would excuse myself and try to sneak under the marquee for a quick letch to fuel my teenage fantasies.

The Clashmore Happy Man festival in County Waterford sticks in my mind as the most eventful, with Bohadoon Festival a close second. I had to wait a couple of years before I could legitimately go to one of the dances but I savoured the atmosphere from within the chip fan. It was a very scary sight to see scores of hungry young men, having had no luck with the women, drunkenly demanding burger and chips. Nerves of steel, speed and a thick skin were required for the job. This ability to cope under pressure undoubtedly helped me in later years whereby, on hairy nights in the restaurant, I would mumble to myself, 'you coped with Joe Dolan at the Happy Man, this is nothing'!

My favourite way of eating potatoes though is to mash them. In 1989 I had lunch at Jamin, Joel Roubochon's ultra famous three star restaurant. I was eating pigs' cheek in a bouillon of truffle and asparagus when the waiter approached with a bowl. Would you like to try our famous pomme purée he asked, somewhat arrogantly. I thought, at the prices you're charging mate, I'm going to eat everything you throw at me. He preciously scooped two spoons of the purée. I tasted it and went straight to heaven. Belle de Fontenay potatoes, steamed to order and mixed with butter and olive oil until almost a sauce consistency. I cannot find words to describe it.

Our mash here in the restaurant, although not nearly as luxurious, gets extra special care. It's certainly not for the weight conscious. Butter, cream, milk, salt, pepper and nutmeg. I omit the olive oil and try to be true to our roots with this particular favourite.

It's important to realise that potatoes come in different varieties and have different seasons. We could make our mash the very same way every day with the same potatoes and get delicious results. Then one day they would just turn into a gluey mass. Then we know it's time to change potatoes.

The flouriest potatoes are British Queens, Kerr's Pinks and Golden Wonders. Roosters and Records are good all-purpose spuds, the former being perfect for chips. Waxy varieties include Pentland Dells, Pentland Ivory and Pentland Crown. A special treat in June is the first Irish earlies, Homeguards, which are perfect boiled or steamed, with as much butter as your wife will allow, some chopped spring onion, sliced ham, a tomato and if you are really decadent, a tiny bit of cream poured over the lot.

## Mash

The two secrets to good mashed potatoes are the quality of the spuds and the generosity of the other ingredients.

We simply boil the spuds and put them through a vegetable mouli to get that finer result but a potato masher of course will do. We boil equal quantities of milk and cream, pour this onto the mash along with generous amounts of real butter. Season with salt, pepper, freshly grated nutmeg and that's it.

## Potato and Parsnip Gratin

This is one of my favourite things ever. Give me this with a daube of beef and I'm yours. If you like you can substitute the parsnip with turnip or celeriac but for me this is the best.

### Serves 4

10 g / ½ oz butter
450 ml / ¾ pint cream
1 clove of garlic, crushed
200 g / 7 oz of parsnips, peeled and thinly sliced
400 g / 14 oz of potatoes, peeled and thinly sliced
150 ml / ¼ pint milk
salt and pepper
grated nutmeg

Preheat the oven to 180°C/Gas 4. Butter a 25 cm / 10" deep ovenproof dish. Bring the cream and garlic to the boil. Arrange the parsnips and potatoes in alternating layers with some of the cream, salt, pepper and nutmeg right the way up to the top of the dish allowing a generous layer of liquid on top of the last layer of potato. If you haven't enough juice top up with some milk. Bake in the oven for 40–45 minutes until the top is crispy and the potato is soft. If you find that it is browning too quickly just turn down the oven.

## Sweet Potatoes with Sesame Seeds

Allow one medium-large sweet potato per person. Peel and cut into three widthways. Then cut the pieces into chip-sized chunks. Sprinkle with a little powdered ginger.

Preheat the oven to 190°C / Gas 5 and heat enough olive oil to cover them in a roasting tray for five minutes. Add the sweet potatoes to the oil. Bake for 30 minutes. At the last minute add a handful of sesame seeds. Stir to coat then bake for another few minutes to brown the seeds. Serve immediately.

## New Potato Salad (to go with anything)

Serves 4 to 6

For the dressing
2 lb scrubbed new potatoes (if medium sized, chop
      into 2 cm pieces)
2 shallots, finely chopped
30 ml / 1 fl oz olive oil
1 teaspoon wholegrain mustard
1 teaspoon Dijon mustard
1 teaspoon honey
1 small clove garlic, crushed
60 ml / 2 fl oz groundnut or sunflower oil
1 splash sherry vinegar
salt and pepper
2 tablespoons chopped parsley
Mix all the above together.

As the name says, use this with anything. Starter, main course, with cold meats, salad plate – it's a good tasty recipe.

Steam or boil the potatoes until cooked and while still warm add the dressing. This will cook the shallots a little and allow the potatoes to absorb the flavour.

# There is nothing better than peeling a freshly steamed potato, lathering it in butter and salt and savouring every mouthful

# Colcannon Hedgehog

Serves 4-6

Cook the potatoes in a covered pan of boiling salted water for 15 minutes until tender. Five minutes before the end of cooking, add the cabbage. Drain and mash the potatoes and cabbage, then beat in the onions, butter and milk, and season well with salt, pepper and the nutmeg, to taste.

Meanwhile, preheat the grill to medium. Arrange the sausages on a grill rack and brush with a little oil, then cook, turning frequently for 10 minutes until cooked through. Add the bacon and black pudding. Brush with oil and grill until crisp, turning once.

Spoon the colcannon onto a large platter and shape into a 'hedgehog', then stab the sausages, bacon and black pudding into the potato. Serve with hot buttered toast and gravy.

Next to mash, colcannon is our most used potato dish. It suits our food, our customers love it and I could never take it off the menu.

This is just a bit of fun in a 'Desperate Dan' sort of way. Good for all the family and the kids can even help making it.

For the colcannon
4 floury potatoes, chopped (Homeguards, Queens or Roosters)
4 large green cabbage leaves, shredded
4 spring onions, chopped
50 g / 2 oz unsalted butter
120 ml / 4 fl oz milk
pinch freshly grated nutmeg

For the hedgehog
8 pork sausages
4 rashers streaky bacon
1 black pudding, cut into 3 cm x ½ cm batons
vegetable oil for grilling
salt and freshly ground black pepper

# Honey and Olive New Potatoes with Marjoram and Crème Fraîche

This is another version of potato salad with a slightly Mediterranean twist. We might serve this with roasted peppers and some grilled fish topped with some of our basil oil.

Boil the potatoes. While they are still warm, fold through the crème fraîche, olive oil, salt, pepper and lemon juice. It doesn't matter if they break up a little. Scatter over the olives, honey and finally the marjoram. (For other potato dishes see Wild Mushrooms, Saffron and Lamb.)

Serves 4

350 g / 12 oz scrubbed, boiled new potatoes
2 tablespoons crème fraîche
60 ml / 2 fl oz olive oil
salt and lots of freshly ground black pepper
squeeze lemon juice
75 g / 3 oz roughly chopped black olives
drizzle of honey
1 tablespoon roughly chopped marjoram or chives

I find prawns visually beautiful. Stacked up outside Parisian brasseries, their arms cast out in front of them in resignation or lazily draped over a seafood platter with luscious mayonnaise waiting to be shelled, dipped and savoured.

Nothing makes me more excited than fresh prawns. They need to be alive to get the most from them or at least not long dead. Fishmongers might have them pre-cooked, so certainly avail of them if you can find them. Just shell them and reheat gently in your chosen sauce or warm butter.

I hate frozen prawns. There just doesn't seem to be any point to them. If they are frozen in the shell, the meat breaks down and becomes like cotton wool. Out of the shell they are likely to be subjected to the most annoying profit-making scam in the world: that of glazing and double glazing in ice thereby increasing their weight. This process, my fishmonger tells me, is supposed to 'protect' them. Now I've never claimed to be the sharpest knife in the drawer but is it not patently obvious when you de-frost these fraudulent ice-cubes that what looked like large, firm and glistening prawns dissolve into scrawny damaged disappointments? The processor walks away with your cash for selling you water at  9.50 a pound.

So fresh is best but they are expensive so maybe save them for a special occasion. Only cook whole prawns for people who don't mind eating with their fingers.

# Only cook whole prawns for people who don't mind eating with their fingers.

## *Red Pepper Soup with Aïoli, Basil and Sautéed Prawns*

This is a real taste of Provence. This visually stunning soup is good hot or cold. You could even serve it as a sauce. The addition of the aïoli, basil and prawns are not strictly necessary but each addition brings the soup to another level. The prawns are served on the side on sticks which allow them to be dipped into the soup.

Sweat the peppers, onion and garlic in the olive oil until soft. Deglaze the pan with the balsamic vinegar. Then add the tomato purée, tomatoes, rosemary, and then the stock. Cook for 15 minutes over a medium heat. Remove the rosemary. Liquidise, season and add the sugar and however many drops of sweet chilli sauce you would like.

When the soup is ready, heat the olive oil in a frying pan. Add the prawns and cook for one minute on each side. Add the garlic butter and smoked paprika and remove the pan from the heat. Roll the prawns around in the butter, season. Add the lemon juice. Skewer with the sticks.
To serve, divide the soup into four warm bowls. Add a spoon of basil oil (see Olive oil), and a drizzle of aïoli (see Garlic) to make a nice pattern (squeezy bottles are good for this) and serve the prawns on the side.
A little crostini of tapenade would make this even more special.

**Serves 4**

2 red peppers, finely chopped
1 onion, finely chopped
3 cloves garlic, finely chopped
60 ml / 2 fl oz olive oil
splash balsamic vinegar
1 tablespoon tomato purée
1 standard tin tomatoes
2 sprigs rosemary, wrapped in muslin
300 ml / 1/2 pint chicken stock
pinch sugar
sweet chilli sauce to taste

**For the prawns**
1 tablespoon olive oil
12 shelled prawn tails and 12 sticks (cocktail sticks)
10 g / 1/2 oz garlic butter
pinch smoked paprika (optional)
squeeze lemon

## Grilled Prawns for a Barbeque

**Serves 4**

24 large raw Dublin Bay prawns (langoustines) in the
  shell
salt and freshly ground black pepper
juice of 1 lemon
4 tablespoons olive oil
1 tablespoon of smoked paprika (optional)

Preheat the grill or barbecue.

Gently prise the head from the body (this can be used for soup or stock) and lay the prawns in their shells on their backs. Use a sharp knife to split them in half cutting from head to tail. Carefully open each prawn out like a butterfly. Season the flesh with salt and pepper. Whisk the lemon juice, olive oil and paprika together with a fork and brush the prawns all over with this mixture. Thread them onto skewers, keeping them flat. Cook for three minutes each side, brushing with the oil and lemon every so often. Serve immediately.

## Spicy Fried Prawns with Guacamole Cream

**Serves 4**

20 to 24 large prawns depending on size, shelled and
  cleaned

**For the chick pea batter**
150 g / 5 oz gram flour (chick pea flour)
pinch salt
pinch sugar
1 teaspoon cumin seeds
1 crushed clove garlic
1 tablespoon white wine vinegar
3 tablespoons thick Greek yoghurt
1 tablespoon mild curry paste
pinch cayenne pepper (optional)

I love anything fried in this batter but prawns are particularly special. Crisp and mildly spicy, it goes really well with the chunky guacamole cream (see Avocados). Eat with plain basmati rice and a wedge of lemon. The prawns can be shallow or deep fried but I prefer to deep fry as you get a crispier result. This could also be a starter, simply served with the guacamole cream.

Mix the gram flour, salt, sugar and cumin seeds and make a well in the centre. Separately mix the garlic, vinegar, yoghurt, curry paste and cayenne pepper and place in the centre of the well. Mix together until you get a thick pourable batter. Add the prawns to the batter and leave to rest for two hours in the fridge. Pre-heat the deep fat fryer to 180°C making sure there is clean oil. Cook the prawns for two to three minutes, depending on size, drain and serve with the guacamole cream and rice.

# Panfried Prawns with Little Gems, Cherry Tomatoes & Sauce Bourride

Bring the chicken stock up to the boil and remove from the heat. Whisk in the aïoli until light and frothy and keep warm.

In a non-stick frying pan, heat the olive oil until it's good and hot. Add the prawns and cook for one minute on each side. Add the cherry tomatoes and garlic butter, salt, pepper and lemon juice. Remove from the heat. The heat from the pan will soften and bring out the flavour of the cherry tomatoes. Divide the lettuce between four bowls, place the prawns and tomatoes on top. Add the chives to the sauce and spoon as much as you like over the prawns.

A bourride sauce is a thinned down warm and fluffy aïoli (see Garlic).

This is drizzled over crunchy baby cos lettuce with some juicy cherry tomatoes. If you add some new potatoes and some blanched whole spring onions, this would make a perfectly acceptable summer main course.

**Serves 4**

For the sauce bourride
4 heaped tablespoons aïoli
300 ml / ½ pint chicken stock
30 ml / 1 fl oz olive oil
24 large prawns, cleaned and shelled
1 punnet cherry tomatoes
50 g / 2 oz garlic butter
salt and pepper
squeeze lemon
2 little gem lettuce, trimmed and washed
1 tablespoon chopped chives

## Other Ways with Prawns

You could sauté some prawns and serve them with red pepper relish (see Chilli) with crème fraîche and either baby spinach or rocket. Add new potatoes and French beans and you have a main course. Or substitute the crayfish for prawns in the risotto of peaches, baby courgettes and crayfish (see peaches). Also the saffron cream sauce (see Saffron) would be fab with it or substitute the lobster for prawns in the ragout of lobster with spring vegetables and mild garlic cream sauce (see Lobster).

# Prunes cooked a little in Armagnac and sugar with the help of a tea bag will give you a rush of surprising pleasure ... they stand out like little black jewels against any background.

Prunes pop up unannounced in a lot of my dishes. I love pairing them with cabbage which, in my view, always benefits from a little sweetness. At the moment we have them nestling under a cannelloni of white chocolate and hazelnut mousse. I know in my heart and soul if we printed prunes on the menu, very few people would choose this dessert, as we Irish seem to have formed a natural association between prunes and our bottoms!

Prunes cooked a little in Armagnac and sugar with the help of a tea bag will give you a rush of surprising pleasure. In this delicious form, I chop them through terrines and parfaits, both sweet and savoury, where they stand out like little black jewels against any background. Couple this with a few green pistachio nuts and you will have a mosaic of colour that will cause your guests to marvel.

These prunes soaked in Armagnac are so deliciously handy that they make a perfect substitute for chutneys or relishes if you don't have time to make your own. Pâtés and terrines will benefit as will cold meats and cheeses by fishing a few of these boys out of their syrup and simply serving. We have a duck plate as a starter: a little crispy drumstick, then a little mould of rillette topped with duck liver parfait. This is served with challah bread and port pickled onions. To finish the presentation we place one shiny prune on top of the parfait, its juices dribbling seductively down the sides just begging to be devoured.

There's a classic old English appetiser, Angels and Devils on horseback. Lightly poached oysters wrapped in streaky bacon and prunes given the same treatment, skewered with cocktail sticks and grilled. The oysters are milky and angelic. The prunes devilishly dark all wrapped in their crispy bacon cloaks. I served these as a starter with a spinach risotto and garnished with orange segments. The colours leap from the plate. Customers are intrigued by the term Angels and Devils and the dish flies out the door.

When buying prunes, get the stoneless ones. Otherwise stoning them can be a nightmare and you will end up cursing and hating them. I find when you are sceptical of an ingredient, the easier it is to prepare, the more likely you are to try it.

## Master Recipe for Prunes in Armagnac

### Makes the equivalent of 3 x 450g / 1 lb jars

150 g / 5 oz sugar

450 ml / 16 fl oz water

1 cinnamon stick

peel of half orange

2 good handfuls of stoned prunes

1 teabag

as much Armagnac or good brandy as you fancy

Bring the sugar and water to the boil. Add the prunes, cinnamon and orange and simmer over a low heat for about 20 minutes until the prunes have swelled and the liquid reduced substantially. Throw in the teabag. Remove after three minutes. Stir in the Armagnac. Cool and refrigerate.

## Risotto of Smoked Chicken, Prunes, Gubbeen Cheese and Curly Kale

### Serves 4

1.5 litres / 2½ pints chicken stock

1 sprig rosemary

50 g / 2 oz butter

1 onion, finely chopped

400 g / 14 oz Arborio rice, rinsed under cold water and drained

2 breasts of smoked chicken, cut into 1 cm dice

10 prunes in Armagnac, each one cut into three

1 good handful curly kale, cut into 2 cm pieces, blanched and refreshed

90 ml / 3 fl oz cream

110 g / 4 oz diced rindless Gubbeen cheese

salt and pepper

25 g / 1 oz toasted walnuts

Bring the stock to a simmer and add the rosemary. In a heavy bottomed pan melt the butter over a low heat and add the onions. Cook for around five minutes until translucent and soft. Add the rice, stir well to ensure all the rice is coated evenly. Start adding the stock, little by little, avoiding the rosemary which will have broken up. Cook the rice until soft to the bite. This may take 20 minutes, stirring all the time, so be patient. Then add all the rest of the ingredients except the walnuts. Season and serve. You might fancy a little Parmesan but remember the Gubbeen. It will be gooey, filling and very delicious. Sprinkle the toasted walnuts over before serving.

# Prune and Armagnac Ice-cream

Bring the milk, cream and vanilla pods to the boil. Whisk the egg yolk and sugar together until thick. Remove the vanilla pods and scrape the seeds into the milk. Pour the milk over the eggs, whisking all the time. Return to the pan and cook over gentle heat, stirring with a wooden spoon until the custard thickens enough to coat the back of the spoon. Pass through a sieve. Chill and reserve.

Place the custard mixture and all the ingredients except the chopped prunes in a bowl and mix together. Place in the freezer and stir every 15 minutes or so. When the ice-cream starts to set, add in the chopped prunes and mix to make sure they are evenly distributed throughout the ice-cream. Continue to stir every 15 to 30 minutes until set.

If you are lucky enough to have an ice-cream machine churn all the ingredients except the prunes until thick. Then fold in the prunes. Transfer to a freezer until ready to use.

This is the most fabulous ice-cream in the whole world.

**Serves 4 to 6**

50 ml / almost 2 fl oz armagnac
12 prunes in Armagnac, diced
3 tablespoons syrup from the prunes

For the custard base
500 ml / 16 fl oz milk
90 ml / 3 fl oz cream
2 split vanilla pods
8 egg yolks
4 oz caster sugar

I would serve this with brandy snaps.

# Prunes in Armagnac with Cream and Italian Meringues

The crispy lightness of the meringues complements the prunes perfectly. Lightly whipped cream is all you need to eat this with. At the restaurant, we make meringue discs with which we sandwich the prunes and whipped cream together.

**Meringues**
3 egg whites
175 g / 6 oz caster sugar
200 ml / 7 fl oz cream whipped
16 prunes in Armagnac

Using an electric beater, beat together the egg whites and sugar in a large bowl set over a pan of gently simmering water (a bain marie). Beat until the mixture forms a thick trail when the whisk is removed. When you reach this stage, immediately remove the bowl from the bain marie and continue to whisk the egg whites for around 2 minutes or until the mixture has cooled down significantly. Using two spoons, spoon 8 meringues onto parchment-lined baking trays, flattening them into disc shapes with the back of a spoon, then bake in the oven at 100°C / Gas 1/2 for 1 hour 45 minutes. Place the meringues on the plate with a dollop of cream and the prunes.

## Terrine of Ham Hock with Prunes, Sage and Onion

I swear this is one of the easiest things you will ever make. Don't be put off by the fact that it's a terrine. It's not worth making this in smaller quantities.

Serves about 10

A 2 lb loaf tin lined with clingfilm that overlaps the edges
2 ham hocks (if you can't get them use 3 oysters of bacon)
1 large onion, finely diced
75 g / 3 oz butter
1 handful fresh sage, finely chopped
salt and black pepper
1 handful of prunes in Armagnac, moderately chopped
1 splash of sherry or cider vinegar, optional

Boil the ham until falling off the bone. Remove from the water, cool and then chop into 2 cm pieces along with most of the fat. This is essential to make it stick together.

Sweat the onion very gently in the butter until it is a golden colour. Then add the sage. There must be no bite to the onions at all. Add a little salt and black pepper to the onions, then add the ham. Now add the chopped prunes and splash of vinegar. Mix everything together and pile into the terrine or loaf tin as tightly as you can. Bring the clingfilm back from the sides and overlap on the top, piercing four or five holes in it. Place the terrine in the fridge for 1 hour to set a little, then take out again and at this point you need to get a piece of wood or strong plastic to use as a press. This should just fit into the top of the tin. (A handy person might knock that up for you). Place a heavy weight (3 or 4 kg) on top (two bags of sugar will do the trick). Refrigerate overnight and turn out. Slice, present and accept acclamation. Serve with toast and chutneys. This keeps for 2-3 days. (Ideal for around Christmas time)

When buying prunes, get the stoneless ones. Otherwise stoning them can be a nightmare and you will end up cursing and hating them ... the easier it is to prepare, the more likely you are to try it.

terrine of ham hock with prunes, sage and onion

Tim my veg man arrives in his van every Wednesday – an Aladdin's cave of shapes and colours. It's pick and mix from the feathery herbs to the baby aubergines and cherry tomatoes. The luminescent **pumpkins** like fat men on a bench, take pride of place.

I don't think I will ever forget Halloween here three years ago. We had a great guy called Richie working for us at the time. I wanted to do a lantern to put in the window – you know, the usual jagged-toothed pumpkin that any six-year-old can do. Don't worry Boss, says Richie, I'll take care of it. Now, as well as being a fine cook, he was notoriously fussy and woe betide any supplier who would try and slip any duff stuff through the door. He carefully chose two suitable pumpkins from our vegetable man, worked on them for 2 afternoons and after work at night. He brought them in on Halloween night and theatrically positioned lamps inside creating a warm glow on the faces, then unveiled his creations to an awestruck staff. I had never seen anything like them, delicately carved with a scalpel, not a jagged edge in sight. One mischievously happy, one benevolently sad. The ironic thing is not one customer paid a blind bit of notice to them. They were so good, no-one thought they could be real and so assumed they were plastic. Eventually we resorted to pointing them out to our customers who congratulated a now dejected Richie.

I look back on that Halloween with a special fondness. Richie has bought a new house in Dublin and the last we heard he was unhappy with the way his wooden floors were put down so he made the builders take them all up again and gave them hell till he was satisfied. That's my boy. Some things never change.

Tim, my veg man, arrives in his van every Wednesday – an Aladdin's cave of shapes and colours. It's pick and mix from the feathery herbs to the baby aubergines and cherry tomatoes. The luminescent pumpkins, like fat men on a bench take pride of place. Two is all I can ever take in a week. There is so much in one I can feed a multitude. To some extent, their size goes against them. Really, you are never going to buy a whole one to feed a small household. An army of appreciative mouths is compulsory. Maybe some enterprising shopkeeper will sell them by the quarter. This I believe would unleash a flurry of pumpkin experimentation.

Spices go wondrously well with pumpkin, especially cumin and ginger. They give it depth of flavour and a complex aroma. I've come across a great dessert recipe from Paul Gaylor, a chef who excels at transforming seemingly mundane vegetables into something magical. He makes a maple glazed pumpkin tarte tatin by smearing butter generously onto a cast iron pan or a flame-proof cake tin. He then mixes sherry vinegar with maple syrup, fresh ginger, ground cinnamon and cumin and spoons this mixture over the butter. He cuts the pumpkin into 1 cm slices and lays these without overlapping onto the maple syrup mixture. The pan is put onto the heat until the syrup starts to caramelise. At that point, remove it from the heat and allow to cool. Preheat the oven to 200°C / Gas 6. Take some puff pastry and roll it to 5 mm thick. This needs to be 2 cm wider than the diameter of the pan. Lay it over the top of the pumpkin and tuck it down into the edges. Brush the pastry with beaten egg and cook for about 15 to 20 minutes until risen and golden. Carefully turn out onto a plate and pour any caramelised juices on top. Serve hot with a spoonful of crème fraîche. Yum, yum, pig's bum.

I am very keen to serve a pumpkin and black pudding risotto. I can just see the colours now, orange, white and black. I probably wouldn't put Parmesan on this as it might aggrieve the black pudding but perhaps a luxurious spoonful of mascarpone at the end might do the trick.

## Honey Roast Pumpkin with Frisée and Feta Salad

This for me is a stunning party main course. The surface of the pumpkin will be golden, crispy and pungent, the inside creamy and satisfying. It needs nothing more than some potatoes, roasted with olive oil, rosemary and garlic along with the garlic bread.

220 g / 8 oz diced pumpkin in 2 cm cubes
60 ml / 2 fl oz olive oil
2 pinches all-spice
salt and pepper
1 heaped tablespoon honey
1 head frisée lettuce, washed and picked
30 ml / 1 fl oz cider vinegar
juice of half an orange
50 g / 2 oz toasted pumpkin seeds or pine nuts
110 g / 4 oz feta cheese, crumbled

Pre-heat your oven to 180°C/Gas 4. Coat the diced pumpkin in olive oil and sprinkle with the all-spice. Place in a roasting tray with four tablespoons of water and seasoning. Roast for 10 minutes, then add the honey and roast for another five. Remove and keep warm. Divide the frisée between four plates. Spoon over the pumpkin. Deglaze the juices in the tray with cider vinegar and the orange juice and pour over the pumpkin and frisée. Divide the pumpkin seeds and feta and serve. If you like you could add strips of crispy bacon to the salad for an extra touch.

# Baked Whole Pumpkin with Farmhouse Cheese, Leeks, Bacon and Cream

Preheat the oven to 160°C / Gas 2½ and place the whole pumpkin in the oven. It doesn't even need a roasting tray at this stage. Cook for 60 to 80 minutes depending on size or until soft. Insert a small knife or skewer through the skin (topside) and into the flesh. It should give way very easily and some flesh should seep through the incision. Remove the pumpkin or if you have more time you could let it cool in the oven – leave the door open to speed things up.

Meanwhile, blanch the leeks until just tender and refresh under cold water. Pan-fry the bacon until crispy and reserve. In a large pot, bring the chicken stock up to a simmer and trim all the rinds from the cheese. Cut the cheese into nuggets or grate if you can. Then drop the cheese into the hot chicken stock. Add the cream to the cheese mixture and cook very gently for 10 minutes until all the cheese has melted. Remove from the heat and blitz with a hand blender. Mind the splashes. When the mixture is cool, squeeze the excess water from the leeks and add them in, then the bacon, then the sage.

Carefully slice the top off your now cool pumpkin. Scoop out the seeds. Preheat the oven to 200°C / Gas 6. Place the hollow pumpkin on a roasting tray and fill with the cheese mixture until almost full. Keep the lid to the side. Place the pumpkin inside the oven. Cook for 20 to 30 minutes until the creamy mixture is forming a golden crust. If this happens too quickly, turn down the oven. Make sure the cream is hot in the middle. Insert a long knife or skewer to test.

Take the utmost care in transferring the pumpkin to a serving dish. This will take two people. At the table, ladle into bowls making sure to scrape some pumpkin flesh with each ladleful.

I do appreciate you will need a large oven for this. If you don't have one, buy a smaller pumpkin and reduce the recipe.

**Serves 6 to 8**

1 large pumpkin
6 large leeks, washed and sliced into 1 cm rounds
300 g / 11 oz rindless streaky bacon
300 ml / ½ pint chicken stock
450 g / 1 lb assorted cheese, Ardrahan, Gubbeen, smoked Gubbeen, cheddar even some blue cheese would go well and give a lovely pungency to this
600 ml / 1 pint cream
1 handful chopped sage

# Salmon

I use wild salmon when it's in season. It goes without saying that it is far better than farmed but I don't want to be élitist because I now think there are fine and acceptable results from commercial fish farming. Be choosey when buying salmon. Look for a deep rich colour with minimum fat content and you're away.

I prefer to poach or steam it, although I love the crispiness attained by roasting it in olive oil. I really don't think fish should be mucked about with. It's not what people want. A while back, we ate our first salmon of the season on a Sunday evening with some friends. I didn't want too much pressure as I spend the rest of the week running around like a nutcase. It was a beautiful day so we made Pimms, followed by poached fillet of salmon, served on a huge platter with new potato salad; a tomato and onion salad dressed with lemon syrup, balsamic vinegar and olive oil; another salad of French beans, pine nuts and bacon; and some organic leaves and soft boiled eggs with Maldon sea salt to conclude the feast. It went down a treat. I nicked some mayonnaise from the restaurant for some creamy indulgence. I appreciate the fact that we have chefs who can whip up something on request so to make your life easier, buy the mayonnaise. We drank a lovely New Zealand sauvignon blanc and ate Waltons style. Five hours later we got up from the table. I was a very happy bunny.

The beauty of doing this sort of thing with salmon is that with the help of some nice tableware, napkins and cutlery and a thoughtful table setting you create an impact as soon as your guests arrive. You can sit at your leisure, the food is not going to go cold and I think good friends will not mind the extra effort involved in that grab it yourself style. I know the weather has its part to play but we just have to be optimistic about that.

As far as the restaurant is concerned I have a few favourite ways to serve salmon. A simple starter would be to poach some salmon, then let it cool and flake it. Add about $1/3$ of the quantity again of chopped smoked salmon but if you really like smoked salmon, use more, I won't chastise you. Then add some chopped dill and chives, crème fraîche and horseradish cream, a pinch of paprika, salt and pepper, maybe some lemon and that's it. Fold everything together gently. Use enough crème fraîche only to bind and horseradish only to taste. As for the salmon, use your judgement here but 400g is loads for four people. Serve with some cucumber and warm toast or if you would like a more formal presentation, press into some ramekins. This mixture is also terrific in sandwiches.

For a main course salmon dish you could serve it grilled, baked or poached with a light curry cream studded with some ginger and raisins.

Tartare sauce as an accompaniment to salmon is always a winner although I temper mine with crème fraîche, lemon syrup and puréed basil to make the flavour less aggressive and more rounded.

The main point when cooking is to bear in

mind that with the exception of pastry or baking, recipes are only guidelines. Cooking should be pleasurable and a labour of love. The best cooks cook by instinct, a little of this, a whisper of that. A true cook deals with nature which is always changing and so we have to change and adapt with it. So dabble would be my advice. If you make something wonderful by yourself, it will be yours, achieved by experience, and the satisfaction will be immense.

## Cream of Sweetcorn Soup with Poached Salmon

This is a flour-based soup, although the blending and subsequent straining of the soup gives a light creamy texture. If you like you can substitute the salmon for chicken, crab or prawns, but the soup us also delicious all on its own.

Melt the butter with the sesame oil and whisk in the flour. Cook on a gentle heat until it is a sandy colour and then add the hot stock bit by bit, whisking into a smooth paste. Keep adding until it's all in and cook out for 10 minutes. Add 350g sweetcorn, reserving 100g for the garnish. Cook for a further two minutes and then add the cream. Liquidise, season and pass through a strainer. To serve put the flaked salmon, pickled ginger and spring onion in bowls. Ladle over the soup and serve.

**Serves 4**

50 g / 2 oz butter
a splash of sesame oil
25 g / 1 oz flour
1.2 litres / 2 pints chicken stock, heated to boiling point
450 g / 1 lb sweetcorn kernels, either tinned or frozen
90 ml / 3 fl oz cream
225 g / 8 oz of poached salmon, flaked
50 g / 2 oz pickled ginger, chopped
1 pinch chopped spring onion per bowl

## Rillettes of Salmon with Crème Fraîche, Horseradish and Herbs

This is something we used to do way back in the 1980s at Chez Nico. It is perfect with toast, brown bread or blinis, accompanied by some pickled cucumber as a starter or on some croûtons as finger food.

Mix all the ingredients together. Serve lightly chilled. (For other recipes for Salmon see under Peas, Cumin, Spinach and Eggs.)

**Serves 4**

225 g / 8 oz poached salmon flaked
175 g / 6 oz smoked salmon (cut into 1/2 cm dice)
3 tablespoons crème fraîche
1 tablespoon creamed horseradish
1 tablespoon chopped dill
1 tablespoon chopped chives
salt and pepper
1 pinch cayenne pepper
1 squeeze lemon juice

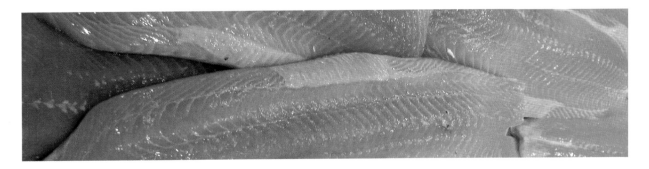

## *Fish and Chip Salad*

I started using batter pieces as croutons one summer when we had a deep fried cod dish on the menu. Long stringy bits would always be lurking in the oil, and when drained and seasoned they would taste fantastic. I was loathe to let them go to waste, so I started doing this salad. Use any batter that is left over for your dinner the next day. You can use any fish you like for this recipe.

**Serves 4**

For the batter
This makes quite a lot of batter but will keep for a day or so in the fridge. You could also use it for deep-frying fish or vegetables.

1/2 cup of self raising flour
1/2 bottle of beer
60 ml / 2 fl oz of sunflower oil for frying

Whisk together to a thickish paste.
Heat the oil in a frying pan. When hot scatter in your batter from a fork. Remove with a slotted spoon onto a kitchen towel when golden and crispy and season.

For the salad

1 tablespoon red wine vinegar
1/2 tablespoon crème fraîche
2 tablespoons olive oil
1 butterleaf lettuce, washed
1/2 red onion finely sliced
225 g / 8 oz poached salmon, flaked

Mix the red wine vinegar, crème fraîche and olive oil together. Turn gently with the lettuce and red onion. Season and arrange on plates. Scatter the salmon and batter bits on top and if you like, some chopped boiled egg and capers.

I use two types of **spinach**, large leaf and baby spinach. Of course there are technical names on these breeds but frankly I don't care. I do care though, that the leaves are fresh and crisp and as green as they can be

I use two types of spinach, large leaf and baby spinach. Of course there are technical names on these breeds but frankly I don't care. I do care though, that the leaves are fresh and crisp and as green as they can be but above all the large leaf spinach should be tender with not much stalk. I have had spinach brought in to me that I would think twice about giving to a goat. The test is if you can eat it easily while raw. The crisp leaf should be crunchy and refreshing in your mouth. It will be meltingly tender when you cook it. Of course I am aware that this tenderness will render your considerable mass of spinach into mere spoonfuls upon cooking but it's worth it so allow for plenty per portion.

Spinach goes with practically everything. You could add a dash of cream and perhaps a hint of English mustard if you were serving it with lamb. Other uses for large leaf spinach would be to put it through pasta and risotto and the occasional soup or if you are making a robust salad, for example spinach and bacon with pears and creamy Roquefort dressing, akin to a Caesar salad – the large leaves are able to bear the weight of the thick creamy dressing.

The baby variety I almost think of as little ladies – perfect for giving a flash of colour and texture to a dish. I never cook this as it would dissolve to nothing so keep it for that special salad: tomato and onion, goat's cheese, beetroot and walnuts or smoked duck with caramelised onions; orzo pasta with bacon, tomato and avocado. It's just one of those ingredients that will bring a dish to life, adding colour. Do be careful with baby spinach though. It bruises easily and doesn't have a long fridge life.

## Buttered Spinach

This is one of the nicest vegetables there is. A beautiful colour and lovely texture, it will go with almost everything. The simplest method of cooking will ensure the best results.

Put one very large handful of washed spinach with some of the water left on the leaves into a pot. Add a good spoonful of garlic butter, salt, pepper and nutmeg. Turn the heat onto full blast and wilt it down for 2 minutes. The excess water on the spinach will evaporate and cook it. The result should be slightly crunchy, buttery with no excess liquid left at the end of the pot.

## Grilled Escalope of Salmon with Spinach Risotto, Horseradish Cream and Poached Eggs

Spinach and salmon. It speaks for itself.

Serves 4

For the horseradish cream
90 ml / 3 fl oz cream whipped
commercial creamed horseradish (jar will do)
tablespoon chopped chives
Add the horseradish and the chives into the whipped cream and reserve.

1 medium onion, finely chopped
50 g / 2 oz butter
2 cloves garlic, crushed
grated nutmeg
400 g / 14 oz risotto rice
1.5 litres / 2$^1$/$_2$ pints chicken stock infused with
    rosemary
2 large handfuls of spinach
8 slices of streaky bacon, baked till crisp and finely
    chopped
4 x 175 g / 4 x 6 oz thinly sliced escalopes of salmon
4 eggs, lightly poached

Sweat the onion in the butter until translucent and add the garlic and nutmeg, then the rice. Turn the rice around in the butter until every grain is covered, then start adding your stock bit by bit, making sure the liquid has been absorbed before adding more. When the rice is almost cooked, add in the spinach. Cook for another 1–2 minutes. Season and if you think you need more liquid add some hot water, then fold in the crispy bacon.

Reserve your risotto, grill the salmon and then distribute your risotto over four plates. Place the salmon on top, then the warm poached eggs and finally the horseradish cream.

If you were serving the risotto without the salmon, either on its own or with some meat – chicken or lamb – you could add a little Parmesan or mascarpone cheese.

## Cream of Spinach and Parmesan Soup

One of the most glorious things about this is the colour. If you are not going to use it straightaway, cool it as quickly as possible so it stays nice and green. Re-heat quickly, don't let it stew, and serve with a few Parmesan curls and a drizzle of olive oil. That's all it needs. This is one occasion where frozen spinach is acceptable but fresh is always preferable. Spinach cooks down to virtually nothing so you will always need more than you think.

Melt the butter in a large pot and cook the leek gently for 2–3 minutes until soft and translucent. Add the garlic, then the flour. Cook for 2 minutes over a low heat, stirring with a wooden spoon all the time. Little by little whisk in the stock to form a smooth paste. When all the stock is in, bring to a simmer, ensuring there are no lumps in the soup. Cook for 10 minutes then add the spinach and the cream. Season then add the nutmeg. Remove from the heat and liquidise or blitz with a hand blender. The heat from the soup will cook the spinach. At this point it may need a squeeze of lemon. Divide into bowls, sprinkle over the Parmesan and drizzle over the olive oil.

**Serves 4**

110 g / 4 oz butter
1 large leek, finely sliced and washed
1 clove garlic, peeled and crushed
25 g / 1 oz flour
1.5 litres / 2½ pints chicken stock
200 g / 7 oz washed spinach or 150 g / 5 oz the frozen type (defrosted)
120 ml / 4 fl oz cream
salt, pepper and nutmeg
squeeze of lemon
50 g / 2 oz grated Parmesan
1 splash olive oil

## Baby Spinach with Smoked Chicken, Blue Cheese & Walnut Dressing

Very few components carefully put together is quite often a success. This dish is an example of that. The spinach is dressed like a Caesar salad. The blue cheese, smoked chicken and pears complement one another perfectly.

Turn the spinach in the dressing, coating nice and thickly. Divide onto 4 plates and arrange the chicken on top. Slice the pear and arrange on top. Then serve.

**Serves 4**

good handful washed young and tender spinach leaves.
2 smoked chicken breasts, thinly sliced
1 ripe pear
1 recipe blue cheese and walnut dressing (see Onions)

223

# Strawberries

Try to imagine summer without strawberries. Impossible isn't it? We may not have a rich culinary history but at least we had strawberries. I use them as an analogy when I am teaching my chefs a starting point for understanding food in general – the central point being the pairing of strawberries and cream. We always knew they go together but how and why. I imagine some chefs in the mid-nineteenth century trying various combinations and feeding them to their nervous families. Strawberries in beer Tuesday night, braised with thrushes Wednesday and so on until they came to cream and the rest is history. Marriages such as these are filed away in cooks' minds as sure-fire winners. Think of others, chocolate and orange, mushrooms and garlic, tomato and basil ... I could go on forever. The more you cook, the more of these natural pairings you build up without you even realising it. It culminates in a wonderful thing called wisdom.

Strawberries are one of the few foods that I can personally call evocative. I did not learn how to cook by clinging onto my mother's apron strings as I know she would be the first to admit that she would burn water, but strawberries remind me of our summer holidays at Clonea Strand (all of three miles away!). Eight children and two parents in two tents, myself the youngest, killed with sunburn and wailing in a corner if I didn't get my way. I was fed on a diet of sausages and strawberries and cream. My sisters tell me the only way to stop me whimpering while the sunburn cream was being applied was to feed me. Some things never change.

My favourite ways with strawberries:
Strawberries and champagne have a natural affinity. Drop a strawberry into a glass before pouring over champagne or sparkling wine. It gives it a delicate fruity flavour. If you are feeling more adventurous, try this strawberry juice as a drink or to freeze in an ice-cube tray to be used instead of a strawberry.

## Gratin of Strawberries

The Italians call this zabaglione and make it with Marsala. I'm using white wine and our lovely local apple juice, Crinnaghtaun. You could substitute the apple juice with some Cointreau if you like.

**Serves 4**

2 punnets strawberries hulled, washed and halved
   for the zabaglione
4 egg yolks
50g / 2 oz  caster sugar
60 ml / 2 fl oz white wine
60 ml / 2 fl oz apple juice

Whisk all the above ingredients in a bowl over gently simmering water until thick and frothy. Pile the strawberries onto four plates. Pre-heat the grill. Spoon the sabayon over the strawberries and grill under a high heat until the sabayon is golden brown and bubbling. This would be lovely with shortbread biscuits.
I normally posh this up with a small basket of strawberry sorbet.

gratin of strawberries

## Strawberry Juice

750 g / 1³/₄ lb strawberries
75 g / 3 oz caster sugar
half lemon, roughly chopped

Place all the ingredients in a bowl and cover with clingfilm. Stand in a bain marie and place in the oven at 90°C/Gas ¹/₄ for 3 hours, taking care it does not boil.
When done, strain through muslin over a bowl. Do not force the last bit through or it will become cloudy. When it is cold, pour into an airtight container and refrigerate until it is ready to use.

## Wimbledon Mess

To make four portions – use your own judgement with quantities

strawberries
broken meringue
whipped cream
red fruit sorbet or broken up ice pop

I think my favourite pairing with strawberries is meringue, as in this dish. Originally called Eton Mess, it was renamed Wimbledon mess when we lived in Wimbledon. Our friend, a chef, had it on his menu during the tennis tournament.
All mixed together and served in a glass. You will know why it is called a mess but it is totally delicious.

## Strawberries with Clotted Cream and Shortbread Biscuits

If you have trouble finding clotted cream, try this cheesecake cream:

25 g / 1 oz caster sugar
225 g / 8 oz  light cream cheese or mascarpone
300 ml / ¹/₂ pint cream lightly whipped
¹/₄ teaspoon vanilla extract

A very heavy, thick cream, indigenous to Devon. Beautiful shortbread biscuits served with strawberries and tea from a china cup. Need I say more.

Beat the sugar into the cream cheese until the sugar has dissolved. Fold in the lightly whipped cream and the vanilla essence. Refrigerate for about an hour before serving.

For the Shortbread

225 g / 8 oz butter
75 g /  caster sugar
450 g / 16 oz flour
15 g /  cornflour

Preheat the oven to 180° c
Grease a baking sheet. Cream the butter and sugar together. Sift the flour and cornflour into the creamed butter/sugar mixture. Work it all together quickly.
Roll the mixture flat (about 1 cm). Mark it into the shapes you want to break it into later and bake for 25 to 30 minutes in the preheated oven until it is golden.

## Strawberry Croissant Crème Brûlée

These are utterly fabulous. They can be refrigerated but they are better at room temperature or just slightly warm. Serve with the toasted almonds and a little crème fraîche.

Pre-heat the oven to 150°C/Gas 2.

Whisk the yolks, Cointreau and sugar together in a bowl. Boil your cream and vanilla. Then pour on top of the yolks, whisking continuously. Distribute the strawberries and broken up croissants evenly between four large ramekins (or small bowls) and pour the cream mixture over them.

Heat a bain marie on the top of the stove bringing the water to just below boiling point. Place the ramekins in the water bath. The water should come halfway up the side of the ramekins.

Cook for 20 minutes until set. Remove from the water bath and allow to come to room temperature.

Sprinkle with sugar and caramelise with a blow torch or under a hot grill.

if you use a vanilla pod, split it lengthways to scrape the seeds into the cream.

4 egg yolks

2 tablespoons Cointreau (optional)

75g / 3 oz caster sugar

600 ml / 1 pint cream

1 teaspoon vanilla extract or better still a vanilla pod

250 g / 9 oz punnet of strawberries, quartered

2 croissants torn up (stale is fine)

1 pinch toasted almonds

a little crème fraîche

50 g / 2 oz dememera sugar for coating the top of the brûlées

Strawberries are one of the few foods that I can personally call evocative ... strawberries remind me of our summer holidays at Clonea Strand

I've got every knife imaginable in my kitchen. Big ones, small ones, serrated, cleavers, parers and peelers and I've had plenty of practice using them. Yet when it comes to turnips I'm convinced that brute force plays an equal part in the successful dissection. Many's the time I've almost left a digit behind on the chopping board so utmost care is needed. This is truly a man's vegetable. Butch and vigorous, this is no pansy. I have always loved them. If we want a plain dinner at home, turnips are usually on the menu with lamb chops or bacon and cabbage. They are honestly Irish and truly part of our culture.

In the restaurant at the moment I simply roast carrots, parsnips and turnips with maple syrup and sage. Honey will do fine also. When they caramelise they take on a lovely lustre and they are crunchy to boot, nothing too flash, just nicely done veg.

A good idea would be to alternate layers of turnip in the classic dauphinoise potatoes. This dish needs the potatoes as turnips themselves have very little starch and tend to be a bit watery. A 50:50 ratio works well. I like taking well-known dishes and putting them back together in a different way. If you have leftover ham try making a risotto with diced turnip and crunchy strips of savoy cabbage. Even better with little cubes of Gubbeen cheese to lubricate everything. Being quite bland, I don't like to introduce turnip to water that often. The water just dilutes the flavour. Steaming gives better results. I also like to spice them. Simply cut the turnip into bite-sized pieces and coat with olive oil and butter. Sprinkle on some ground cumin and ginger and a sprinkling of water or stock and a couple of spoonfuls of demerara sugar and pop them in a hot oven, turning every so often to get a nice caramelisation. The final touch, however, is a squeeze of orange juice to cut through the sugar. These turnips would be delicious with some yoghurt and toasted almonds and could nearly be eaten on their own, otherwise marinade some skinless chicken fillets (see Cumin) in natural yoghurt overnight with some crushed garlic. Put them on a buttered tray and put them in a 180°C / Gas 4 oven until cooked. Put these on top of the turnips and scatter with chopped coriander.

I've also made a coconut and curry stew with all sorts of veg that my organic man brings to me. The turnip is a particular star of this concoction, proudly nestled amongst the various greens and luscious creaminess of the sauce.

I have always loved them. If we want a plain dinner at home, turnips are usually on the menu with lamb chops or bacon and cabbage. They are honestly Irish and truly part of our culture.

## Cream of Turnip, Saffron and Almond Soup

There are some seemingly ordinary ingredients that merely by association with more elegant sophisticated influences take on some of their glamour. Saffron is one ingredient that elevates all associated with it into the stratosphere.

Cook the leek in the butter until translucent and soft. Add in the turnip and stock and cook for 10–15 minutes or until the turnip is soft. Add the saffron, rosemary and cream and cook gently for another 10 minutes. It might be a good idea to wrap the rosemary in muslin as it tends to break up. Remove the rosemary, blitz or liquidise with the honey and pass through a sieve. Return to a clean pot. Season and serve in warm bowls, garnished with almonds and crème fraîche.

**Serves 4**

1 large leek, washed and finely diced
50 g / 2 oz butter
1 medium turnip, peeled and finely diced
1.5 litres / 2½ pints ham stock (from a previously boiled ham – never throw anything out) but chicken stock will do
1 pinch saffron strands
1 sprig rosemary
90 ml / 3 fl oz cream
1 tablespoon honey
handful toasted almonds
2 tablespoons crème fraîche to garnish

# Steamed Scallops with Turnip, Brown Butter and Citrus Vinaigrette

This is earthy, yet luxurious. I steam the scallops with nothing more than salt and pepper because the sauce is so flavourful and butterladen. The bitterness of the turnip is offset by the sweet citrussy flavour of the vinaigrette. This will be perfect with some angel hair pasta or new potatoes

**Serves 4**

125 g / 4$^1$/$_2$ oz butter

2 tablespoons sliced almonds

2 tablespoons orange juice

1 tablespoon lemon juice

1 grated orange zest

$^1$/$_2$ turnip, diced into 1 cm cubes, poached in chicken stock

salt and pepper

2 little gems or baby cos lettuce

1 tablespoon chopped coriander

5 or 6 clean scallops per person depending on size

Melt the butter and cook gently over a medium heat until golden brown.

Remove from the heat, allow to cool a little and add the almonds, orange juice, lemon juice, orange zest and turnips. Be careful – it might spit. Season and reserve.

The scallops

Steam for two minutes or until slightly firm. Distribute the lettuce onto plates. Add the coriander to the vinaigrette and warm slightly. Place the scallops on top of the lettuce and drizzle over the dressing.

Note: This butter pretty much goes with any white fish, salmon or trout.

# Crispy Turnip, Chèvre and Apricot Pies

**Serves 4**

You might think this is a strange combination but the sweetness of the apricots complements the tanginess of the cheese and the bitterness of the turnip.

8 sheets filo pastry

melted butter for brushing

half turnip diced into half centimetres and steamed

6 dried apricots soaked and halved

1 small chèvre log or other goat's cheese, crumbled

handful baby spinach leaves

3 eggs

120 ml / 4 fl oz milk

230 ml / 8 fl oz cream

salt and pepper

Preheat an oven to 160°C/Gas 2$^1$/$_2$..

One by one brush the filo pastry sheets lightly with butter and fold over into a square. You will use two per pie. Butter some muffin tins or large Yorkshire pie moulds and press one sheet of filo into four different moulds. Return with the other sheet, alternating the corners to form a star shape leaving plenty of excess on the sides which you will scrunch to form a lip.

In a bowl mix the turnip, apricot, goat's cheese and spinach and spoon 2/3 of the way up in each pie. Mix the eggs, milk and cream and season. Pour over the cheese mixture and bake for 15 minutes until set. Serve hot or cold.

steamed scallops with turnip, brown butter and citrus vinaigrette

# Afterword

Chefs that don't eat annoy me. Not that they don't eat full stop but they go out to eat either rarely or not at all. At the risk of sounding like a boring old fart, the trainees I come across now don't have the same interest. I'm as guilty as the next guy when it comes to junk food but I can't stress enough that a fundamental part of learning about food is eating in other people's restaurants. OK, it can be expensive but where are their priorities? It's important to keep up with the scene, who has the good reputations and why? The proof is in the eating.

Regularly my chefs thrust a freshly made sauce or soup at me to taste. They know me well enough by now only to offer it to me when they consider it finished and they are satisfied with it. If they are in trouble, that's no problem, we'll finish it together. Flavour is my thing. Blandness is inexcusable but it can be fixed with a little imagination. Over flavouring is the problem and this happens a lot. Chefs who don't eat out don't have an understanding of a complete dish. One spoon of sauce is not enough to judge a whole dish. They have to question how does the sauce relate to the main ingredient? If one spoon is so powerful that it makes your gums and tastebuds go into a frenzy, what are four or five spoons going to do? In cases like this I usually get them to try three or four spoonfuls of said sauce for themselves until the full impact hits them and then no more need be said.

It's quite simple, the more you put into it, the more you get out of it. When I am truly impressed with someone's cooking it makes me want to cook more, to get better, to question why I never tried this or that. The really good ones make me reflect on my whole outlook and despair at my failings.

I enjoy restaurants. It's a pleasure to have something served up to you having been on the other side of the fence all week. If you can learn from it all the better. My work is my hobby. To some people it may sound sad but really, when you think of it, I am lucky. How many people hate their jobs? If I am bored with something I change it, every day if I wish. Each day something new, isn't that wonderful? If you are excited with what you do, the day flies by despite the bone crunching hours on your feet. The feeling of elation when someone compliments your work, equally when someone complains, my heart sinks and I am left feeling disappointed for the customer and myself. That's it you see, you are only as good as your last meal. There's always a new restaurant that's just opened to try so every meal has to be cooked with care. We can't afford to take our eye off the ball.

When I was a commis, some friends of mine who had been saving for a couple of months flew over to Switzerland to eat at Freddy Giradet in his restaurant in Crissier. I was broke at the time but I was extremely envious of them. Giradet was the pre-eminent chef of the 1980s in the way that Robouchon was of the 1990s and Gordon Ramsey is now. Upon their return they pronounced it worth every penny. These boys were a dedicated bunch and later, one of them, Tony Wright, became the youngest chef in Britain to have a Michelin Star in Mallory Court near Birmingham. Another is now running a sandwich bar having given up the game in pursuit of a better quality of life. There is no doubt there are easier ways to make a living and it's a marathon, not a sprint and it certainly won't suit everyone. I don't blame them, but the one thing that will make the long hours acceptable is to love what you do and if your are going to do it you may as well do the best you can and eating is what makes sense of it all. We eat to live and we eat good food for pleasure, and when you understand the pleasure that is derived from something executed beautifully then it should help you to cook beautifully.

So fine, eat frozen pizza if you want to, but save your money. Go to a nice restaurant every once in a while. Relax, don't pick holes and enjoy the experience with your friends. Take it all in. Applaud the things you like and the things you don't like, simply do it better when you have your own place.